CONTEMPORARY SOCIAL RESEARCH SERIES
General Editor: MARTIN BULMER

9

Introduction to Causal Analysis

CONTEMPORARY SOCIAL RESEARCH SERIES

Introduction to Causal Analysis

Exploring Survey Data by Crosstabulation

OTTAR HELLEVIK

London
GEORGE ALLEN & UNWIN
Boston   Sydney

George Allen & Unwin (Publishers) Ltd,
40 Museum Street, London WC1A 1LU, UK

George Allen & Unwin (Publishers) Ltd,
Park Lane, Hemel Hempstead, Herts HP2 4TE, UK

Allen & Unwin Inc.,
9 Winchester Terrace, Winchester, Mass. 01890, USA

George Allen & Unwin Australia Pty Ltd,
8 Napier Street, North Sydney, NSW 2060, Australia

First published in 1984

British Library Cataloguing in Publication Data

Hellevik, Ottar
    Introduction to causal analysis. –
(Contemporary social research series; 9)
1. Social sciences – Statistical methods
I. Title   II. Series
300'.1'51953   H61
ISBN 0-04-312019-9
ISBN 0-04-312020-2 Pbk

Library of Congress Cataloging in Publication Data

Hellevik, Ottar.
    Introduction to causal analysis.
(Contemporary social research series; 9)
Bibliography: p.
Includes index.
1. Social sciences – Research – Addresses, essays, lectures.
2. Social surveys – Addresses, essays, lectures.
I. Title.   II. Title: Causal analysis.
III. Title: Crosstabulation.   IV. Series.
H62.H37633   1984   300'.72   84-6192
ISBN 0-04-312019-9
ISBN 0-04-312020-2 (pbk.)

Set in 10 on 12 point Times by
Graphicraft Typesetters Limited, Hong Kong
and printed in Great Britain
by Billing and Sons Ltd, London and Worcester

Contents

List of Tables

List of Figures

Foreword

Statisticians, like theologians, are generally concerned with the here and now only to the extent it reflects the unknown and unknowable – that is, the professionals focus on problems of estimation (sampling error), while we amateurs sweat over what these particular data are trying to say. This division of labour is sensible. They know how to whip out theorems and we know what we are trying to find out. Furthermore, in social science our sample sizes are so generous (inefficient), our measurements are so equivocal and our need for precision is so modest that research workers can live comfortably with estimators that would shock a statistician.

Because of this difference, a research worker's list of desirable statistical properties may differ considerably from those in statistical textbooks. In my opinion – and my opinion is that the main reason for writing a preface is to wallow in opinions – a good statistical system for contemporary social research has three properties:

it is at ease with plebian categorical data as well as aristocratic interval-level scales;

it treats multivariate data as a causal system or network, not as a wagonload of coefficients;

it can be grasped by beginners such as students and deputy ministers.

The categorical imperative, as it were, is familiar. So many variables of interest to social science are categorical (sex, region, political party, marital status, religious preference, and so on) that we must have techniques to handle them.

The network approach needs some justification. My argument turns on market strategy for social science. If we are to survive, we must provide something of use and most probably it is information about relationships among variables. So far, the ones we have found are neither astonishing to common sense nor awesome in magnitude. Merely documenting disappointing magnitudes for relationships everyone knew already is not likely to make us indispensable. What we can do, however, is to show how social reality is constructed of non-obvious, intricate chains, whose individual links are not-terribly-exciting relationships. This means systems analysis.

The third criterion boils down to accessibility. Outside continental

Europe accessibility is a desirable trait in any intellectual work. But I believe it is particularly important for quantitative social science. For example, in the United States there are very roughly as many social scientists (about 143,000) as natural scientists (about 352,000). But for every natural scientist there are three engineers (a total of about 1,111,000). For social scientists there are virtually no engineers or brokers or middlemen. Consequently, if social science is to be communicated and its findings are to be used, the original investigator must do the job. A penchant for arcane and inscrutable research techniques is not likely to facilitate this task.

Some widely known and elegant approaches fail these three tests completely. Analysis of Variance (ANOVA) is an example. It becomes rather upset when the independent variables are related to each other, which is the essence of the systems approach; it trembles with anxiety when faced with the bizarre variances of categorical data; its central mystery, sums of squares, defies explanation to either students or ministers. Consequently, social scientists other than experimental psychologists have drifted to sophisticated regression ('econometrics', 'structural equation models') or contingency table techniques, plain (Lazarsfeld) or fancy (Goodman).

Regression clearly dominates and what O. D. Duncan called the 'protean beauty of its algebra' continues to amaze. Lord knows, it handles systems, and its central concepts (for instance, slopes) are amazingly clear to beginners. But regression is not at ease with categorical data. Not that it is impossible to handle categories with regression (see Chapter 9), but the machinery creaks and its Holy Grail, variance explained, tends to leak when the dependent variable is qualitative.

In the last decade the methodological *avant-garde*, at least in the US social science, has shifted to the Goodman approach or 'loglinear models' (see Chapter 10). By definition this approach loves qualitative data and it is at ease with multivariate designs. But multivariate is not the same as 'systems analysis' in which the research worker untangles the causal links and shows how they operate. As you will learn in this book, the loglinear approach is a total bust when it comes to systems analysis. What it is wonderful for is interaction effects (Chapter 8). Somehow there is a deep tension between neat handling of interactions and neat handling of systems properties. Loglinear methods are a spectacular advance in handling the former and a spectacular retreat in handling the latter. Do loglinear methods meet the third criterion of accessibility? Make up your own mind after reading Chapter 10. My opinion is that the chapter is surprisingly clear but is a triumph of writing skills over recalcitrant materials.

There remains the 'percentage table' approach central to this book. On my checklist the percentage approach comes off well. These methods are designed for categorical data. As you will see in Chapters 1–7, they are amenable to systems analysis. Are they accessible? You must judge. I found the volume amazingly readable and concrete. Readers with no prior quantitative background should be able to analyse tabular data with considerable sophistication after studying this book.

Not that it is all easy stuff. Chapters 8–10 deal with complex issues (though not mathematically demanding ones). The advanced student of contingency tables will find novel and interesting ideas there, the beginner will find an accessible introduction to some problems that still trouble methodologists. I do not agree with everything in these chapters – Hellevik fails to appreciate the airtight logic and ultimate triumph of my own scheme for stewing up conditional tables, but even on this transcendent issue he is clear and fair!

Nor is this the ultimate scheme for social science data analysis. Eventually we need one that does everything promised here, and also (*a*) handles polytomies (many categories per variable) with less clutter, (*b*) includes a persuasive equivalent to R^2 or variance explained and (*c*) integrates interactions into systems analysis.

Pending that millennium, I am happy to recommend this book. The beginner will find a lucid and practical introduction to causal thinking and its application to contingency tables. The specialist will discover original insights into the problems of interactions and estimating partial effects. (But I still believe I am correct about weighting by conditional sampling variances.)

JAMES A. DAVIS
Harvard University
Cambridge, Mass.
May 1983

Editor's Preface

The structure of the social sciences combines two separate elements, theory and empirical evidence. Both are necessary for successful social understanding; one without the other is barren. The Contemporary Social Research series is concerned with the means by which this structure is maintained and kept standing solid and upright, a job performed by the methodology of social research.

The series is intended to provide concise introductions to significant methodological topics. Broadly conceived, research methodology deals with the general grounds for the validity of social scientific propositions. How do we know what we do know about the social world? More narrowly, it deals with the questions 'how do we actually acquire new knowledge about the world in which we live?', 'what are the strategies and techniques by means of which social science data are collected and analysed?' The series will seek to answer such questions through the examination of specific areas of methodology.

Why is such a series necessary? There exist many solid, indeed massive, methodology textbooks, which most undergraduates in sociology, psychology and the social sciences acquire familiarity with in the course of their studies. The aim of this series is different. It focuses upon specific topics, procedures, methods of analysis and methodological problems to provide a readable introduction to its subject. Each book contains annotated suggestions for further reading. The intended audience includes the advanced undergraduate, the graduate student, the working social researcher seeking to familiarise himself with new areas, and the non-specialist who wishes to enlarge his knowledge of social research. Research methodology need not be remote and inaccessible. Some prior knowledge of statistics will be useful, but only certain titles in the series will make strong statistical demands upon the reader. The series is concerned above all to demonstrate the general importance and centrality of research methodology to social science.

Ottar Hellevik's *Introduction to Causal Analysis* provides a fresh perspective upon a standard analytic procedure, multivariate analysis by means of crosstabulations in the classic manner of Stouffer and Lazarsfeld. The author emphasises the benefits to be gained from the use of simplified causal diagrams, and the analysis of percentage differences in tables, by comparison with more elaborate statistical procedures. His elegant text provides a convincing approach to causal modelling with social survey data.

MARTIN BULMER
*The London School of Economics
and Political Science*

Author's Preface

In pioneering analyses of survey data, such as *The People's Choice* (Lazarsfeld *et al.* 1944) or *The American Soldier* (Stouffer *et al.* 1949), percentage tables were the principal tools in the statistical analysis. Even today, most students are introduced to the logic and procedures of quantitative analysis by working with crosstabulations. Inspired by the contribution of Lazarsfeld and collaborators, bivariate relationships are controlled for third variables, and the results interpreted within a causal framework.

Over the last decade sophisticated techniques of analysis have, however, taken over in research reports and more advanced courses in statistics. One of the most exciting is *path analysis*, where the causal perspective of the Columbia tradition has been further developed with regard to both the complexity of the models and the accuracy of the results of the decomposition of statistical relationships. The strength of path analysis is that it stimulates theoretical reflection and helps to clarify one's assumptions about the social phenomenon under study, at the same time providing a statistical technique that allows one to pursue these ideas in the empirical analysis.

The application of path analysis in social research has been hampered, however, for practical as well as pedagogical reasons. Regression analysis, which is used to establish the size of causal effects, requires data at a high level of measurement, while sociologists and political scientists often have to work with crudely measured variables, and therefore may regard the path analytic approach as irrelevant to their research problems. Others may have been discouraged by the technical and often unnecessarily complicated way in which path analysis is presented, preventing those unfamiliar with multivariate regression from discovering the simple logic that underlies the model construction and analysis design.

In this book diagrams are used instead of the equivalent structural equations to present causal models. In the empirical analyses crosstabulations and differences in proportions are used instead of regression coefficients, giving highly similar or identical results. Thus the problems with regard to measurement level are avoided, and the simple procedures of crosstabular analysis make the basic ideas of path analysis easily accessible and intuitively meaningful for students with no prior statistical training. Right from the start of introductory courses in quantitative analysis the crosstabular approach combined with causal models allows the student to work on problems of substantive interest.

Relative to the new sophisticated techniques for non-metric variables, such as loglinear models, our comparatively simple instrument has two important assets. First of all, the technique is rapidly mastered by a student, and the rationale behind it easily grasped. Secondly, the results and the assumptions on which they rest may be presented to a wider public in a non-technical way, allowing for a critical appraisal of their implications. Today a student may have the discomforting experience of labouring hard – and sometimes even in vain – to master a sophisticated statistical technique, and end up finding it impossible to communicate meaningfully with anyone outside a tiny circle of colleagues.

The book introduces students to how they may go about constructing causal models, how the implications of the assumptions made in a model can be deduced and how the empirical analysis is to be performed. The main types of problem faced when interpreting results are also discussed. Each chapter contains a summary, a glossary and problems with which readers may test their understanding of the ideas presented in the text.

Readers may find Chapters 8–10, in particular the last two, a bit harder to get through than the first seven chapters. They are not essential for learning how to perform a causal analysis by means of crosstabulations, but put this approach in perspective by relating it to other approaches.

In the long process which started in 1978 with a couple of articles in the Norwegian social science journal, followed by several courses at Scandinavian universities, a Norwegian textbook published in 1980, and finally a sabbatical year 1981–2 at the Department of Sociology, Harvard University, where I gave a course and wrote the major part of the manuscript for this book, a number of people have contributed invaluable encouragement, advice and criticism. It is not possible to list all the students and colleagues involved, but some must be singled out for particular mention. Gudmund R. Iversen helped me with statistical problems during his sabbatical stay at Oslo, a role taken over by Herdis Thorén Amundsen after he left. Throughout the process I have benefited greatly from the writings, lectures, correspondence and discussions with my sponsor at Harvard, James A. Davis. Among all the others, I would especially like to thank Hubert M. Blalock, Karl Erik Brofoss and Gudmund Hernes for their encouragement along the way. Comments from series editor Martin Bulmer and reviewers at George Allen & Unwin influenced the final version of the manuscript.

OTTAR HELLEVIK
*Department of Political Science,
University of Oslo*

Introduction to Causal Analysis

1

Introduction

1.1 Quantitative Analysis, or What Difference Does a Difference Make?

As individuals we may often find ourselves preoccupied with questions like 'will my university training enhance my chances of getting a well-paid job?', or 'does the fact that I'm a woman affect my political career?'

Among social scientists, the study of how one difference relates to another is a favourite pastime. Long ago Emile Durkheim in a pioneering empirical analysis asked whether the suicide rate varied between different religious groups. Today political scientists may wonder if differences in religious affiliation go together with differences in party preference.

To answer questions like these a social scientist will systematically collect for a set of individuals information on the properties where they may differ, such as religion and choice of party in the last example. Or to put it in the tribe's own lingo the researcher collects data showing which values the units have on the relevant variables. A *unit* is the object under study (a person, an organisation, a book). A *variable* (for instance, party choice) is a property where the units may take on different characteristics called *values* (Democrat or Republican; Labour, Liberal, or Conservative; or whatever the alternatives are in the country we are considering).

As an illustration of such a research enterprise, we shall use a study of court decisions in a district of Norway (Aubert 1964). Looking at all defendants in criminal cases for a ten-year period the researchers in each case recorded the occupation and income of the defendant, whether he had previously been convicted, the nature of the offence for which he was tried, and so on.

The information thus collected can be presented as a *data matrix*, where the units (defendants) are listed along the side of the matrix and the variables at the top. In each cell the value that the actual unit has on the variable in question is entered, as shown in Figure 1.1. This (fictitious) data matrix tells us that the first defendant is a

| Units | Variables | | | | | |
Units	Occupation	Income	Previous convictions	Offence	Verdict	Sentence	•••
Defendant 1	White collar	50,000	None	Embezzlement	Guilty	Suspended	•••
Defendant 2	Out of work	3,000	Three	Larceny	Guilty	6 months' jail	•••
Defendant 3	Blue collar	20,000	None	Drunk driving	Not guilty	—	•••
• • •	• • •	• • •	• • •	• • •	• • •	• • •	•••

Figure 1.1   *Data matrix.*

white-collar worker with a clean record on trial for embezzlement.

One purpose of compiling such a data matrix is to study the *relationships between the variables*, whether a certain value on one variable tends to be combined with specific values on others. Are, for instance, defendants who differ with regard to previous convictions given different sentences by the courts? In a *quantitative analysis* this question is answered by counting how often the various combinations of values on the variables occur in the data matrix. If the matrix is of a moderate size, this may be done with the help of paper and pencil, but usually the information in the data matrix is fed into a computer which takes care of the counting.

The set of units whose value combinations we are counting may consist of all units we are interested in making statements about, the entire *population* of units. Or it may constitute a selection of units from this population, a *sample*. To obtain comparable information about the units their values on the various variables are *measured* in an accurately specified way. As the variables in the data matrix exemplify, the measurement procedures range from the quite primitive to the very elaborate. In some cases measurement implies nothing more than assigning values to the units telling us which are similar and which different with regard to the variable in question (the offence variable). Nothing is said about which is higher or stronger (ranking), or about *how* different (distance). But measurement may also imply locating the units on a measurement scale where distances can be expressed by means of a unit of measurement (the income variable).

For the last kind of variables, which may be called *metric* variables, very sophisticated statistical techniques may be used to analyse what relationships exist between variables in the data matrix. In many fields of social science, however, most variables can only be measured in the more primitive sense of the word. For these *non-metric* variables, the arsenal of statistical techniques has been more restricted. Analysis by means of percentage tables used to be the most common procedure. Recently more sophisticated techniques have been developed, however, with those referred to as loglinear models attracting particular attention.

This book deals primarily with quantitative analysis of relationships between non-metric variables (also called categorical or attribute variables, or variables with nominal or ordinal levels of measurement). The analysis is carried out on the basis of theoretical assumptions concerning the causal relations between the variables, expressed by means of diagrams where the postulated influences are depicted as arrows pointing from cause to effect variable.

The causal models are similar to those used in path analysis, a technique where relationships between metric variables are analysed by means of multivariate regression. Our discussion of model construction and analysis design may, therefore, also serve as an introduction to path analysis. Compared with regression analysis, we shall use a much simpler procedure for measuring the effect of one variable on another, basically an extension of percentage table analysis.

In the rest of this chapter a brief example of what is meant by causal analysis by means of crosstabulations is given. As our point of departure we shall take an ordinary percentage table analysis, and then proceed to show how the analysis may be carried further by adopting an explicit causal framework.

1.2 Crosstabulations and Differences in Proportions

In Figure 1.2 a selection from the data matrix of the study of Norwegian court decisions is given. The units are the 216 men who were convicted of larceny, and the variables social status (a composite measure based on occupation and income), criminal record (whether they had been previously convicted or not) and the severity of the sentence they received. To save space each single defendant has not been separately listed. Instead the matrix has been contracted by grouping together units with similar value combinations. The number of units in each group is listed to the right of the matrix.

How often is a convicted thief sent to prison? By counting the occurrences of the value 'severe sentence' we find the number to be

Units		Variables			Frequency
		Social status	Record	Sentence	(No. of units)
Defendant	1 ... 25	High	Criminal	Severe	25
Defendant	26 ... 40	High	Criminal	Lenient	15
Defendant	41, 42	High	Clean	Severe	2
Defendant	43 ... 64	High	Clean	Lenient	22
Defendant	65 ... 159	Low	Criminal	Severe	95
Defendant	160 ... 181	Low	Criminal	Lenient	22
Defendant	182 ... 198	Low	Clean	Severe	17
Defendant	199 ... 216	Low	Clean	Lenient	18

Social status: composite measure based on occupation and income.
Severe sentence: jail or detention in institution.
Lenient: fine or suspended sentence.

Figure 1.2   *Data matrix for men convicted of larceny (see Aubert 1966: 138).*

139. A more lenient reaction – fine or suspended sentence – occurs in 77 cases (Table 1.1). These are the *absolute frequencies* for the two values of the sentence variable. By dividing each of the frequencies with their sum, and multiplying by 100, we find their relative share of the total number of units expressed as a *percentage*. If we omit multiplying by 100, we get the corresponding *proportion*. While the absolute figure of 139 in itself conveys little information, the proportion of 0·64 immediately tells us that just below two-thirds of all defendants were sentenced to imprisonment.

A proportion may be interpreted as the *probability* that a unit from our data matrix will have the value in question. If we randomly draw units from the matrix, the probability that a given defendant will have received a severe sentence is defined as the long-run proportion of times that this result occurs. Probabilities vary between 0 and 1, between certainty that a result will *not* occur and certainty that it *will*. If none of the defendants in our data matrix had been severely sentenced, the probability of drawing one with this value would obviously be 0. If all had been severely sentenced, the corresponding probability would be 1.

Usually calculation of univariate distributions is just the first step in an analysis, an introduction to the study of relationships between variables. Suppose that we – as were the researchers who carried out this project – are interested in the relationship between social status

Table 1.1   *Univariate Frequency Distribution: Severity of Sentence*

Data matrix   Frequencies   Univariate frequency distribution

Status	Record	Sentence		
Hi	Cr	Se	25	25
Hi	Cr	Le	15	15
Hi	Cl	Se	2	2
Hi	Cl	Le	22	22
Lo	Cr	Se	95	95
Lo	Cr	Le	22	22
Lo	Cl	Se	17	17
Lo	Cl	Le	18	18
			139	77

Sentence	Absolute frequencies	Percentages	Proportions
Severe	139	64	0·64
Lenient	77	36	0·36
Sum	216	100	1·00

Table 1.2   *Bivariate Frequency Distribution: Status and Sentence*

Data matrix   Frequencies   Absolute frequencies   Proportions

Status	Record	Sentence				
Hi	Cr	Se	25	25		
Hi	Cr	Le	15		15	
Hi	Cl	Se	2	2		
Hi	Cl	Le	22		22	
Lo	Cr	Se	95			95
Lo	Cr	Le	22			22
Lo	Cl	Se	17		17	
Lo	Cl	Le	18			18
			27	37	112	40

	Social status			Social status		
Sentence	High	Low	Sum	High	Low	Differences
Severe	27	112	139	0·42	0·74	−0·32
Lenient	37	40	77	0·58	0·26	0·32
Sum	64	152	216	1·00	1·00	0·00

and sentence. Does the probability of being given a jail sentence differ between high-status and low-status defendants? To answer this question we count how often the four combinations of values on these two variables occur in the data matrix (Table 1.2).

Table 1.2 is a *bivariate crosstabulation*. The values of the variables are listed horizontally or vertically, rendering a matrix where the number of occurrences for each value combination may be entered. The two variables have different roles in the analysis. Social status, which is the characteristic used to sort the units into groups we want to compare, is referred to as the *independent variable*. The comparison is made with regard to what kind of sentence the defendants receive, making sentence the *dependent variable*. The task is made easier by using relative frequencies, since differences in the size of the groups mean that the absolute figures cannot be directly compared.

Looking at Table 1.2 we see that a higher proportion of offenders with low status than with high status is sent to jail. As a measure of the degree of *statistical association* between the two variables, we may calculate the difference between the proportion having a certain value on the dependent variable within each of the two groups defined by the independent variable. The *difference in proportions* in our case is 0·32, showing that the probability of a severe or lenient sentence is clearly different depending on which group we are considering, high-status or low-status defendants.

To be more specific, it is a high social status which means a lower probability of being sent to jail. If we decide to define a severe sentence as the 'high' value on this variable, and likewise for high status on the other, we may say that the relationship between the two variables is a *negative* one. Having a high value on the independent variable goes together with a low probability, comparatively speaking, of having the high value on the dependent variable.

If the value on the independent variable made no difference for the probability of a severe sentence, that is, if the difference in proportions had been zero, we say that there is no statistical association between the variables. The association reaches its maximum when the probability of a severe sentence is 0 in one group and 1 in the other, that is, when the difference in proportions equals 1 (or -1).

Returning to the data matrix we may also be interested in whether a clean or criminal record makes any difference for the chances of a severe sentence. In Table 1.3 a bivariate analysis similar to the one above is carried out with record as independent and sentence as dependent variable. Defining a criminal record as the high value we find a *positive* association between the two variables of 0·44. The difference in the probability of a severe punishment turns out to be somewhat greater when we compare groups with different records than is the case when we differentiate according to social status.

Some crosstabular analyses do not move beyond studying bivariate

Table 1.3   *Bivariate Frequency Distribution: Record and Sentence*

Status	Record	Sentence	Frequencies		
Hi	Cr	Se	25	25	
Hi	Cr	Le	15		15
Hi	Cl	Se	2		2
Hi	Cl	Le	22		
Lo	Cr	Se	95	95	22
Lo	Cr	Le	22	22	
Lo	Cl	Se	17		17
Lo	Cl	Le	18		18
			120	37 19	40

	Absolute frequencies			Proportions		
	Criminal record			Criminal Record		Differ-ences
Sentence	Criminal	Clean	Sum	Criminal	Clean	
Severe	120	19	139	0·76	0·32	0·44
Lenient	37	40	77	0·24	0·68	−0·44
Sum	157	59	216	1·00	1·00	0·00

relationships. If we suspect, however, that the independent variables may be associated between themselves, a multivariate analysis is in order. We may, for instance, wonder if the difference between high- and low-status defendants with regard to punishment has something to do with differences between the two groups when it comes to prior conflicts with the law. If we compare high- and low-status defendants who all have the same value on the record variable, either clean or criminal, perhaps we would find that they are similar with regard to the risk of a severe sentence? To see whether this is actually the case or not we set up a *trivariate table*, with sentence as the dependent variable, and social status and record as independent variables (Table 1.4).

Comparing the four groups we get by combining values on the two independent variables we find marked differences in the probability of a severe sentence. Worst off are low-status defendants with a criminal past, where the proportion sent to jail is 0·81. At the other extreme we find high-status defendants with a clean record, where the risk of a jail sentence is as low as 0·08. The remaining groups fall somewhere in between these two.

We now turn our attention to the question of what each of the independent variables contributes to the variation between the groups. To assess the association between social status and sentence we this time must calculate *two* differences in proportions, between high- and low-status defendants who have a clean record, and likewise for defendants with a criminal record. Record here functions as a *control variable*, whose value is kept *constant* each time we calculate the association between status and sentence.

Among defendants with a clean record, we find that a high status decreases the probability of a jail sentence with 0·41 compared with

Table 1.4 *Trivariate Frequency Distribution: Status, Record and Sentence*

Data matrix			Frequencies		Absolute frequencies				Proportions			
Status	Record	Sentence		Social status	High Criminal		Low Criminal		High Criminal		Low Criminal	
						Clean		Clean		Clean		Clean
Hi	Cr	Se	25	Record								
Hi	Cr	Le	15	Sentence								
Hi	Cl	Se	2	Severe	25	2	95	17	0·63	0·08	0·81	0·49
Hi	Cl	Le	22	Lenient	15	22	22	18	0·37	0·92	0·09	0·51
Lo	Cr	Se	95	Sum	40	24	117	35	1·00	1·00	1·00	1·00
Lo	Cr	Le	22									
Lo	Cl	Se	17									
Lo	Cl	Le	18									

low status, while the corresponding figure is 0·18 among defendants with a criminal record. These figures represent the *partial associations* between status and sentence, controlling for criminal record. The term partial is used because each coefficient applies to a part of the total data matrix, namely, those units with a specific value on the control variable.

Table 1.5, which is a simplified version of Table 1.4, just giving the proportions for one of the values on the dependent variable, shows the partial associations between each of the independent variables and the dependent variable.

Table 1.5   *Proportion Receiving a Severe Sentence, Depending on Social Status and Criminal Record*

Criminal record	Social status High	Low	Difference (partial associations for social status)
Criminal	0·63	0·81	−0·18
Clean	0·08	0·49	−0·41
Difference (partial associations for criminal record)	0·55	0·32	

Table 1.5 tells us that the size of the partial associations between an independent variable and sentence is different according to which value we keep constant on the control variable. This is called *statistical interaction* between the independent variables. In other cases the degree of association turns out to be the same regardless of which value the units have on the control variable. It may be weaker, stronger, or similar to what we found in the bivariate table before introducing the control variable. Comparing Table 1.5 with Tables 1.2 and 1.3 we see that for both independent variables one partial association is stronger and the other weaker than the bivariate association with the dependent variable.

So far, we have looked at two bivariate and one trivariate table. Even with our diminutive data matrix containing only three variables, this far from exhausts the possibilities. The bivariate relationship between social status and record has not been examined, and we in all the tables may alternate the roles as dependent and independent variables. All taken together, we may calculate six different bivariate and three different trivariate tables containing relative frequencies. The above exercises should suffice, however, to show how a cross-tabular-analysis is conducted. The procedures used are quite simple, leaving nothing mysterious about how the results are reached. The proportions and differences in proportions have intuitively meaningful interpretations as probabilities and differences in probabilities of having a certain value on the dependent variable for units with specified values on an independent variable.

Such appealing properties notwithstanding, in a contingency table analysis (as with other techniques), one may soon find certain questions cropping up which have no straightforward answer immediately to hand.

First of all, we have the question of *analysis design*. Which variables will it be of interest to combine in a table, and which variable is in each case to serve as dependent variable? Do we, for instance, need to calculate the bivariate association between status and sentence if we already have studied this relationship in the trivariate table for status, record and sentence?

Secondly, we have the question of a *measure of overall association* between two variables when we control for others and the partial associations turn out to be different. Without interaction, the identical partial associations immediately give us a measure of the degree of association between independent and dependent variable net of any influence from the control variables. With differing partial associations, the question is whether we may calculate some kind of average measuring overall association, or if we have to refer to all the separate partial measures when we are describing the relationship between the two variables. As the number of control variables, and thereby the number of partial associations increases, the last solution becomes very cumbersome.

Finally, we have the question of *theoretical interpretation* of the results. Why do we find a difference in probability for having a certain value on the dependent variable between units with different values on an independent variable? What does it mean that a relationship between two variables changes when we control for a third variable?

As will be illustrated for the example involving social status, record and sentence in the next paragraph, and then discussed in more detail throughout the rest of the book, answers to the above questions may be found by adopting a causal framework for our crosstable analysis.

1.3 Causal Analysis by Means of Contingency Tables

When we are trying to make sense of what is going on around us, the notions of cause and effect are important tools. Regularities observed in the flow of events are interpreted as a result of a prior event influencing a latter. Also for social scientists working on a research problem, such ideas usually play a prominent role, even if they are not always explicitly stated. In what is called a causal (or path) analysis, however, the assumptions concerning how the variables influence each other are accurately specified by means of a *causal model*. Such models may take on various forms, as for instance algebraic equations. We shall use *causal diagrams*, where the variables are represented by boxes and the influences by arrows pointing from the causal to the effect variable. If we assume that whether a defendant has a clean or criminal record will affect what kind of sentence he is given by the court, we will draw the causal diagram shown in Figure 1.3.

What about the causal relationship between the third variable, social status, and the two others? One of the ideas underlying the study of Norwegian court decisions was that the social status of a defendant might be of consequence for the sentence he was given by the court. In Figure 1.4 this assumption is represented by an arrow linking status with sentence, broken to symbolise a *negative* influence (high status is supposed to decrease the risk .of a severe – that is, 'high' – sentence). The broken arrow linking status with record symbolises that high status is assumed to reduce the probability of getting repeatedly into conflict with the law (alternatively, the sign may be indicated by a + or −).

A causal model like the one in Figure 1.4, of course, constitutes a drastic simplification compared to the social phenomena it portrays.

Figure 1.3   *Bivariate causal model.*

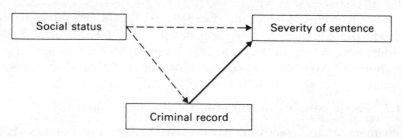

Figure 1.4   *Trivariate causal model.*

Just a few aspects of a complex process have been singled out for attention. For the variables included, one out of several alternative ways of conceiving the causal influences to flow has been selected. Using our imagination it is not very difficult to come up with other models whose assumptions of causal relationships may seem just as reasonable as the ones we have postulated. We shall postpone the discussion of model development to Chapter 3, however, and for the moment just take it for granted that our model is a reasonable representation of the central aspects of the real-world phenomena we are studying.

In the model social status is a *causal variable* and sentence an *effect variable*. Record serves in both capacities, it is a causal variable in relation to sentence, and an effect variable in relation to social status. Its position in the model may be described as *intervening* between the two other variables.

What, then, are the implications of the causal assumptions put forward in our model? With regard to social status, the model says that when a defendant faces the court, his chances of getting away with a lenient sentence will depend *directly* upon whether he has a high or a low status. In addition, his social status has an *indirect effect* on the sentence through his record. Both effects are negative, that is, reducing the probability of a jail sentence for high-status defendants compared with low-status defendants. With regard to the indirect effect, the lower risk of recidivism works to the advantage of high-status defendants, since a criminal record means increased chances of a severe sentence.

Turning to the relation between record and sentence our model postulates that in addition to the direct effect there will exist some amount of statistical association which is a result of both variables having a common cause, the *prior variable* status. A disproportionately large number of the recidivists according to our model will come from the low-status category of defendants. Since low status in itself is supposed to increase the risk of a jail sentence, the difference in social composition between defendants with a clean record and defendants with a criminal past necessarily will contribute to the difference in the probability of a severe sentence between the two groups. A part of the statistical association between record and sentence is thus created by the status variable, instead of being a causal effect of record on sentence. Such *non-causal association* is often referred to as *spurious effect*, it may look like a causal effect without in fact being so.

The above discussion shows how the model provides us with a

tentative answer to the question of why we find statistical association between the variables. Provided the assumptions of the model are adequate – a problem we shall return to later – the association between social status and sentence is explained as a result of status influencing sentence, directly and indirectly through the intervening variable record. The association between record and sentence is interpreted as partly a result of a direct effect of record on sentence, and partly as spurious effect which is created by the prior variable status.

So far, this has been a theoretical discussion of the relationship between the variables. To carry the analysis further by establishing the relative importance of the components of direct, indirect, or spurious effect we have to turn to the empirical data. This leads us to the question of design for the analysis. What tables do we need to find the various components?

In the preceding section we calculated the bivariate association between each of the independent variables and the dependent variable. The result may be called *gross association*, since it includes both association directly attributable to the independent variable itself, and association resulting from both variables being related to other variables. When we in the trivariate table control for one such variable, we find the *net association* between independent and dependent variable, meaning association net of any influence from the control variable which is kept constant. The difference between gross and net association tells us how much differences with regard to value on the control variable between the groups with high and low value on the independent variable contributed to the difference in probability for a high value on the dependent variable. Or in other words, the contribution made by the control variable to the gross association between independent and dependent variable.

According to our model, the only variables influencing the sentence given to men convicted of larceny is their social status and criminal record. The direct effect each of these variables has on sentence is defined as the association net of all other causal variables, which in this case means the association we find in the trivariate table. The difference between gross and net association, which we find by comparing the results from the bivariate and the trivariate tables, gives us the component due to the control variable. Since record in our model is an intervening variable between status and sentence, this component is interpreted as an indirect effect with regard to the relationship between status and sentence, and as a spurious effect when it comes to the relationship between record and sentence.

We have now seen what tables we have to calculate in order to find the components which according to our model the association between an independent and the dependent variable consists of. However, one problem remains, namely, that of deciding the size of the net association. If the partial associations found in the trivariate table had been of the same magnitude, let us say 0·26 each for social status and 0·40 each for the two partial associations between record and sentence, we would immediately have had the measure of net association we are looking for. Things did not turn out to be that easy for us, however, the trivariate table left us with two dissimilar partial associations for each independent variable.

In trying to establish the direct effect of social status on sentence by controlling for record we found a strong effect among defendants with a clean record, and a weaker effect among the recidivists. To arrive at a single measure for the data matrix taken as a whole on the basis of these two effects from separate parts of the matrix some kind of average seems to be what we need. The overall effect of status controlling for record must lie somewhere in between the two partial effects. But what kind of average will do the job?

The simplest thing would be to calculate an average as this is ordinarily done, by adding together the partial effects and dividing by the number of effects. For social status, the result would be $(0·18 + 0·41)/2 = 0·30$. This is an *unweighted* average, all partial effects are given equal weight when calculating the average. If the control groups are of dissimilar size, however, the unweighted average is badly suited for our purpose.

This is most easily demonstrated by constructing a data matrix where the independent variables are not associated with each other. If the proportions of first-timers and recidivists were the same among high-status and low-status defendants, social status and record would be unrelated, and the arrow between these two variables in Figure 1.3 should be deleted. This implies that the association between status and sentence consists of one component only, namely, direct effect. In this case a multivariate analysis is superfluous in order to establish the direct effect, which is given by the bivariate association. A multivariate analysis will, however, show whether there is interaction between the independent variables or not. In the case of interaction we may calculate an average of the partial effects, which with unrelated independent variables ought to coincide with the gross association from the bivariate table.

In Table 1.6 the fictitious frequencies have been arranged so as to make the two independent variables unrelated. The table contains absolute as well as relative figures, displaying the bivariate relationship between status and sentence in addition to the trivariate frequencies. The gross association is -0.26, while the partial associations are -0.20 and -0.40. This gives an unweighted average of -0.30, which obviously is unsuited as a measure of the overall effect of status net of record, since it deviates from the gross association with which the net association in this case with unrelated independent variables ought to coincide.

Table 1.6   *Fictitious Trivariate Table for Social Status, Record and Sentence, with No Association between Status and Record*

| Social status | High | | | Low | | |
Record	Criminal	Clean	Total	Criminal	Clean	Total
Sentence						
Severe	42	3	45	112	30	142
Lenient	28	27	55	28	30	58
Sum	70	30	100	140	60	200
Proportion severe	0·60	0·10	0·45	0·80	0·50	0·71

What is wrong with the unweighted average? Evidently it lies too close to the partial effect of status among defendants with a clean record, and too far from that of the recidivists (Figure 1.5). The absolute figures in the table reveal that the former control group is more than twice as large as the latter. It would seem reasonable to

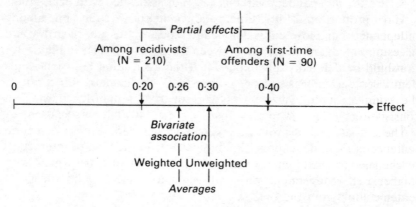

Figure 1.5   *Partial and average effects of social status on sentence (from Table 1.6).*

take this difference in size into account when we calculate the overall effect. By weighting each partial effect with the relative share of all units belonging to this control group, we get a measure of net effect where the contribution of each partial effect is proportionate with the number of units it applies to.

Calculating this size-weighted average we get the following net effect for social status: $(-0.20) \times (70 + 140)/300 + (-0.40) \times (30 + 60)/300 = (-0.20) \times 0.70 + (-0.40) \times 0.30 = -0.26$. This time we have obtained the desired result, a net association which is identical with the gross association.

Returning to the actual empirical data in Table 1.4 we shall calculate the net association for each independent variable by means of this weighting procedure. The results are given in Table 1.7.

Table 1.7   *Net Association with Sentence for Social Status and Criminal Record (Calculated on the Basis of Table 1.4)*

	Social status	*Criminal record*
Partial associations	$0.63 - 0.81 = -0.18$ $0.08 - 0.41 = -0.33$	$0.63 - 0.08 = 0.55$ $0.81 - 0.49 = 0.32$
Weight (share of all units)	$(40 + 117)/216 = 0.73$ $(24 + 35)/216 = 0.27$	$(40 + 24)/216 = 0.30$ $(117 + 35)/216 = 0.70$
Net association as weighted average	$(-0.18) \times 0.73 = -0.13$ $(-0.41) \times 0.27 = -0.11$ $\overline{-0.24}$	$0.55 \times 0.30 = 0.17$ $0.32 \times 0.70 = 0.22$ $\overline{0.39}$

Having thus calculated both gross and net association for the independent variables in our causal model, we have the information necessary to make a causal interpretation of the statistical relationships between each of the independent variables and the dependent variable. Table 1.8 states the results with regard to the size of the components that each relationship according to our model consists of.

The major part of the association between social status and sentence is explained as a direct effect of status upon the decision reached by the court, while the indirect effect via record contributes a smaller part. For record, the impact of status on the relationship with sentence is slight, rendering the spurious effect only one-eighth the size of the direct effect which a criminal record has on the risk of being sentenced to imprisonment.

Table 1.8 *Results of the Causal Analysis*

Components of the association with sentence:	Social status	Criminal record
Gross association: GA (bivariate relationship)	−0·32	0·44
Causal effect (CE) (association net of prior variables)	−0·32	0·39
Direct effect (DE) (association net of all causal variables)	−0·24	0·39
Indirect effect (IE) (association due to intervening variables = CE − DE)	−0·08	0
Spurious effect (SE) (association due to prior variables = GA − CE)	0	0·05

This concludes our introductory exposition of what a causal analysis by means of crosstables implies. In the chapters which follow possible refinements and extensions will be discussed, as well as various problems not yet touched upon.

1.4 A Note on Terminology

The literature on statistical analysis swarms with concepts referring to aspects of the relationship between variables. A few words on how the terms we have applied relate to others commonly used might be in order, especially concerning the one instance where we deviate from the established practice.

Synonymous with statistical association between two variables, terms like correlation and statistical dependence often are used. When we study the relationship without taking other variables into account, we in addition to bivariate or gross association also will see references to zero-order correlation. Controlling for other variables we have called the association between independent and dependent variable within each control group partial association. Here the common terms are conditional or within-group association. The term partial correlation elsewhere refers to the summary measure for overall association after controlling for other variables, in other words, what we have termed net (or overall) association.

Table 1.9 summarises the discussion, with the terms used in this book set off in italics.

With regard to the terms describing the various kinds of causal effect, no such diversity in usage exists. The terms (total) causal effect, direct, indirect, or spurious effect are used in the same sense in

Table 1.9   *Terms for Statistical Association/Correlation*

	Bivariate association	Association after control for other variable(s)
Association applying to the entire data matrix	*Gross association* *(Bivariate association)* Zero-order correlation	*Net association* *(Overall association)* Partial correlation
Association applying to a part of the data matrix		*Partial association* Conditional association Within-group association

the literature on path analysis as we have defined them. It may be noted that the distinction made in path analysis, but not utilised here, between exogenous and endogenous variables, refers to whether a variable is influenced by other variables in the model (endogenous) or not (exogenous). In our model social status would have been an exogenous variable, whereas record and sentence are endogenous variables.

Summary

The question whether individuals, groups, nations, or other units that are different with regard to one characteristic also differ with regard to other variables, may be answered by means of a quantitative analysis. For a specified set of units, their values on the variables are measured, and the relationship between the variables is studied through a statistical analysis of the tendency for certain combinations of values to occur more often than others.

Several alternative approaches to such an analysis exist. The one discussed in this book, designed for non-metric variables, analyses the relationship between two variables by means of crosstabulations. The independent variable is used to sort the units into separate groups, which then are compared with regard to the proportion having a specific value on the dependent variable. The degree of association between the variables is measured as the difference in proportions.

The bivariate table gives the gross association between the two variables. By controlling for other variables in a multivariate table we find the components of this association which are due to the control variable(s) being related to the first two variables.

On the basis of a causal model which expresses our assumptions concerning the causal relations between the variables, we may explain the gross association between a pair of variables as a result of the independent variable influencing the probability of attaining a certain value on the dependent variable, directly or indirectly through intervening variables, or as a spurious effect created by prior variables.

Glossary

ASSOCIATION (statistical *a*): difference in the proportion of units with a certain value on the dependent variable between groups which differ with regard to value on independent variable.

BIVARIATE ASSOCIATION/TABLE: a./t. involving two variables.

CAUSAL DIAGRAM: graphic presentation of causal model by means of boxes (variables) and arrows (influence relations).

CAUSAL EFFECT (total CE): net association between independent and dependent variable controlled for prior variables in the causal model.

CAUSAL MODEL: specification of causal relationships assumed to exist within a set of variables.

CAUSAL VARIABLE: variable assumed to influence other variable(s).

CONTROL GROUP: set of units with identical value on one (or more) control variable(s), for which a partial association between two other variables is calculated.

CONTROL VARIABLE: variable whose value is kept constant when the partial associations between two other variables are calculated.

DEPENDENT VARIABLE: variable for which the proportion of units having certain values is calculated.

DIRECT EFFECT: net association between two variables controlled for all other variables influencing the dependent variable in the causal model.

EFFECT VARIABLE: variable assumed to be influenced by other variable(s).

GROSS ASSOCIATION: bivariate association between two variables.

INDEPENDENT VARIABLE: variable used to sort the units into groups, which are compared with regard to distribution on dependent variable.

INDIRECT EFFECT: component of the association between two variables which is due to intervening variables in the causal model (= difference between causal and direct effect).

INTERACTION (statistical *i*): varying partial associations between control groups.

INTERVENING VARIABLE: variable located between two other variables in the causal model, assumed to be influenced by the first variable, and itself influence the second, thus mediating indirect effect between them.

MULTIVARIATE ASSOCIATION/TABLE: a./t. involving three or more variables.

NEGATIVE ASSOCIATION/EFFECT: high value on independent variable goes together with low (reduces the) probability for a high value on dependent variable.

NET ASSOCIATION: weighted average summarising the partial associations between two variables after control for other variable(s).

PARTIAL ASSOCIATION: association between two variables within a
control group.
POSITIVE ASSOCIATION/EFFECT: high value on independent variable
goes together with high (increases the) probability for a high value on the
dependent variable.
PRIOR VARIABLE: variable located prior to two other variables in the
causal model, assumed to influence them both, thus creating spurious
effect between them.
PROBABILITY: the long-run proportion of times that an event occurs.
SPURIOUS EFFECT: component of the association between two variables
which is due to prior variables in the causal model (= difference between
gross association and causal effect).
TRIVARIATE ASSOCIATION/TABLE: a./t. involving three variables.
UNIT: the research object about which information is collected.
VALUES: the different characteristics units may exhibit with regard to a
variable.
VARIABLE: property of the units with regard to which they may differ.

Exercises

1.1 What Difference Does Sex and Occupation Make for Income?
For readers with a limited experience when it comes to quantitative
social research, the first assignment provides a taste of the process
leading from social phenomena to the kind of tables we will work
with in the rest of the book. The do-it-yourself project kit comes
complete with a piece of social reality, a data matrix and tabulation
form to be filled in and causal diagram and tables waiting for your
results.

The crowd of people represent men and women in the working
population, engaged in manual or non-manual occupations, or
blue-collars (shaded) and white-collars as they are sometimes re
ferred to. Those with a happy grin are the ones rewarded with a high
income, while the low-income earners look less content. The distribution of these characteristics among our research objects has not been
decided at random, it in fact mirrors quite closely the one found in a
sample of American citizens interviewed in 1977, with each person in
the diagram representing ten identical persons from the survey
(Gilbert 1981: 28–30).

Does it make any difference for the difference in income whether
you are male or female, white collar or blue collar? A visual
inspection of the crowd will not get us far towards an answer to this
question, a more systematic approach is necessary. For each person
the value on each of the three variables sex (male/female), occupation (white collar/blue collar), and income (high/low) is to be entered
in the cells of the data matrix. Then we can proceed to register how

Unit	SEX	OCC.	INC.
1	M	B	H
2	M	B	L
3	F	W	H
4			
5			
6			
7			
8			
9			
10			
11			
12			
13			
14			
15			
16			
17			
18			
19			
20			
21			
22			
23			

(Additional grid cells numbered 24–48, 49–73, and 74–98 follow, all blank.)

SEX	OCC.	INC.	*HHt* //...		Sum
Male	White Collar	High			
		Low			
	Blue Collar	High	/		
		Low	/		
Female	White Collar	High	/		
		Low			
	Blue Collar	High			
		Low			

often each combination of the three values occurs in the matrix by means of the tabulation form beneath the matrix. The first three persons have already been entered into the data matrix and tabulation form, so there are just 95 more to go!

When you know with what frequency each combination occurs, you have the information you need to carry out a causal analysis of the relationship between sex, occupation and income. First, you have to decide how the variables are to be entered into the causal model on which you base the analysis. Then it's a matter of finding the relevant proportions and differences in proportions in order to establish the size of the causal components you are looking for.

Thus, you will finally be in a position to say something about what

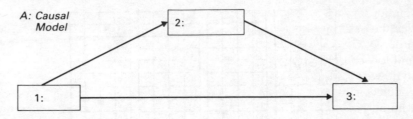

A: Causal Model

B: Bivariate association for 1:   & 3:

Absolute frequencies		Proportions	
3:	1:	1:	
			Differences
------	------	------	------
Sum			

C: Bivariate association for 2:   & 3:

Absolute frequencies		Proportions	
3:	2:	2:	
			Differences
------	------	------	------
Sum			

D: Trivariate association for 1:   ,2:   & 3:

Absolute frequencies				Proportions			
1:							
2:							
3:							
---	---	---	---	---	---	---	---
Sum							

E: Proportion on 3: depending on 1 & 2

2:     1:   Difference

Difference

F: Causal decomposition of bivariate associations

Components in association between	1: & 3:	2: & 3:
Gross association:		
Causal effect: . . . . Direct effect: . . . . Indirect effect: . . . . Spurious effect:		

difference a difference in sex or occupation does make for the income differences – and how.

1.2 Sex and Legislative Career

In the elections to the Norwegian Parliament in 1973 and 1977 the proportion of female representatives increased markedly, from less than one-tenth in the 1960s to 0·16 and then 0·24 (Skard 1980). When the leadership positions within the assembly are filled, seniority is an important although not decisive factor, which necessarily works to the disadvantage of the recently arrived female representatives. An interesting question is whether the sex of a representative in itself influences the chances for recruitment to high-ranking positions. Are female representatives favoured to compensate for their lack of seniority, or are there on the contrary indications of direct discrimination against them?

The data matrix gives information on sex, seniority and rank for representatives from the two major Norwegian parties for the period 1973–81. Specify a causal model for the three variables, and analyse the relationship between sex and rank, and between seniority and rank, within each of the parties.

Sex	Seniority	Rank	Labour Party	Conservatives
Male	High	High	41	23
Male	High	Low	46	15
Male	Low	High	0	1
Male	Low	Low	21	14
Female	High	High	11	4
Female	High	Low	5	6
Female	Low	High	4	1
Female	Low	Low	10	6

Seniority is measured as number of sessions attended (high: 4 or more, low: 0–3). Rank refers to whether or not a representative has been elected to a leadership position in the Storting (Parliament) or one of its two sections, in a standing committee or a party group.

1.3 Opinions about Promotion Opportunity in the American Army

Below a table based on a chart from the seminal study of army life during the Second World War, *The American Soldier: Adjustment during Army Life* (Stouffer et al. 1949: 253; also printed in Lazarsfeld and Rosenberg 1955: 143), shows how satisfaction with promotion opportunities seems to depend on expectations rather than actual openings. Within the categories where the probability of promotion was highest (education high, Service Air Corps), the percentage finding the chances for promotion for an able soldier 'very good' is the lowest. Here there is nothing spectacular about being promoted, while not to earn a rating is felt to be more of a failure.

Use the information in the table to perform a causal analysis of the relation between education, rank and opinion on promotion for each of the two branches of service separately.

Opinion about Promotion Opportunity (white enlisted men in the army 1 to 2 years, continental United States. Military Police data from representative cross-section of MPs, 1944; Air Corps data are a segment from a representative cross-section of all white EM 1944)

Question: '*Do you think a soldier with ability has a good chance for promotion in the army?*'

Branch: Rank: Education:	Military Police				Air Corps			
	Noncoms		PVTs/PFCs		Noncoms		PVTs/PFCs	
	Low (%)	High (%)	Low (%)	High (%)	Low (%)	High (%)	Low (%)	High (%)
Very good	58	27	33	21	30	19	20	7
Fairly good	29	45	35	36	39	44	42	27
Undecided	5	8	9	12	10	3	5	6
Not much/none	8	20	23	31	21	34	33	60
Sum	100	100	100	100	100	100	100	100
(N)	(165)	(241)	(707)	(470)	(70)	(152)	(79)	(123)

1.4 Analyse a Table of Your Own Choosing

An inexhaustible data source for causal analyses is the multivariate tables found in research monographs and journals. Look through the literature for a trivariate percentage table which in your opinion provides an interesting basis for a causal analysis. A prerequisite is that the table gives information on the bases for the percentages (the number of units within each group), so that you can reconstruct the bivariate tables you need to establish gross associations.

Specify a causal model for the variables in the table, perform the analysis and comment on the results.

2

The Meaning and Measurement of Causal Effect

2.1 Theoretical Definitions of Causal Effect

Most social scientists applying causal reasoning to empirical research problems probably do not worry much about the extensive philosophical debate concerning this concept. Cause, effect and similar terms seem clear enough as used in everyday language. Being pressed for a theoretical definition of what is meant by a causal variable, the following two examples may be taken as representative of the likely answers. The first comes from a classic in the sociological literature on causal analysis, the second from one of the most widely used computer packages today:

> If X is a cause of Y, we have in mind that a change in X produces a change in Y, and not merely that a change in X is followed by or associated with a change in Y. (Blalock 1961: 9)

> X_1 is a cause of X_0 if and only if X_0 can be changed by *manipulating* X_1 and X_1 alone . . . It [the notion of causality] implies the notion of possible manipulation. (Nie *et al.* 1975: 384)

The conception of a causal effect as an immediate change in Y when X is manipulated or changes, is tied to the classical experimental situation. For the same reasons which restrict the use of experiments in most fields of social research, such a notion does not cover the actual use of the concept of a causal variable. Important sociological variables, such as marital or occupational status, to take two examples from the individual level, cannot be changed according to the wishes of the researcher. For other variables, such as sex or place of birth, it is not only manipulation that is out of the question, individuals do not change value at all. Finally, the time which elapses from the assignment of value on the causal variable (place of birth) until the effect may be registered (on the educational level attained) can be of considerable length.

That a variable like sex cannot be manipulated or changed at all, does not prevent sociologists from asserting that the sex of a person influences other aspects of his or her existence. This probably is done on the basis of a conception of some kind of social process resulting in the assignment or change of the value on a dependent variable Y, where the course of this process is supposed to be different depending upon whether the individual is male or female. In other words, the probability of attaining a certain value on Y is influenced by the value held on X.

Instead of an effect of a change in X, we in this case may talk about the effect of a *substitution*, how the outcome of the social process is influenced when a unit of analysis (in our case a person) is substituted for another who is alike in all relevant aspects except for a different value on X. How will, for instance, the process leading up to the decision reached by the court in a criminal case be altered if we substitute a defendant with low social status with another who has high status, but otherwise is identical with the first defendant with regard to all characteristics that may influence the outcome of the process?

The phrase 'alike in all relevant aspects' needs further clarification. It refers to variables whose values are obtained or changed *prior* to the value on X, and which also influence the process determining the value on Y. Since X cannot have any influence 'backwards' in time on these variables, we have to make sure that the units with different value on X to be substituted for each other are similar with regard to the prior variables. Otherwise their effect on Y will be mixed up with the effect of the substitution with regard to X.

Concerning variables whose value is determined *after* X but prior to Y in time, we do not require similar values for the units which are substituted. On the contrary, acquiring dissimilar values on these variables, which in turn influence the probability of obtaining a certain value on Y, is an example of how X may influence the outcome of the social process under investigation, in this case *indirectly* through intervening variables.

The difference in probability resulting from a substitution of units which are similar with regard to both prior and intervening variables, constitutes the *direct effect* of X on Y.

Figure 2.1 represents an attempt at a graphic illustration of this discussion of how the concepts of cause and effect may be linked to a social process where the outcome – which value the units obtain on the effect variable – depends upon what values they have on a set of prior variables.

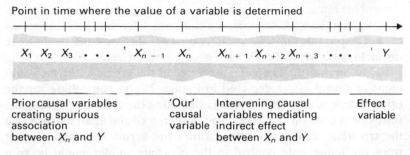

Point in time where the value of a variable is determined

X_1 X_2 X_3 . . . X_{n-1} X_n X_{n+1} X_{n+2} X_{n+3} . . . Y

| Prior causal variables creating spurious association between X_n and Y | 'Our' causal variable | Intervening causal variables mediating indirect effect between X_n and Y | Effect variable |

Figure 2.1   *Causal process.*

The effect on the outcome of a social process of a substitution of units which are identical with regard to other causal variables than X is a theoretical conception which cannot be directly observed in the real world. To obtain an empirical measure of causal effect we compare the distribution on Y for units which differ with regard to value on X. Disturbing influences from other variables we may try to avoid by keeping these variables constant, as illustrated in Chapter 1. But what happens if this control is incomplete, if relevant variables are left out? Is it possible to adopt other approaches in our effort to obtain an empirical measure of causal effect that is not contaminated by other variables? These questions are discussed in the next section.

2.2   Measuring Causal Effect: the Control Problem

If we had conducted the analysis of court decisions in Chapter 1 on the basis of a bivariate model where either social status or record had been left out, the results reached would have been misleading. The model would have been incorrect in the sense that a *relevant variable* was missing. By this is meant a variable which is associated with (at least) two of the variables in a model, that is, acts as a prior or intervening variable in relation to variables included in the model.

If we had calculated the direct effect of record on sentence without controlling for social status, the result would have included a component of spurious effect in addition to the direct effect. Inadequate control for prior variables thus contaminates our measure of causal effect.

If we had calculated the direct effect of social status on sentence without controlling for record, that is, failed to control for an intervening variable, a component of what we take to be direct effect actually is indirect effect. Ordinarily we would consider a failure to control for intervening variables as a less serious error than shortcomings in the control for prior variables. Clearly, the distinction between spurious and causal effect is of greater importance than the distinction between the two kinds of causal effect.

In our analysis in Chapter 1 we avoided the errors in the measurement of causal effect depicted in Figure 2.2 by controlling for the other independent variable when calculating the effect of either social status or record on sentence. The outcome of the analysis based on the trivariate model also showed that the errors that would result from the inadequate control in the bivariate model would be of a moderate size. For both causal variables, the major part of the bivariate association with sentence comes out as a direct effect in the trivariate analysis. This we would not know, however, without the proper control for the prior or intervening variable.

This points to the general problem of multivariate analysis. We can never be certain that we have controlled for all relevant variables, or know for sure what the consequences of possible omissions are for the results we have reached. No matter how reasonable the trivariate model for status, record and sentence may seem to us, there may still be variables we have overlooked. And even if we are able to control for one, or two or more additional variables, the possibility still exists that a variable for which we lack data or have not at all thought about does influence our measure of the causal effect of X on Y. This situation is illustrated in Figure 2.3.

In practice our confidence in the results of a multivariate analysis will depend on our ability to control for what we consider to be the most likely confounding variables. There is another approach to the

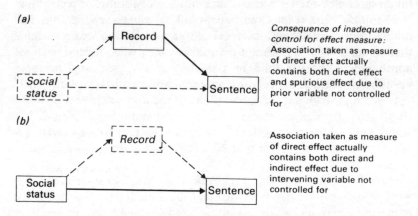

Figure 2.2   *Implications of failure to control for prior or intervening variable.*

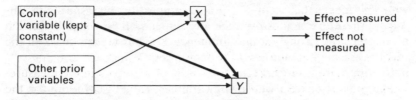

Figure 2.3   *Multivariate analysis with statistical control.*

control problem, however, by means of which we may eliminate completely the risk of contaminating influence from prior variables, be they known or unknown to us. This approach, called the *experimental design*, is first and foremost utilised in the natural sciences.

In order to perform an experiment, a researcher must be able to control the assignment of values on the causal variable X to the units to be studied. Or as it is known in the scientific jargon, he must be able to *manipulate X*. In this way he can make sure that what units get a high and what units a low value on X is randomly decided, so that no other characteristic of the units has any influence on their chances of acquiring any specific value on this variable.

In its simplest form an experiment is carried out by distributing the units in two groups (the experimental group and the control group) by means of a random selection procedure. The researcher then takes the necessary steps to provide the units in the experimental group with a high value on X, and the units in the control group with a low value. The difference thereafter found between the two groups in the proportion of units which has a high value on the effect variable Y is taken as a measure of the causal influence of X on Y.

The implications of such a procedure are shown in Figure 2.4. The random selection of units to the two groups has the effect of making them similar with regard to all prior variables. There will be approximately corresponding proportions of men and women, vegetarians and meateaters, extroverts and introverts, or what have

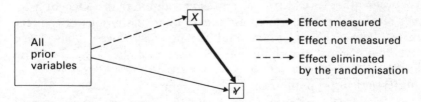

Figure 2.4   *Experiment with control through randomisation.*

you. This means that no prior variable can possibly be associated with X, and therefore cannot produce any association between X and Y, no matter how strongly it may influence Y. Thus we are guaranteed that the association measured between X and Y in an experiment will not contain any spurious effect.

This way of dealing with prior variables, called *randomisation*, is extremely effective in that all such variables are taken care of through the random assignment of value on the causal variable. In contrast to a multivariate analysis, we do not need to have data on a variable we wish to control for, or even be aware of its existence. Why, then, are experiments so rare in most fields of social research?

As pointed out in the preceding section, some variables have fixed values, such as the sex of a person or the location of a city, and therefore cannot be randomly assigned to the units. Other variables will not be manipulable for practical or ethical reasons. We might, for instance, contemplate an experimental study of the impact of the social status of a defendant on the decision reached by the court by withholding the correct information on his social situation from the court, and instead provide him with a randomly decided status. Possible scientific merits notwithstanding, the prospects for being allowed by the legal authorities to interfere with the court proceedings in this way would seem bleak.

Even in situations where randomisation is feasible, the precautions necessary for carrying out an experiment may require creating an artificial social setting for the kind of social process we want to investigate. The very act of removing the influence from prior variables on the causal variable implies a situation which deviates from the ordinary social setting where they would be related. We might, for instance, conduct simulated trials in which students with a randomly assigned status acted as defendants. The question is how much the results of such an experiment would tell us about the real-life court proceedings in which we are interested.

An advantage of multivariate analysis in relation to the classical experimental design is the information it supplies on the relationship between other variables in the model in addition to the effect of X on Y, making it possible to assess the amount of spurious or indirect effect between X and Y. In a multivariate analysis we will also learn whether X interacts with the control variables in their effect on Y, by providing us with a set of partial associations and not just one difference in proportions as in the experiment.

If the partial associations actually are dissimilar, we find the overall effect of X by weighting each partial effect by the relative size of the control group for which it applies. If the relative sizes of the control groups in the sample of units we analyse should happen not to be representative of the population of units about which we want to make statements, we would use the correct proportions for the population as weights. Such a correction is impossible in an experiment where the set of units are not representative of the population. A look at the research literature reveals that this is often the case. Participants in experiments tend to be students, conscripts, or other captive groups more easily accessible and controllable for a researcher than a representative sample from the population.

A problem in multivariate analysis is that to control for other variables by means of control groups may require a large number of units. With two dichotomous variables we get four control groups, with three control variables eight groups, and so on, each of which is further divided into two groups according to value on the independent variable when we calculate the association with the dependent variable. Experiments are less 'unit-consuming', all we need is to have large enough experimental and control groups to keep the expected random differences between the two groups within acceptable limits.

Scarcity of available units has sometimes led researchers to adopt a design resembling an experiment in some ways in situations where randomisation is impossible. In experiments a procedure called *matching* may be used to reduce the amount of random differences between experimental and control groups. The units are compared with regard to a set of variables, and pairs of units with identical value combinations are picked out. Within each pair one unit is randomly selected to the experimental group, the other goes to the control group. With regard to the matched variables, the two groups will be exactly identical; with regard to other prior variables, there will only be random differences, smaller the larger the number of units.

If someone other than the researcher controls the assignment of value on X, such as the prosecuting authority with regard to information on criminal records, the randomisation part of the above procedure may have to be omitted. The matching, however, may still be used. From units with dissimilar values on X (for instance, record), we select pairs of units which are similar with regard to other variables we want to control for (for instance, social status). The two matched groups are then compared with regard to the dependent variable. The matched variables cannot possibly have contributed to the association thus found between X and Y, since they will be unrelated to X. Unmatched prior variables will still be a source of contaminating influence on our measure for the causal effect of X on Y, however. (See Figure 2.5.)

Still another approach to the control problem may be encountered in investigations where the number of units studied is particularly low. The analysis may be *restricted* to units with a specific value on one or more control variables, which in this way are turned into *constants* in the data matrix. Since these control variables will be unrelated to both X and Y, they cannot possibly influence the association measured between the two variables in the restricted data matrix. (See Figure 2.6.)

In the study of court decisions this control technique was actually used in combination with the multivariate analysis. The nature of the offence obviously is of prime importance when the court decides how a defendant is to be punished. We also find differences between social groups with regard to the nature of the crimes typically committed by members of a group. A difference in the probability of a severe sentence between defendants with high and low social status may, therefore, be a result of differences in the nature of the offence for which they were convicted – in other words, be an indirect rather than a direct effect of status on sentence. To control for the nature of the offence through a multivariate analysis was impossible in this study due to the low number of occurrences for most kinds of crimes. Instead the analysis was restricted to the one category where the number of units was large enough to permit a trivariate analysis of the

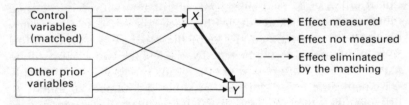

Figure 2.5   *Control through matching.*

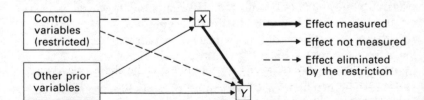

Figure 2.6   *Control through restriction.*

relationships between status, record and sentence, namely, men convicted of larceny. The low number of female defendants explains why the researchers chose to control for sex in addition to offence by means of restriction.

Obviously, all studies may be said to incorporate an element of 'restriction' in the design, as the selection of units to be analysed necessarily will have to be limited in time and space. We may, for instance, study a sample of voters from one nation in a particular election year. Or court decisions within a district of Norway for a ten-year period. Restriction as a special technique for controlling for possibly confounding variables means turning variables which, in fact, do vary for the population which is investigated into constants by excluding all other units than those with a specified value from the analysis.

The research designs relying on matching or restriction to control for prior variables, may be said to combine the drawbacks of both the experiment and the multivariate analysis with few of their advantages. The existence of confounding prior variables cannot be excluded, and we are deprived of information on spurious or indirect effects, or on statistical interaction. In situations where lack of control over the causal variable makes randomisation impossible, and scarcity of units hampers the application of multivariate analysis, they may still prove useful.

The purpose of this discussion has been to explicate the rationale behind the use of multivariate crosstable analysis to measure the causal effect of one variable upon another. The references to the other approaches to the control problem have been intended to highlight the characteristics of the multivariate analysis, its strong as well as weak points. It should be mentioned that more complex experimental designs may be used to overcome some of the problems discussed above with reference to the classical two-group design, for instance, to study interaction between causal variables. Readers interested in this approach to the control problem should consult such excellent texts as Campbell and Stanley (1963) or Cook and Campbell (1979).

Summary

Causal effect has traditionally been defined as the change produced in one variable Y when another variable X is manipulated by the researcher or changes for other reasons. To be able to consider also fixed variables as having causal effect it is suggested causal effect is defined in relation to the substitution of units which differ with regard to X, but are alike with regard to variables determined prior to X in the social process resulting in the assignment of value on Y. The causal effect of X on Y is understood as the impact of the substitution on this process, resulting in a change in the probability of obtaining a certain value on Y.

Empirically we may seek to measure the causal effect of X on Y by taking the difference in proportions from a crosstable which has X as independent and Y as the dependent variable. Similarity with regard to prior variables is approached by controlling for variables deemed to be relevant.

Other approaches intending to prevent prior variables from contaminating the empirical measure of causal effect work through eliminating the influence of all prior variables on X (randomisation), of some prior variables on X (matching), or on X as well as Y (restriction). Compared to a multivariate crosstable analysis these approaches provide less information on the relationship between X and Y.

Glossary

CAUSAL EFFECT: change in the probability of obtaining a certain value on the effect variable resulting from a substitution of units with dissimilar values on the causal variable and similar values on prior variables (theoretical definition).

CONSTANT: variable whose range is restricted to just one value for the set of units to be analysed.

DICHOTOMY (dichotomous variable): variable with two values.

EXPERIMENT: investigation where the researcher manipulates the causal variable in order to avoid influence from other variables on its relationship with the effect variable.

FIXED VARIABLE: variable where the value of each single unit never changes.

MANIPULATION: the researcher decides (by a random procedure) which value the units are assigned on a causal variable.

MATCHING: selection of units to two groups so as to make them similar with regard to the distribution on one or more control variables, while different with regard to value on the causal variable.

RANDOMISATION: control for prior variables through random selection of units to groups which are assigned different value on the causal variable.

RESTRICTION: control for other variable(s) through restricting the analysis to units with a specific value on the control variable(s).

STATISTICAL CONTROL: control for other variable(s) through multivariate analysis where a partial association between causal and effect variable is calculated for each (combination of) value(s) on the control variable(s).

SUBSTITUTION: exchange of one unit for another with a different value on the causal variable but similar values on prior variables.

Exercises

2.1 Sex Differences in Legislative Career – Direct or Indirect Effect?

The analysis of the Conservative Party in assignment 1.2 showed a direct effect of sex on rank in Parliament when controlling for seniority. We may imagine that the male-dominated party leadership would deny all charges of direct discrimination against female representatives, and instead would claim that the two groups are different with regard to other variables of importance for recruitment to leadership positions.

Discuss possible intervening variables between sex and rank that we might wish to control for, in addition to seniority, in order to increase our confidence in the empirical measure of the direct effect of sex.

2.2 Effect of Criminal Stereotype on Conviction of Homicide Defendants

An American study of the adjudication of homicide defendants concluded that conformity to a popular stereotype of the violent offender (that is, having personal or social characteristics which suggest participation in a culture where the violent response is thought to be normal) has important consequences for the course and final outcome of the judicial process. In the analysis several possible prior or intervening variables with regard to the relationship between conformity to stereotype (called 'the normal primitive') and final conviction were controlled for.

What potential prior variables would you suggest to control for in order to ascertain the causal effect of conformity to the criminal stereotype? What possible intervening variables should be considered in order to find the direct effect of this variable on the final conviction?

2.3 Government Involvement and Income Inequality

A crossnational study of 32 nations sought to assess the importance of direct government involvement in the economy on the degree of income inequality by an analysis on the basis of a four-variable model, which in addition to these two variables incorporated one prior and one intervening variable. What might the prior variable and the intervening variable be, would you suggest?

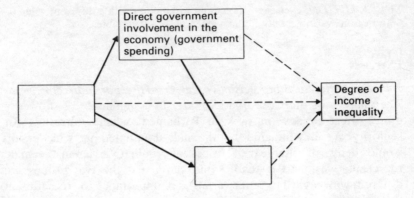

2.4   Pick Your Own Control Problem

Choose a relationship between two variables where you assume one to have a causal effect on the other. Discuss which prior and intervening variables you would like to control for in an empirical study designed to measure this causal effect.

3
Developing Causal Models

3.1 The Choice of Variables

The ingredients used in making a causal model are of two kinds, variables and their relationships. In the next section we shall take a closer look at the various kinds of possible relationships between pairs of variables. But, first, a few words on the selection of variables for a model may be in order. Above all, this is of course a question of knowledge and imagination with regard to the specific social phenomena whose essential features we are trying to capture in the model. Some general guidelines may, however, be indicated.

The basic principle is that of *simplicity*. The variables should be kept as few as possible. There will, of course, be a tradeoff here between simplicity and *realism* of the model. But if the number of variables can be kept down, a theoretical model which is more surveyable, and an empirical analysis which is more manageable, are gained. The more variables included in the model, the larger the number of units required in the analysis to permit the necessary controls when calculating effects. In practice we will often find ourselves confined to work with data matrices of such moderate sizes that we are restricted to operate with models of no more than five, four, or even three variables. This points to the necessity of choosing the variables with care.

When we are considering what variables will be most useful for our model, the answer will depend on the purpose of the analysis. We may distinguish between two different kinds of research problem, which give rise to different criteria for the selection of variables.

In some cases the point of departure for a causal analysis is a bivariate association between a pair of variables. The purpose of the analysis is to *explain why the two variables are related*. By constructing a causal model incorporating variables which are prior to or intervening between the original pair, and performing an empirical analysis based on this model, we may explain the gross association by *decomposing* it into spurious effect due to the prior variables, indirect effect due to the intervening variables, and direct effect.

In selecting variables to accompany the original pair in the model we will look for variables which are highly associated with them both. If a control variable is weakly associated with one of the pair, it cannot possibly produce a spurious or indirect effect of any importance between the two, and thus contribute very little to an explanation of the gross association. (If for any reason there had been strong expectations to the contrary, such a negative result would of course be of interest.)

In other cases the research problem is defined as *explaining the variation in the effect variable*, without having singled out one causal variable for particular attention. In this case we would select causal variables with strong direct effects, since it is the sum of direct effects which constitute the *explanatory power* of the model. Explaining variation in the effect variable is a question of defining groups by means of a set of causal variables which are as different as possible with regard to the proportion of units having a specific value on the effect variable. The amount of variation is displayed in the multivariate table where the units are sorted into groups according to values on all causal variables and compared with regard to distribution on the effect variable. It is the same set of proportions we use to find the direct effects of the variables. In this context indirect or spurious effects are irrelevant.

This means that for this research purpose one will be looking for causal variables which are highly associated with the effect variable, while at the same time weakly associated among themselves. Thus the major part of their association with the effect variable will be a direct effect, rather than spurious or indirect effect due to the other causal variables. (Even better than little or no association between the independent variables is association of the opposite sign as the direct effects on the dependent variable. In this case the direct effects will be larger than the corresponding bivariate associations, since the spurious or indirect effect components are of the opposite sign; compare Exercise 1.1 and Section 4.2 in Chapter 4.)

To illustrate, if we want to explain the association between sex and an effect variable, we would consider occupation, which is highly related to sex, rather than age, which is weakly related, for inclusion in the model. But if our research purpose is to explain the variation in the effect variable, the age variable might be our first choice, provided that the causal variables have gross associations with the effect variable which are of a similar size.

3.2   Relations between Variables

So far, we have just worked with one-way arrows, symbolising a relationship where we assume that the value of a unit on one of the variables is always obtained or changed prior to the value on the other variable. Any causal influence between the two variables would then necessarily have to flow from the former to the latter variable.

We may, however, conceive of quite different kinds of relationship between a pair of variables. There may be no association at all between them, which would be the case with for instance sex and nationality for individuals. Or they may be associated, but without being in our opinion causally related. Such a *non-causal relationship* may be due to both variables having a common cause, or just be a product of chance, and is represented by a curved line (Figure 3.1). The favourite example in methodology textbooks is the association reportedly found between the number of storks and the number of childbirths per family in Danish counties. Another case of greater

Relationship between pair of variables	Time ordering (assumed) for the determination of value on variables	Graphic symbol ——— positive – – – – negative
No association	Irrelevant	X Y
Non-causal association	Irrelevant	 X ⌒ Y
One-way causation	X before Y	 X ⟶ Y
Two-way sequential causation	First X, then Y, then X, etc.	 X ⟞⌒ Y
Two-way simultaneous causation	X and Y simultaneous	 X ⟷ Y
Ambiguous relationship	Uncertain	 X ⌒ Y

Figure 3.1   *Types of relationships between pairs of variables.*

sociological relevance is the tendency for spouses to be of the same social or ethnic origin.

When we suspect a pair of variables to be causally related, the influence in some cases will seem to flow both ways, not just from one variable to the other. We may distinguish between two kinds of such *reciprocal causation* on the basis of whether we are able to study separately the influences running in each direction or not. When our data permit us to locate the effects in opposite directions to separate time intervals, we may talk about *sequential two-way causation*. Otherwise, we have a case of *two-way simultaneous causation*.

When two variables influence each other mutually, the causal process will be of a quite different nature depending upon whether the effects are of the same or of opposite signs. When the variables influence each other in the same direction, that is, both signs positive or both signs negative, we have a case of *positive feedback*. The relationship between prices and wages might serve as an example. Increased wages lead to an increase in prices, which again pushes up wages, and so on. Or to take an example from international politics, the arms race. When nation A increases its armament level, this induces nation B to increase its armament efforts, which in turn makes nation A increase, and so on (Figure 3.2).

The mutually reinforcing influences in a positive feedback cycle make for an unstable situation, the prices and wages will soar to

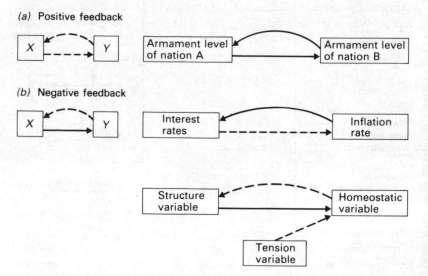

Figure 3.2   *Models with positive or negative feedback.*

higher and higher levels if other causal forces are not brought to bear. Or to take a more gratifying example, a decrease in the armament level of one nation will set off a process of disarmament according to the positive feedback model.

When the variables have reached their extreme values, the mutually reinforcing influences will keep them there unless other variables have counteracting effects. We have a situation which may be termed a *vicious* or a *beneficial circle*, depending upon the characteristics of the case and our normative standards. A vicious-circle argumentation has, for instance, been used to explain the lack of improvement in the economic situation of developing countries, or the preservation of status differences in a political system with equal rights of participation. Low social status implies lack of political resources, which decreases the probability of being politically active, which means decreased probability of exerting any influence on the decisions made by public authorities on the distribution of scarce goods, resulting in a decreased probability of obtaining resources, and so on, round and round in this circle where the variables influence each other indirectly (Martinussen 1977).

When the reciprocal influences are of opposite signs, we have a case of *negative feedback*. This time the variables have a stabilising effect on each other. If a change occurs in one of the variables, this will have an effect on the other variable so as to release a counteracting influence on the first variable. If, due to for instance a decrease in exports, the level of unemployment increases, this in some economies will set off an increase in the level of government expenditures, which in turn will lead to decreased unemployment, thus counteracting the original change in the unemployment variable.

The negative feedback model may be used to define what is meant by a *functionalist explanation* (Stinchcombe 1968). A tension variable (price of imported raw materials) increases, producing a change in a homeostatic variable (inflation rate). This influences the level of a structure variable (interest rates), which releases a counteracting effect on the homeostatic variable, bringing it back to the level before the disturbance.

The last type of relationship shown in Figure 3.1, the curved arrow symbolising an *ambiguous relationship*, is used whenever the researcher is unable to decide what assumption to make concerning the relationship between a pair of variables. Whether the association is non-causal or causal, and eventually in what direction the influence flows, is left open.

This completes our survey of alternative forms of relationships between pairs of variables. We shall now go on to consider the different types of models that may be constructed by combining the various kinds of relationships.

3.3   Types of Models

In order to perform a causal analysis we have to decide on which variables to include, and how we suppose them to influence each other. The assumptions concerning relevant variables and their causal ordering are the minimal assumptions required of any causal model. In addition, we are free to make assumptions concerning the sign or size of the direct effects of a model. We may, for instance, delete an arrow from the diagram, indicating that we assume no direct influence to take place between the pair of variables involved. Or we may indicate that we expect an effect to be positive or negative.

A model where just the minimal assumptions are made, may be called a *general model*. In the diagram the variables assumed to be relevant are arranged according to their causal priority from the left to the right (or from the top down), and all possible effects from prior to later variables are drawn with no indication of sign.

If we make further specifications concerning the sign or size of a relationship, the model may be called *specific*. One general model may give rise to several different specific models – such is the case for the trivariate model involving the sex, seniority and rank of legislators (see Exercise 1.2). By assuming the direct effect of sex on rank to be alternatively positive, zero, or negative, we have specified models with direct discrimination against the women, irrelevance of sex as recruitment criterion, or direct favouring of the women in the recruitment to leadership positions.

In the pioneering work of Paul F. Lazarsfeld on causal analysis by means of crosstables (1955) the focus is on trivariate models made specific by deleting one of the three direct effects of the general model. In this context ideas and concepts central in a causal analysis were developed. Figure 3.3 gives examples of the different types of models you get when a direct effect is assumed – or turns out in the empirical analysis – to be absent.

The specific models of Figure 3.3 may be considered as extreme cases when we move from a strong to a gradually weaker direct effect. In practice the complete absense of an effect will rarely be found, so that the association between X or Y and Z will be mainly, but not wholly, an indirect or a spurious effect.

(a) General model

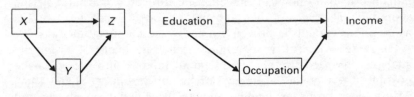

(b) The intervening variable/indirect effect model

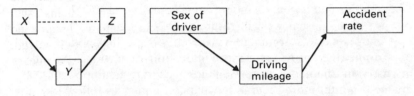

(c) The prior variable/spurious effect model

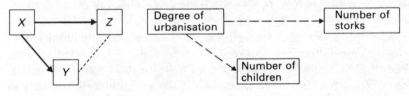

(d) The independent causes model

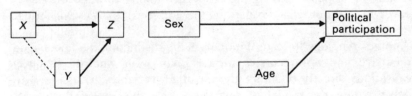

Figure 3.3 *General and specific trivariate models.*

The results of the empirical analysis may show that the assumptions made concerning the sign or size of direct effects were wrong. A specific model is thus *testable*, that is, liable to being disconfirmed by the empirical results. The results will not, however, tell us whether a relevant variable has been left out of the model, or whether an influence actually flows in the opposite direction of what we have supposed. This means that a general model is not testable, its assumptions cannot be proven wrong by the empirical analysis.

On these grounds it is sometimes argued in favour of basing the analyses on specific rather than general models, in order to make possible a test of the 'adequacy' or 'fit' of the model (Land 1969: 34–6). Since such a test involves only the specified direct effects, and not the assumptions made with regard to relevant variables and causal ordering, its scope is rather narrow. We are operating within the framework of one particular general model, and the question is whether alternative general models may be more reasonable than the one we have chosen (we will return to this in Chapter 7).

A more decisive argument in favour of specific models is the opportunity they provide for more interesting deductions. As will be discussed in Chapter 4, by making more accurate assumptions we are enabled to infer more accurately what consequences follow logically from the assumptions.

Specifying models may also be said to increase the readability of the theoretical discussion introducing the empirical analysis. It may be rather dull fare for a reader when the researcher just puts together a general model for a more or less arbitrary selection of variables, and moves swiftly on to the analysis. If we can argue convincingly the case for assuming a direct effect to be absent, or to have a certain sign, it may stimulate the reader's appetite for the empirical analysis to come. If we are even able to justify the possibility of alternative specific models with interesting implications – are the female representatives compensated for their lack of seniority, or are they rather discriminated against? (Exercise 1.2) – we may succeed in creating a feeling of suspense leaving the reader skimming through the pages eager to find out what revelations the empirical analysis will bring.

Another typology for causal models is the distinction made between recursive and non-recursive models, based on whether two-way causation, directly or indirectly via other variables, is assumed to occur within the model or not. In a *recursive model* the causal ordering of the variables is completely transitive, excluding the possibility of reciprocal causation. In a *non-recursive model* the variables are not transitively ordered, allowing a variable to be at the same time influencing and influenced by another variable.

To illustrate this distinction we shall return to the trivariate model discussed in Chapter 1, linking social status, criminal record and sentence (Figure 3.4(*a*)). This is a recursive model. Some readers may have reacted however, against the relationship assumed to exist between social status and record. The dictum 'crime doesn't pay' indicates that in addition to social status influencing the probability of recidivism, recidivism will have a detrimental effect on the social status of a person. An unstable occupational career and a low income

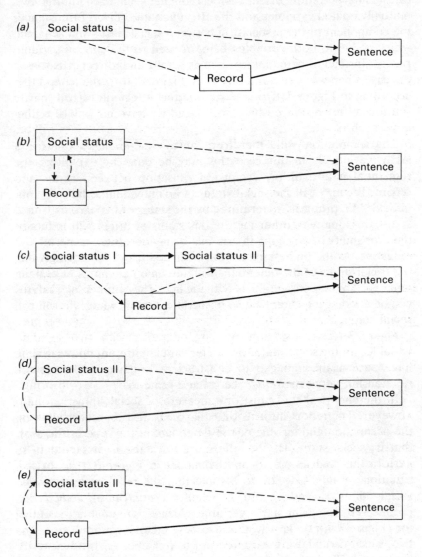

Figure 3.4   *Recursive and non-recursive models.*

at the time of the trial may in many cases be the result of past criminal conduct and conflicts with the law. These considerations may lead us to construct the model depicted in Figure 3.4(*b*). The assumption of two-way causation between social status and record renders the model non-recursive.

With a non-recursive model, we can no longer obtain a complete causal interpretation of the association between each of the two mutually related variables and the effect variable. Take, for instance, the component of the association between social status and sentence which is due to both variables being related to the control variable record. Instead of being interpreted as wholly an indirect effect, as is the case when we base our analysis on Figure 3.4(*a*), the component according to Figure 3.4(*b*) is partly indirect effect via record, partly spurious effect produced by record. And we have no way of telling how much of each.

The temptation will, therefore, always be great to opt for a recursive model. In our case this may be done by exploiting the sequential nature of the reciprocal causation between status and record. We may call the social status of an individual as he starts out in adult life, primarily determined by the status of his parents, social status I. Along with other factors this status of origin will influence the probability of engaging in criminal behaviour, being exposed and punished. At the time of the trial investigated in our research project the social status of the defendant will among other things have been influenced by any past conflicts with the law. The original social status will be another important cause of the later status, which we will call social status II.

Figure 3.4(*c*) shows how we, by operating with two separate variables for the social status of a defendant at different points in time have once again managed to construct a recursive model for the relationship between status, record and sentence.

In the empirical study just one measure of social status is found, however. The report informs that this measure is based on data on the occupation and income of the defendant at the time of the trial, that is, social status II. We, therefore, lack the necessary data to perform an analysis based on the model in Figure 3.4(*c*). In this situation we might decide to assume that the relationship between social status II and record is wholly a non-causal association, produced by the prior status variable which we are unable to control for (Figure 3.4(*d*)). This would also be a recursive model, since the two causal variables are assumed not to influence each other at all.

Or we might decide to leave the whole question of the relationship between social status and record open, by setting up the model shown in Figure 3.4(*e*). Since an ambiguous relation does not exclude the possibility for two-way causation, this model must be considered non-recursive.

3.4 Models as Tools for Text Interpretation

A major asset of causal models is their clarity, once put forward no doubt need exist regarding which variables are assumed to influence each other and how. The same thing cannot be said about social science prose in general. When we read the discussions by different authors of some topic, or even by the same author, we may find it hard to gain a clear understanding of exactly how the social phenomena described are conceived to be related. One way of trying to cope with such a situation is to make an effort at expressing the reasoning of the author(s) by means of a causal model.

The first step in this endeavour will be to read carefully through the text, looking for references to variables and their relationships. After having compiled a list of variables and relationships, the need for collapsing or splitting up variables must be considered. The use of different terms for identical or highly similar concepts is to be avoided for the sake of simplicity. In instances where the same term is used with different connotations, clarity will be increased by defining a different term to cover each separate meaning.

On the basis of the revised list of variables, and the allusions made to relationships between variables, we may present the reasoning implicit in the text in the form of a causal diagram. Finally, we may consider revising the resulting model by altering the direction or sign of a causal effect, by adding or deleting effects, or by adding new variables to the model or removing old ones.

The task of interpreting a text can sometimes be a very difficult one, and the discussion of what an author really meant can go on forever. Instead of pondering the hidden meanings of the text, it may be wise to choose a reasonable interpretation, and then devote the major part of one's effort to an elaboration of this model.

To illustrate how causal models may be used as a tool for text interpretation we shall make use of a short excerpt from the highly stimulating book *Exit, Voice, and Loyalty. Responses to Decline in Firms, Organizations, and States*, by Albert O. Hirschman (1970). The theme of the book is how purchasers of a commodity (or members of an organisation) can express dislike of the firm's product (the organisation's policy) in two different ways, by the use of *exit* or *voice*. They can cease to buy the product (leave the organisation), or complain to the firm (take action within the organisation).

As regards the choice between exit and voice in the event of dissatisfaction, Hirschman states that the former is often preferred, because there is less uncertainty tied to the outcome of the action, and less effort demanded in carrying it through. To change party allegiance is, for example, an easy way out compared with effecting a redirection of a particular party's policy. In this situation *loyalty* comes in as a factor enhancing the chances for a lively internal debate, in that it reduces the inclination to withdraw as soon as dissatisfaction occurs. Hirschman illustrates this point with a discussion of the difference between two-party and multiparty systems (pp. 83–4):

> there should be the possibility of exit, but exit should not be too easy or too attractive as soon as deteroriation of one's own organization sets in.
>
> The correctness of this proposition can be illustrated by the extent to which parties are responsive to the voice of the membership. The parties of totalitarian one-party systems have been notoriously unresponsive – as have been the parties of multi-party systems. In the former case, the absence of the possibility of either voice or exit spelled absolute control of the party machinery by whatever leadership dominated the party. But in the second case, with both exit and voice freely available, internal democracy does not get much of a chance to develop either because, with many parties in the field, members will usually find it tempting to go over to some other party in the case of disagreement. Thus they will not fight for 'change from within'. In this connection it may be significant that Michels' 'Iron Law of Oligarchy' according to which all parties (and other large-scale organizations) are invariably ruled by self-serving oligarchies was based on first-hand acquaintance primarily with the multi-party systems of Continental Western Europe. The best possible arrangement for the development of party responsiveness to the feelings of the members may then be a system with just a very few parties, whose distance from each other is wide, but not unbridgeable. In this situation, exit remains possible, but the decision to exit will not be taken lightheartedly. Hence voice will be a frequent reaction to discontent with the ways things are going and members will fight to make their voice effective. This prediction of our theory is confirmed by the lively internal struggles characteristic of parties existing in two-party systems, however far they may be from being truly democratic.

The discussion involves units at three different levels, individual members, parties and political systems. If we confine our attention to characteristics of political systems referred to in the text, at least the following four can be found: the *number of parties* within the political system, the amount of *exit* or *voice* resorted to by the members of parties, the *responsiveness* of the party leaders to membership opinion. Disregarding one-party systems it is stated that many parties increase the level of exit compared with few parties, a high rate of exit reduces the amount of voice, and little internal debate (voice) reduces the responsiveness of the leaders to the preferences of the members. One way of expressing the reasoning in the text is thus the causal model in Figure 3.5(*a*).

If we reread the excerpt once more to see if there is anything else implied in the text than what is already included in the model, one

(a) Original model based on the excerpt from Hirschman's book

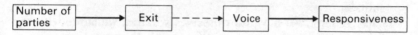

(b) Model extended with two variables

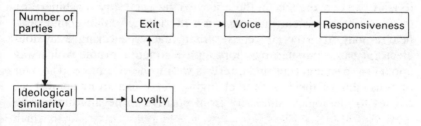

(c) Revised version of extended model

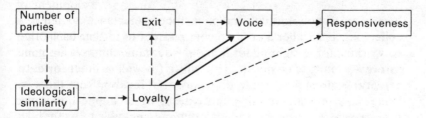

Figure 3.5   *Models for the relationship between number of parties and responsiveness of party leaders.*

aspect that may be taken up is the relation between the number of parties and the inclination to withdraw. Hirschman's argumentation may seem to include an assumption to the effect that the more parties there are, the more will they *resemble each other ideologically*. Further, an implicit assumption might be that the more similar the parties are in terms of policies pursued, the less *loyalty* will the members feel towards them. As previously mentioned, Hirschman elsewhere in the book argues that the more loyal a member feels, the less likely he is to exit.

We may thus extend the causal chain of the original model with two new variables (Figure 3.5(*b*)). With an increasing number of parties, the ideological similarity of the parties is assumed to increase, and a high degree of similarity between the parties will reduce the amount of loyalty towards the party among the members. If we decide that the model as it now stands captures the essence of the author's reasoning, it is time to consider whether revisions in our opinion may be needed.

As a beginning, we may ask ourselves whether we agree with the signs given to the direct effects in the model. Is it not, for example, conceivable that the relationship between the number of parties and ideological similarity is negative? In a two-party system the fight for the voter in the middle in order to gain a majority of the vote seems to lead to a convergence in the policy of the contestants. Few parties in a multiparty system may entertain the idea of coming anywhere near a majority, the object is rather that of securing a reliable electoral basis, pursued by adopting a distinctive profile which will appeal to special groups and interests within the electorate. This line of reasoning is the basis for changing the effect from number of parties to ideological similarity from positive to negative in Figure 3.5(*c*).

We may further consider whether additional direct effects can be envisaged. One reviewer of Hirschman's book criticises his understanding of how loyalty works (Barry 1974: 98):

> loyalty does not normally mean a mere reluctance to leave a collectivity but rather a positive commitment to further its welfare by working for it, fighting for it and – where one thinks it has gone astray – seeking to change it. Thus voice (as well as other forms of activity) is already built into the concept of loyalty. Reluctance to leave is not central, but is in many cases a logical implication of the requirements of loyalty since it is often only possible to further the welfare of a collectivity while belonging to it.

One way of expressing this point of view in our model is to add an arrow going from loyalty directly to voice. Another possible objection to Hirschman's argument is that he only takes into consideration the aggregate result of the decisions reached by the members on whether to use voice when explaining the degree of leadership responsiveness. In deciding whether to conform to or neglect the majority view as they perceive it the assessment of possible reactions from the members will necessarily play a part in the deliberations of the leaders. Fear that unpopular decisions will lead to a massive exit may in itself help to ensure responsiveness to the members' wishes, independently of how actively they make use of their voice in order to promote these wishes. While thus loyalty may induce responsiveness indirectly through stimulating the use of voice, it may have a negative direct effect on responsiveness by making it easier for the leadership to ignore the danger of a possible exit of dissatisfied members (Figure 3.5(c)).

Finally, a case of reciprocal causation has been indicated in the revised model. It would seem reasonable to assume that when members engage in the internal debate in an attempt to influence the policy of the party, an increase in the attachment felt towards the party will result. We thus get a direct effect from voice to loyalty, rendering the final result a non-recursive model.

Hirschman assumed the parties of a two-party system to be more responsive than those of a multiparty system. What will the relationship between these two variables be like according to the revised model we have ended up with? If you feel uncertain about the answer, Chapter 4 on making deductions on the basis of causal models may be of help.

Summary

When constructing a model, the number of variables should be kept as low as considerations of its realism permit. The choice of variables will depend upon the purpose of the analysis, whether we want to explain the association between a pair of variables or the variation in an effect variable.

In describing the relationship between a pair of variables we in addition to one-way causation may assume the absence of any association, or association which is non-causal, or two-way simultaneous or sequential influence with positive or negative feedback, or – if we feel unable to make any definite assumptions with regard to the nature of the relationship – characterise it as ambiguous.

Models may be classified as general or specific depending upon whether the assumptions made are restricted to what variables to include in the model and how to order them, or in addition specifications with regard to the sign or size of effects are made. The distinction between recursive and non-recursive models is based on whether the possibility of reciprocal causation may be excluded or not.

Glossary

AMBIGUOUS RELATIONSHIP: association between a pair of variables where no assumption of the causal nature of the relationship is made.

CAUSAL ORDERING: ranking of the variables according to their time priority, establishing the direction of possible causal influence between them.

EXPLANATORY POWER: sum of all direct effects in the model on a variable.

GENERAL MODEL: model where only the minimum required assumptions concerning what variables to include and how to order them are made.

NEGATIVE FEEDBACK: reciprocal influences which have opposite signs.

NON-CAUSAL RELATIONSHIP: association between a pair of variables which is explicitly assumed not to be the result of causal influence between them.

NON-RECURSIVE MODEL: model where reciprocal influence may occur.

ONE-WAY CAUSATION: relationship between a pair of variables where the causal influence is assumed to flow in one direction only.

POSITIVE FEEDBACK: reciprocal influences which have identical signs.

RECURSIVE MODEL: model where reciprocal influences cannot occur.

SEQUENTIAL CAUSATION: two-way causation where the reciprocal influences may be separated in time.

SIMULTANEOUS CAUSATION: two-way causation where the reciprocal influences cannot be separated in time.

SPECIFIC MODEL: model where assumptions concerning the sign or size of effects are made.

TWO-WAY CAUSATION: reciprocal influences between a pair of variables.

Exercises

3.1 Robert Michels and the Iron Law of Oligarchy

The book *Political Parties* by Robert Michels, first published in Germany in 1911, is a classic in the study of the internal processes in parties and organisations. Here the Iron Law of Oligarchy, the inevitability with which the development of large-scale working-class organisations produces a group of leaders which use the organisation to further its own interests at the expense of the members, is forcefully put forward. The argumentation for this thesis is extensive and replete with empirical illustrations, but can hardly be said to excel with regard to rigour and precision. It has, for instance, been asserted that the very concept of oligarchy is used in at least ten different senses in the 300-page book (Linz 1968). The result has been widely divergent opinions on what Michels actually meant (May 1965).

Below, an excerpt from the book (1966: 108–9) is given. Try to express the causal reasoning contained in the verbose discussion by Michels in the form of a causal model:

> But the level of instruction among the leaders of working-class origin is no longer the same as that of their former workmates. The party mechanism, which, through the abundance of paid and honorary posts at its disposal, offers a career to the workers, and which consequently exercises a powerful attractive force, determines the transformation of a number of proletarians with considerable intellectual gifts into employees whose mode of life becomes that of the petty bourgeois. This change of condition at once creates the need and provides the opportunity for acquisition, at the expense of the mass, of more elaborate instruction and a clearer view of existing social relationships. Whilst their occupation and the needs of daily life render it impossible for the masses to attain a profound knowledge of the social machinery, and above all of the working of the political machine, the leader of working-class origin is enabled, thanks to his new situation, to make himself intimately familiar with all the technical details of public life, and thus to increase his superiority over the rank and file. In proportion as the profession of politician becomes a more complicated one, and in proportion as the rules of social legislation become more numerous, it is necessary for one who would understand politics to possess wider experience and more extensive knowledge. Thus the gulf between the leaders and the rest of the party becomes ever wider, until the moment arrives in which the leaders lose all true sense of solidarity with the class from which they have sprung, and there ensues a new class-division between ex-proletarian captains and proletarian common soldiers. When the workers choose leaders for themselves, they are with their own hands creating new masters whose principal means of domination is found in their better instructed minds.

3.2 Hypotheses on Social Differences in Political Participation

Texts will be more or less lucid and precise in their discussion of a problem. If Michels represents one extreme of this continuum, we may let an excerpt from the book *Human Behavior. An Inventory of Scientific Findings*, by Berelson and Steiner, exemplify the other (1964). The book attempts a survey of well-substantiated findings in the behavioural sciences, in the form of a systematic list of hypotheses. Below, is a selection taken from the section on political institutions (pp. 423–5, references to the research literature have been deleted).

Draw a causal diagram to represent the hypotheses. Discuss how this model might be revised.

If you were to select two independent variables from this model to perform an analysis with the purpose of explaining as much of the variation in political participation as possible, which two would you consider?

If you were interested in explaining the relationship between place of residence and political participation, which one of the other causal variables in the model would you suggest to include in a trivariate analysis?

C 13   The higher a person's socioeconomic and educational level – especially the latter – the higher his political interest, participation, and voting turnout.

C 14   Men are more politically active than women.

C 15   Middle-age groups are more active politically than young adults or the old.

C 16   Urban residents are somewhat more active politically than rural residents, especially with regard to national affairs.

3.3   Choose Your Own Text for Interpretation

Select one or more articles or books on a topic of your choice. Set up a list of the variables used in the discussion, and the relationships suggested between the variables. Develop a causal model to represent the text(s) surveyed. Discuss if, and eventually how, the resulting model might be revised.

4

Deductions from Causal Models

In Chapter 3 we saw how causal models may serve as instruments for clarifying our thoughts about the influences at work in a social process, by forcing us to make explicit what variables we believe to be relevant and what kind of relationship they have to each other. Once these assumptions, embodied in the final version of our causal model, are made, consequences with regard to the statistical association between the variables can be deduced.

Deduction means finding out what implications logically follow from our assumptions, what we have in fact already assumed but are not yet aware of. In this chapter we will be concerned with how to make correct deductions so as to arrive at results that are *logically valid*. Whether they are also *empirically tenable*, is another matter to be settled by the outcome of empirical analyses.

As will be demonstrated in the last section of this chapter, it is easy to deceive oneself when making deductions. A proposition on the relationship between two variables which seems to be a necessary consequence of our assumptions may turn out to be invalidly deduced. By basing our deductions on causal models, we may avoid such pitfalls.

4.1 The Sign of Spurious or Indirect Effects

In all causal models assumptions with regard to what variables to include and how they are ordered causally are made. By assuming that all relevant variables have been included, so that no variable outside the model which affects one of the variables in the model will at the same time be related to other variables in the model, we can deduce that the relationship between variables in the model will not be affected by outside variables. This assumption permits us to forget about other variables when making further deductions on the basis of the model.

On the basis of the assumptions concerning the causal ordering of the variables we can deduce what kind of effect a variable can produce between other variables in the model, spurious if it is prior to them, indirect if it is intervening.

If a model has been made specific by additional assumptions concerning the sign of direct effects in the model, more interesting implications with regard to the sign of indirect or spurious effects can be deduced by applying the *sign rule:*

> *The sign of an indirect effect of* X *on* Y *equals the product of the signs of each of the direct effects included in the chain of effects between intervening variables linking* X *and* Y.

> *The sign of a spurious effect between* X *and* Y *equals the product of the signs of the effect which the prior variable has on each of the two variables* X *and* Y.

When we multiply two effects with similar signs (both positive or both negative), the result is positive. When the effects are of opposite signs, the product becomes negative:

> *Generally speaking, the product will be positive when there is an even number of negative effects (0, 2, 4, etc.), and negative when the number is odd (1, 3, 5, etc.).*

If the rationale for this rule is not intuitively evident, some examples may be helpful. In Figure 4.1 three models with varying constellations with regard to the signs assumed for the direct effects are displayed.

If we consider the *indirect effects* in Figure 4.1, it would seem obvious that an increase in the probability of a high income caused by having 'high' education will benefit the men if they have a greater chance of acquiring high education than the women. In other words, two positive direct effects in a path produce a positive indirect effect (Figure 4.1(*a*)). Or that, if being in a hospital reduces one's risk of dying, the reduced probability of being hospitalised for healthy people actually implies an increase in their mortality risk. Two negative direct effects result in a positive indirect effect (Figure 4.1(*b*)).

The growth in the educational system means that the older generation had less opportunity of obtaining high education than the younger generation. If high education increases the chances of having a high income, this works to the disadvantage of older people. In

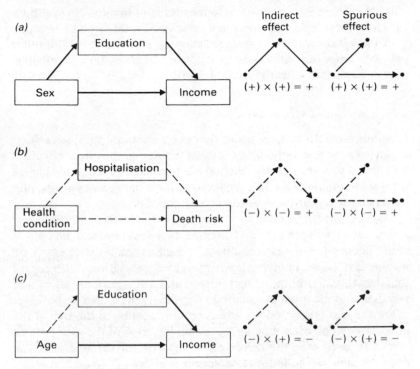

Figure 4.1   *Deduction of sign of indirect or spurious effect.*

other words, a path with a negative and a positive direct effect produces a negative indirect effect (Figure 4.1(c)).

Turning to the signs of *spurious effects* we may start by considering the two positive effects from the prior variable sex in Figure 4.1(a). These two effects imply that we frequently will find a high education combined with a high income (in males), and likewise a low education combined with a low income (in females). In other words, there will be a positive association between education and income which is a result of the effects of the sex variable, a non-causal association. Similarly, since good health reduces the chances of going to hospital as well as the risk of dying, a tendency for positive values to be combined for the latter two variables will result (healthy people stay out of hospitals, and alive). In other words, two negative effects from the prior variable produce a positive spurious effect (Figure 4.1(b)).

If on the other hand being of age means a reduced probability for having a high education, and at the same time an increased probability for a high income (due to seniority), the implication will be a tendency for a high value on the education variable to be combined with a low income (among younger people), and vice versa (for older people). Opposite influences from prior variables thus result in a negative spurious effect (Figure 4.1(c)).

4.2   The Sign of Gross Associations

It is thus possible to deduce the sign of indirect and spurious effects on the basis of assumptions concerning the sign of the direct effects in a model. From the results reached we may then proceed to deduce what sign is implied for the gross association between two variables by adding together its constituent components.

Looking at the model in Figure 4.1(a) the sign of the gross associations between sex and income or education and income is easily deduced. For sex, the direct as well as the indirect effect on income is positive, implying a positive gross association. With regard to education, both the direct effect and the spurious effect are positive, and the gross association accordingly must also be positive.

For the two other models, however, the question of the sign of the gross association cannot be answered on the basis of the assumptions made. In each case the direct effect of a causal variable is of the opposite sign as the indirect or spurious effect. The result reached when summing the components of a gross association will, therefore, depend on which of the components is the stronger. In the next section we shall discuss how the size of a spurious or indirect effect can be deduced if we are willing to make explicit assumptions regarding not only the sign, but also the size of the direct effects of the model.

Even as they stand, however, the models in Figure 4.1(b) and (c) have interesting implications. We can deduce that the direct effect of a causal variable will be larger than the gross association with the effect variable, in contrast to the situation in Figure 4.1(a), where the direct effect will be smaller. This means that failing to control for the prior or intervening variable (that is, erroneously taking the gross association as a measure of the direct effect) will for the first model lead us to *exaggerate* its size, while for variables in the last two models we will *underrate* it.

In the empirical world there seems to be a tendency for variables to affect each other in such a way as to produce spurious or indirect effects of the same sign as the direct effect of a causal variable. We have the situation depicted in the model in Figure 4.1(a), where the direct effect is smaller than the gross association. Although they may be rare, situations of the kind exemplified in the last two models, where the variables affect each other in such a way as to produce components of opposite signs, imply results which may be surprising and therefore of great interest. A causal variable seemingly unrelated to an effect variable (or strangely related, as hospitalisation with a high risk of death) turns out to have a causal impact which did not show up in the gross association due to the influence of a prior *'suppressor'* variable. Or a small causal effect turns out to be the result of direct and indirect effects balancing each other by working in opposite directions.

4.3 The Size of Spurious or Indirect Effects and Gross Associations

As will be demonstrated in Chapter 5 on designs for causal analysis, it is not only the *sign* of an indirect or spurious effect that can be found by multiplication of direct effects, but also the *size*. Strictly speaking we are guaranteed completely accurate results only when using standardised regression coefficients to measure the direct effects, a problem we will return to in Chapters 8 and 9. But also with the kind of effect measures we are using, weighted averages of proportion differences, we will in most cases come quite close.

If we are willing to make assumptions concerning the strength of the direct effects in our model, we can thus deduce the approximate size of an indirect or spurious effect. Adding together the relevant components we arrive at the implied size of the gross association. We will, however, seldom be in a position to make such accurate assumptions with regard to the effects in the model with any reasonable justification, thus rendering the deduced consequences of limited interest.

One instance where deductions concerning the size of an indirect or spurious effect may be useful, however, is a situation where we want to appraise the consequences of leaving a variable we believe to be relevant out of the model on which we base the analysis, for lack of data or other reasons. Perhaps prior empirical studies exist which provide guidelines for the assumptions we make with regard to the unknown effects. Or we may just specify a set of alternative assumptions, and deduce the resulting component in the association between other variables in the model under each alternative. In this way we may form an opinion on how the shortcomings of the model will influence the results of the analysis.

As an illustration, we may take the case of a missing intervening variable where we assume one of the direct effects in the path to be of the size 0·5, and the other 0·4. This implies an indirect effect of 0·2, indicating that if the intervening variable had been included in the analysis, the direct effect would be 0·2 lower than what we actually found. Often we may have good reasons for setting the upper limits of the unknown effects lower than the above example, indicating that the errors resulting from leaving the variable out of the analysis will be minor.

4.4   Exploiting the Potentials of Deductive Reasoning: an Illustration

As one becomes familiarised with the rules for making deductions from causal models some readers may find the procedures so straightforward and the results so obvious that the entire enterprise seems like a rather dull formal exercise. A closer look at the scientific literature will reveal, however, that even some of the best works would have profited from utilising the possibilities for causal deductions. The seemingly 'trivial' results are not always as easily seen as one might have imagined.

As an illustration we shall take an issue in the prolonged debate within political science on the relationship between social status and political participation in democracies. Numerous empirical studies from a wide range of countries have invariably shown members of high-status groups to be more active in politics than low-status citizens. This was also the conclusion of one study based on interviews with a representative sample of Norwegians (Martinussen 1977). The picture painted of a socially biased political participation constituting a threat to democratic values has since been challenged by another book (Lafferty 1981).

The critique opens with a discussion of whether bivariate differences in proportions of magnitudes from 0·10 to 0·20 between social status variables and various political activities can reasonably be termed strong and regarded as a threat to political equality. For our purpose of demonstrating the utility of deductive reasoning, the next question is the interesting one. Given these bivariate associations, what kind of relationships between the status variables themselves would be most beneficial for political equality?

To put it more concretely: if we have found a bivariate association between, say, education and membership in parties of 0·25, and between income and membership of 0·20, would the relationship between education and income be of any consequence for the social bias in party membership?

The participants in the debate seem to take it for granted that positively correlated status variables would aggravate the problem of social bias in political participation. The reason for this may be that *positively related* status variables implies that resources will tend to be *cumulated* in the hands of some people, while others lack them completely. If a high education tends to go together with a high income, a substantial part of the population will have the benefit of possessing both these resources for political participation, while another group is totally deprived of resources by combining a low education with a low income.

Unrelated status variables would mean that a high status on one variable did not affect the chances of being well-off on the other variable as well. Such an *unsystematic* distribution of resources would, compared to the cumulative pattern, increase the number of people possessing just one resource, and reduce the size of the two extreme groups of people with either two or no resources.

If the status variables had been *negatively* related, the combination of one high and one low value on the two variables would be the dominant pattern, with just a few people being better or worse off with regard to resource possession. We would have a *dispersed* distribution, where the lack of one kind of resource tends to be compensated by access to the other.

The dispersed distribution is clearly the most egalitarian, placing the major part of the population on an equal footing with regard to resources for political participation. The cumulative pattern in contrast implies that large groups will differ markedly when it comes to control over resources. There thus may seem to be little reason for questioning the contention that positively related resources is the pattern most detrimental to the prospects for attaining a socially unbiased political participation.

At this point a warning-bell ought to sound in the mind of a person well acquainted with causal deductions. There is more to the problem than the matter of distribution of resources considered so far. The nature of the association between the independent variables will, as we have seen, also affect what happens to their relationship with the dependent variable as we turn from the bivariate association to association controlled for the other independent variables.

By assuming a *positive association* between education and income we are able to deduce that the direct effect of each variable on political participation will be smaller than the original bivariate associations of 0·25 and 0·20. Small direct effects further mean that the extreme groups with either two or no resources will not be so far apart with regard to the level of participation, as the advantages of resource possession for participation will be modest.

The assumption of *negatively related* status variables on the other hand implies that the variables function as what we have called 'suppressors', meaning that the direct effects will turn out larger than the bivariate associations. Individuals possessing both a high education and a high income will thus have a much higher probability for participation than those lacking both resources.

Figure 4.2 provides a numerical illustration of the main points in the above reasoning, in the form of three fictitious trivariate distributions on two resource variables (R_1 and R_2) and a political activity variable (A). (In the trivariate tables – see Figure 4.2(a) – a high value on any of the variables is designated 1, a low value 0; P_A stands for the proportion of units with a high value on the activity variable.)

Figure 4.2(b) shows that the three cases are identical with regard to the bivariate associations between each of the resource variables and the activity variable (0·25 and 0·20). They differ, however, with regard to the relationship between the two resources. To the left we have a case of positive association (difference in proportions of 0·50), in the middle unrelated resources (0·00) and to the right a situation with negative association (−0·50). (All of these associations are found by collapsing the trivariate table – see Figure 4.2(a) – into the relevant bivariate tables, as the reader may check out.)

In Figure 4.2(c) the implications of each pattern with regard to access to resources are displayed by showing the proportion of all units having two, one, or zero high values on the resource variables. With a positive correlation between R_1 and R_2, the two extreme groups far outnumber the group in the middle with individuals possessing just one resource, contrary to the situation with negative association, where the middle group is the dominant one.

Figure 4.2(d) highlights the other aspect of our discussion, what happens to the relationship between resources and activity when we perform a trivariate analysis to establish the direct effects. (You find the direct effects by calculating the partial effects from the proportions at the bottom of each table in Figure 4.2(a). As you will see, the task has been simplified by making the partials for each independent variable come out identical.)

The results displayed are in accordance with our deductions. With unrelated resource variables, each direct effect equals the corresponding bivariate association (situation in the middle). A positive association between the resource variables will reduce their direct effects on activity compared to the bivariate associations (to the left),

Cumulated resources   Unrelated resources   Dispersed resources

(a) Trivariate distribution for two resource and one activity variable

R_1	0		1	
R_2	0	1	0	1
A 1	112	50	62	225
0	263	75	63	150
Sum	375	125	125	375
P_A	0.30	0.40	0.50	0.60

R_1	0		1	
R_2	0	1	0	1
A 1	56	106	118	168
0	194	144	132	82
Sum	250	250	250	250
P_A	0.22	0.42	0.47	0.67

R_1	0		1	
R_2	0	1	0	1
A 1	0	162	175	112
0	125	213	200	13
Sum	125	375	375	125
P_A	0.00	0.43	0.47	0.90

(b) Bivariate associations

	R_1	R_2
R_2	0.50	—
A	0.25	0.20

	R_1	R_2
R_2	0.00	—
A	0.25	0.20

	R_1	R_2
R_2	−0.50	—
A	0.25	0.20

(c) Distribution of resources

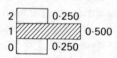

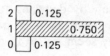

(d) Causal model with direct effects

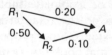

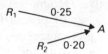

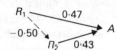

(e) Group sizes and level of participation

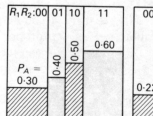

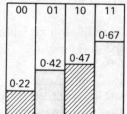

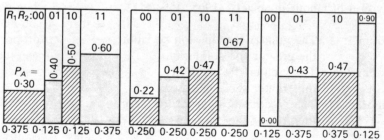

Figure 4.2 *Distribution of resources and political participation.*

while a negative association means that the direct effects increase in strength.

Finally, Figure 4.2(*e*) combines the two aspects of the discussion. The distribution of the population on the resource variables is indicated by the width of the bars, while the effect of resources on the level of participation is given by the differences in height between the shaded parts of the bars. Given a set of bivariate associations between resources and activity, resource cumulation means that the groups of privileged or of deprived citizens will be large, but not too different with regard to the proportion participating in politics. Resource dispersion gives the opposite pattern, relatively few fall in one of the extreme groups with regard to resource possession, but for those who do, there is a tremendous distance in the level of participation between the haves and the have-nots.

We thus seem to be facing a choice between two evils from the point of view of political equality, making a definite conclusion as to whether resource cumulation or dispersion poses the greatest problem for democratic values hard to draw. We were able to reach this result by deducing the consequences of assumptions made in the debate on political participation, consequences which the debaters may seem not to have been aware of.

4.5   A Digression on Axiomatic Theory

In social science deduction has traditionally been tied to systems of propositions called deductive (Homans 1964) or axiomatic theory (Zetterberg 1954). From a set of propositions on the relationship between pairs of variables called postulates or axioms, other propositions called theorems are derived. In the influential book *On Theory and Verification in Sociology* Hans Zetterberg provides us with the following typical example, derived from Durkheim's discussion of the division of labour in society (1965: 159–61):

axiom 1:   The greater the division of labor,
             the greater the solidarity.
axiom 2:   The greater the solidarity,
             the greater the consensus.
theorem 1:   The greater the division of labor,
             the greater the consensus.

Zetterberg presents other axioms and derives more theorems, but as an example of deduction by means of axiomatic theory, the above propositions will suffice. The logical structure of the deduction looks similar to the sign rule we have discussed earlier in this chapter. On the basis of two assumptions of positive relationships between pairs of variables where one variable is part of both pairs, a positive relationship between the remaining two variables is derived.

Such a deduction may appear to be perfectly valid. We may have the feeling that if we accept the assertions made in the axioms, the theorem must necessarily be true. Costner and Leik (1964) demonstrated, however, that contrary to this impression the derived theorem does *not* follow with logical necessity from the axioms. Unless we are prepared to make additional assumptions specifying the association between the variables of the axioms to be extraordinarily strong (between 0·7 and 0·8 or higher), any kind of association between the variables of the theorem – positive, zero, or negative – is in fact compatible with the axioms. It is simply impossible to say anything definite concerning the relationship between division of labour and consensus on the basis of the axioms as stated by Zetterberg.

A simple way of showing why this is so is to transform the axioms into a causal model. When doing this, we make the important observation that nothing about influence, effect, or any other allusions to causality is said in the axioms. If we restrict ourselves to one-way causation, two different interpretations are therefore compatible with each axiom. Division of labour may affect solidarity, or the influence may flow in the opposite direction, to take the first axiom.

If we choose to interpret the axioms so as to make the first variable the causal variable and the second the effect variable, we arrive at the model shown in Figure 4.3(*a*). We have a causal chain where division of labour influences consensus indirectly via solidarity. Assuming that prior or intervening variables related to two or more of those in the model do not exist, by means of the sign rule we can deduce that the association between division of labour and consensus will be positive.

By choosing other causal interpretations of the axioms we may come up with quite different models, however. In Figure 4.3(*b*) the causal direction has been reversed for the second axiom. From the assumption that two variables both influence a third variable, nothing can be deduced with regard to the relationship between them. In the model the variables are assumed to be unrelated. They might also have been positively or negatively related, without violating the assumptions of the axioms.

This goes to show that when the axioms are formulated in terms of association between variables, ambiguities arise which make the

(a) Causal chain interpretation: deduction valid

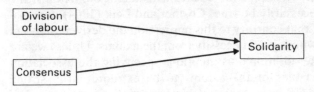

(b) Independent causes interpretation: deduction invalid

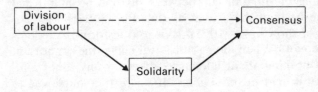

(c) Opposite direct and indirect effects interpretation: deduction invalid

(d) Similar direct and indirect effects interpretation: deduction valid

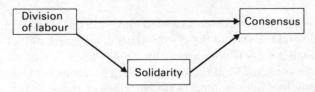

Figure 4.3   *Alternative causal interpretations of Zetterberg's axioms and*
validity of deduced theorem.

axioms unsuitable as a basis for arriving at deductions. Thus it would
seem to solve our problems if we reformulate the propositions in
causal terms:

axiom 1:   an increase in the division of labour
             will lead to an increase in solidarity.
axiom 2:   an increase in solidarity
             will lead to an increase in consensus.
theorem 1:   the greater the division of labour,
             the greater the consensus.

With the new axioms, the causal model in Figure 4.3(*b*) can be ruled out, since the effect from consensus to solidarity in the model violates the assumption of the second axiom. This does not, however, put an end to our problems. Even with the causal axioms, ambiguities remain which mean that the theorem cannot be said to be a necessary consequence of the assumptions made in the axioms.

This time the problem lies in the fact that nothing is said in the axioms about a possible causal relationship between division of labour and consensus. This may be interpreted as signifying an absence of any direct effect, in which case we are back to the causal chain depicted in the model in figure 4.3(*a*) and the theorem is a valid deduction. There is nothing in the axioms that prevents us, however, from assuming a direct effect from division of labour to consensus. If this effect is negative – an assumption that increased division of labour will lead to a decrease in consensus does not appear unreasonable – we have the situation shown in Figure 4.3(*c*). Once again, we have a causal model fully compatible with the assumptions of the axioms, where the derived theorem by no means necessarily follows. Whether the association between division of labour and consensus will be positive, negative, or equal to zero, will depend upon the strength of the opposing direct and indirect effects between the two variables in Figure 4.3(*c*).

If we add an axiom stating the absence of any direct effect between division of labour and consensus (Figure 4.3(*a*)), or that there is a positive direct effect (Figure 4.3(*d*)), we have arrived at causal models where a positive association between the two variables can be deduced. The two original axioms, even when formulated in causal terms, are insufficient as a basis for deducing the theorem.

The conclusion would seem to be obvious: causal models are better instruments for making deductions than axiomatic or deductive theories. When constructing a causal model, we are forced to make explicit our assumptions with regard to the causal relationship between all of the variables, thus precluding the kind of ambiguities that frustrated our efforts at making deductions on the basis of axiomatic propositions.

Summary

Deduction means deriving the logical implications of the assumptions we have made when constructing a causal model. On the basis of assumptions concerning the signs of the direct effects in a model we can deduce what kind of indirect or spurious effect is produced between a pair of variables. The sign of an indirect effect is deduced by multiplying the sign of the direct effects which constitute the indirect path. The sign of a spurious effect is found by multiplying the effects from the prior variable on to each of the two variables in question. If we specify the strength of direct effects, the approximate size of indirect or spurious effects can be deduced in the same way.

Alternative ways of formulating one's assumptions, such as axiomatic theory, may be plagued with ambiguities making it less suited than causal models as an instrument for making logically valid deductions.

Glossary

AXIOM: proposition which is used as a basis for making deductions.

DEDUCTION: deriving of the logical implications of a set of assumptions (for example, those embodied in a causal model or a set of axioms).

PROPOSITION: statement about the relationship between variables.

SIGN RULE: rule for deducing the sign of indirect or spurious effects on the basis of the sign of direct effects.

SUPPRESSOR VARIABLE: prior variable which produces spurious effect of opposite sign as the causal effect between a pair of variables, or intervening variable mediating indirect effect of opposite sign as direct effect.

TENABLE PROPOSITION: proposition which is in accordance with the results of empirical analyses.

THEOREM: proposition derived from axioms.

VALID PROPOSITION: proposition which follows logically from a set of assumptions.

Exercises

4.1   The Relationship between Number of Parties and Responsiveness of Party Leadership

Show that the relationship between number of parties and responsiveness of party leadership actually is negative in the model in Figure 3.5(*b*), as Hirschman (1970) assumed it to be.

In Figure 3.5(*c*) what is the relationship between number of parties and loyalty of members? What is the sign of the indirect effect of loyalty on responsiveness? What is the total causal effect of loyalty on responsiveness? And finally, what can we say about the relationship between number of parties and responsiveness of party leaders on the basis of the assumptions of Figure 3.5(*c*)?

4.2   Does the Fire Department Help or Hurt?

In the local newspaper a critic of the proposal to increase the appropriations for the Fire Department has produced statistics showing an increase in the damages caused by a fire as the number of fire engines turning up increases. In the capacity of public relations officer of the department your task is to convince the readers of the newspaper that the assistance of the Fire Department actually does help instead of hurt. There seems to be nothing wrong with the statistics, however. Along what lines will you argue in your reply?

4.3 Deducing a Missing Piece of Information
A research report may not always contain all the information on results of the analysis we are interested in. Sometimes it will be possible to find the missing piece by means of deduction, definitely a quicker way of obtaining it than writing to the author.

In a study of elections to Parliament in Denmark and Norway it was found that a slightly higher proportion of male than of female candidates were elected in Norway. The difference in proportions was 0·06 (Foverskov 1978). Another variable found to have great impact on success in the elections was the kind of list position occupied by the candidate (the implications of the proportional representation electoral system is discussed in Section 7.3, where another aspect of this study is considered). When controlled for list position, the effect of sex on election success was 0·07. The effect of a favourable list position on election success, controlled for sex, was 0·45.

In the article nothing is said about the relationship between sex and list position, a result we might be interested in, to see if the parties seem to favour men or women when they rank the candidates on their list. On the basis of the above information what can we say about the effect of sex on the chances of obtaining a favourable list position?

4.4 Make Deductions from Your Own Models
Suggest variables which may fit into the models diagrammed below. Deduce the sign of indirect and spurious effects within each of the models. What can be said about the gross associations between the causal variables and the effect variable?

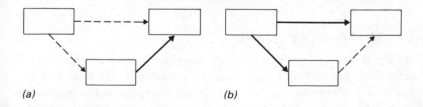

(a)   (b)

5

Designs for Causal Analyses

Causal models are helpful not only for efforts to clarify and develop one's theoretical understanding of a social phenomenon, or deduce the implications of this understanding. When we are to perform the empirical analysis, clear guidelines for how to proceed are provided by the models. The question of design is a question of which statistical relationships we need to establish, and how by means of them we can calculate the various causal components.

Our scheme for causal analysis is different from path analysis in that we use contingency tables and differences in proportions instead of regression analysis to measure effects. With regard to the *design for analysis*, what effects we have to find and how to use them, there is no difference. In the literature on path analysis two different designs, that is, two different ways of arriving at the same results, are used. The most common is the one we shall call the *effect transmittance design*, where indirect or spurious effects are found by multiplication of direct effects. In Chapter 1 we applied the other design, the *effect change design*, when we found the various causal components by studying the changes in association between two variables resulting from controlling for other variables.

In this chapter by means of a four-variable model we shall demonstrate the general features of the two designs, and discuss when to use which. In order to focus the attention solely on the question of design the empirical data have been somewhat modified to avoid statistical interaction, which is the subject of Chapter 8. The results of the analysis are the same for the modified and the real data, however, with regard to the size of the causal components.

5.1 The Effect Change Design

An interest of students of voting behaviour has been the importance of influences during adolescence and early adulthood for shaping one's political preferences. In the pioneering Norwegian election study from 1957 a four-variable table with the independent variables father's occupation, father's vote, and respondent's own occupation, and the dependent variable own vote is presented (Valen and Katz 1964: 177). On the basis of this table the data matrix in Table 5.1 has been constructed.

To perform a causal analysis of the relationships between the variables in the data matrix we have to decide how the variables are to be ordered causally, in which direction we will assume possible causal influences to flow between them. Here the answer to this question seems straightforward, father's occupation prior to father's vote which in turn comes prior to own occupation, and finally own vote. Assuming that we have not overlooked other relevant variables we thus arrive at the general model diagrammed in Figure 5.1.

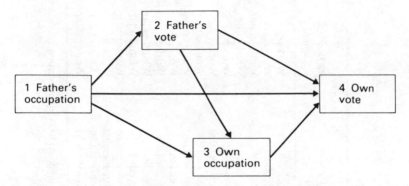

Figure 5.1   *Factors influencing the choice of party*

Table 5.2 contains the tables we have to prepare in order to find the effects needed for the causal decomposition of associations. We start out with three bivariate tables, between each of the first three variables in the model as independent variable and the fourth one as dependent variable (steps 1.1, 1.2 and 1.3 in the analysis). Then we proceed with a trivariate table, involving variable 1 and 2 as independent variables, while the fourth variable still serves as dependent variable (step 2). Finally, we have a four-variable table where the third causal variable has been added to the list of independent variables (step 3).

To arrive at the frequencies in the bivariate table for father's occupation and own vote (step 1.1) we add together the number of units from the data matrix which have the same combination of values on these two variables. The combination father a worker and own vote socialist is found in 126 + 21 + 39 + 8 = 194 cases. A

Table 5.1   Data Matrix for Sample of Norwegian Voters

Units (in ordered sequence)	*1 Father's occupation*	*2 Father's vote*	*3 Own occupation*	*4 Own vote*	Number of units
1...126	Worker	Socialist	Worker	Socialist	126
127...135	Worker	Socialist	Worker	Non-socialist	9
136...156	Worker	Socialist	White collar	Socialist	21
157...173	Worker	Socialist	White collar	Non-socialist	17
174...212	Worker	Non-socialist	Worker	Socialist	39
213...239	Worker	Non-socialist	Worker	Non-socialist	27
240...247	Worker	Non-socialist	White collar	Socialist	8
248...278	Worker	Non-socialist	White collar	Non-socialist	31
279...305	Farmer/white collar	Socialist	Worker	Socialist	27
306...310	Farmer/white collar	Socialist	Worker	Non-socialist	5
311...319	Farmer/white collar	Socialist	White collar	Socialist	9
320...330	Farmer/white collar	Socialist	White collar	Non-socialist	11
331...397	Farmer/white collar	Non-socialist	Worker	Socialist	67
398...467	Farmer/white collar	Non-socialist	Worker	Non-socialist	70
468...484	Farmer/white collar	Non-socialist	White collar	Socialist	17
485...621	Farmer/white collar	Non-socialist	White collar	Non-socialist	137

Note: Based on table 6.23 in Valen and Katz (1964: 177), modified to avoid interaction between the first three variables in their effect on the fourth variable.

Table 5.2 The Effect Change Design: Steps in the Analysis

Step	1 Father's occupation	2 Father's vote	3 Own occupation	4 Own vote Proportion socialist	Effect of independent variable X_1	X_2	X_3
1.1	Worker			$\dfrac{194}{278} = 0.70$			
	Farmer/ white collar			$\dfrac{120}{343} = 0.35$	0.35		
1.2		Socialist		$\dfrac{183}{225} = 0.81$			
		Non-socialist		$\dfrac{131}{396} = 0.33$		0.48	

Table 5.2 – contd

Step	1 Father's occupation	2 Father's vote	3 Own occupation	4 Own vote Proportion socialist	Effect of independent variable		
					X_1	X_2	X_3
1.3			Worker	$\dfrac{259}{370} = 0.70$			
			White collar	$\dfrac{55}{251} = 0.22$			0.48
2	Worker	Socialist		$\dfrac{147}{173} = 0.85$			
		Non-socialist		$\dfrac{47}{105} = 0.45$	0.16	0.40	
	Farmer/ white collar	Socialist		$\dfrac{36}{52} = 0.69$			
		Non-socialist		$\dfrac{84}{291} = 0.29$	0.16	0.40	

3							
Worker	Socialist	Worker	$\frac{126}{135} = 0.93$	0.09	0.34	0.38	
		White collar	$\frac{21}{38} = 0.55$				
	Non-socialist	Worker	$\frac{39}{66} = 0.59$	0.10	0.34	0.38	
		White collar	$\frac{8}{39} = 0.21$				
Farmer/ white collar	Socialist	Worker	$\frac{27}{32} = 0.84$	0.10	0.35	0.39	
		White collar	$\frac{9}{20} = 0.45$				
	Non-socialist	Worker	$\frac{67}{137} = 0.49$	0.10	0.34	0.38	
		White collar	$\frac{17}{154} = 0.11$				

working father combined with a non-socialist vote occurs $9+17+27+31 = 84$ times. This renders the proportion voting socialist among the offspring of workers equal to $194/(194 + 84) = 194/278 = 0.70$, as shown under step 1.1 in Table 5.2.

By similarly summing frequencies in the lower half of the matrix we find that 120 out of 343 children of farmers or white-collar workers vote socialist. This gives a proportion of socialists of 0.35, and a difference in proportions as compared to the children of workers of $0.70 - 0.35 = 0.35$.

Having thus looked into the details of how the bivariate association between father's occupation and own vote is computed, the reader should have no trouble in checking up on the frequencies, proportions and differences in proportions for the other associations. We will, therefore, turn our attention to the question of how the results in Table 5.2 are to be interpreted.

We shall start by considering the relationship between X_1 (father's occupation) and X_4 (own vote). The bivariate association between the two variables (step 1.1) is 0.35. Controlled for X_2 (father's vote) the association drops to 0.16 (step 2). When we in addition to X_2 also control for X_3 (own occupation) in step 3, a further drop in the association to 0.10 occurs.

We see that the effect of father's occupation on own vote changes as a result of the control for the other two variables. To get the meaning of these changes in effect it may be useful to consider each outcome as a result of analyses based on different causal models, as shown in Figure 5.2. In step 1.1 the implicit causal model is one where X_1 is the only variable affecting X_4. In step 2 we introduce another causal variable, X_2. The change in the effect of X_1 on X_4, $a - b = 0.38 - 0.16 = 0.19$, is a result of controlling for X_2. Father's vote, in other words, has contributed a component of 0.19 to the gross

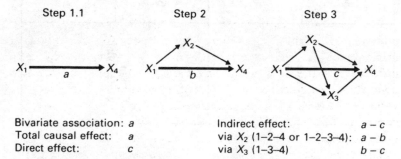

Step 1.1	Step 2	Step 3

Bivariate association:	a		Indirect effect:	$a - c$
Total causal effect:	a		via X_2 (1–2–4 or 1–2–3–4):	$a - b$
Direct effect:	c		via X_3 (1–3–4)	$b - c$

Figure 5.2 *Finding the causal components for the first variable.*

association between father's occupation and own vote, which we remove by controlling for X_2 when finding the effect of X_1 on X_4.

How is the component of $0·19$ in the association between X_1 and X_4 which is due to X_2 to be interpreted causally? Since father's vote is an intervening variable between father's occupation and own vote, its contribution to the association between these two variables will be to mediate *indirect effect*. We have thus found the indirect effect of X_1 on X_4 going via X_2 by noting the change in the effect of X_1 on X_4 brought about by the control for X_2.

Shifting from the model with X_1 and X_2 influencing X_4 (step 2), to the model which also includes X_3 as a causal variable (step 3), the change in the effect of X_1 on X_4 is $b - c = 0·16 - 0·10 = 0·06$. Since the change in effect is a result of changing the model by adding X_3, we have found a component in the association between father's occupation and own vote which is due to the intervening variable own occupation, and accordingly is an *indirect effect*.

The complete model of step 3 has three indirect paths leading from X_1 to X_4, the two-link path from X_1 to X_2 to X_4, the three-link path via both intervening variables X_1 to X_2 to X_3 to X_4, and the two-link path from X_1 to X_3 to X_4. The component of indirect effect found by controlling for X_2 ($a - b = 0·19$) contains all indirect effect going via X_2, that is, indirect effect resulting from X_1 influencing X_2 which in turn affects X_4, either directly or indirectly via X_3. The change in the effect of X_1 on X_4 brought about by adding X_3 to the model ($b - c = 0·06$) gives the indirect effect caused by X_1 influencing X_3 directly, and X_3 in turn influencing X_4.

If we were looking for a quick way of establishing the *total indirect effect*, without bothering about through which paths this effect flows, we might skip step 2, and just compare the effect of X_1 on X_4 with no other variables included in the model with the corresponding effect where both independent variables have been added: $a - c = 0·35 - 0·10 = 0·25$.

We have now seen how we find the indirect effect due to intervening variables by studying how the association between the original pair of variables changes when the intervening variables are introduced in the model. The *direct effect* of father's occupation on own vote is defined as the association remaining after all other variables influencing own vote in the complete model have been controlled for. The direct effect, in other words, equals the association found in the four-variable table (step 3), that is, $c = 0·10$.

The *total causal effect* is defined as the association net of all prior variables in the model. Father's occupation is the first variable of our model, thus there are no prior variables to control for. The total causal effect accordingly equals the bivariate association found in step 1.1: $a = 0.35$. This, of course, equals the sum of the components of direct and indirect effect: $0.10 + 0.25 = 0.35$. And correspondingly, with no prior variables in the model, we will have no *spurious effect* between father's occupation and own vote.

Turning to the relationship between X_2 (father's vote) and X_4 (own vote) Table 5.2 shows a bivariate association of 0.48 (step 1.2). Controlling for X_1 the association drops to 0.40 (step 2), while the additional control for X_3 results in a further drop to 0.34 (step 3). In Figure 5.3 the three models which may be seen as underlying each step in the analysis are diagrammed.

The difference between the effect of X_2 on X_4 without controls (d) and the effect after controlling for the prior variable $X_1(e)$, $0.48 - 0.40 = 0.08$, gives the component in the association between father's vote and own vote resulting from both variables being influenced by father's occupation. The causal interpretation of this component, which is due to a *prior variable*, is *spurious effect*.

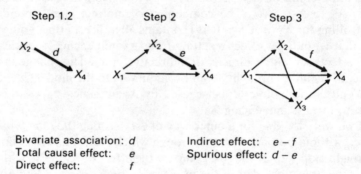

Figure 5.3   *Finding the causal components for the second variable.*

By controlling for the intervening variable X_3 in step 3, and noting the change in effect for X_2 on X_4 $(e - f)$, we get at the component in the association between father's vote and own vote mediated by own occupation: $0.40 - 0.34 = 0.06$. We have thus found the component of *indirect effect* in the relationship between father's vote and own vote.

As always, we find the *direct effect* of father's vote on own vote by controlling for all other causal variables in the complete model (step 3): $f = 0.34$.

For father's vote, the result of the decomposition of the bivariate association with own vote of 0·48 is thus a spurious component due to father's occupation of 0·08, and a *total causal effect* of 0·40, composed of a direct effect of 0·34 and an indirect effect via own occupation of 0·06.

Finally, considering the relationship between X_3 (own occupation) and X_4 (own vote), we notice that this causal variable is absent from the trivariate table in step 2. We have a bivariate association with own vote of $g = 0·48$, which controlled for the two prior variables in step 3 changes to an association of $h = 0·38$.

The difference between the two effects ($g - h$ in Figure 5.4) gives us the amount of *spurious effect* in the relationship between own occupation and own vote created by the prior variables father's occupation and father's vote: 0·10. The effect of 0·38 remaining after removing the spurious effect is the *direct effect* of own occupation. As the model includes no intervening variables between X_3 and X_4, there can be no indirect effect, and 0·38 thus constitutes the *total causal effect* of own occupation on own vote.

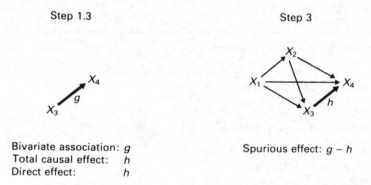

Step 1.3   Step 3

Bivariate association: *g*
Total causal effect: *h*
Direct effect: *h*

Spurious effect: *g − h*

Figure 5.4   *Finding the causal components for the third variable*

Table 5.3 recapitulates the main points of the above discussion of the effect change design. The upper part contains the results from Table 5.2, which right away give the size of the total causal effect and the direct effect. For each variable, the *total causal* effect is found as its effect when we control for prior variables, that is, in step 1 for the first variable, step 2 for the second and step 3 for the third variable. The *direct effect* is the result from the last step, where the effect of each variable is controlled for all other causal variables.

The two remaining components of the causal interpretation presented in the middle section of Table 5.3, indirect effect and spurious

Table 5.3 Causal Interpretation of the Changes in Association between the Independent Variables and Own Vote

Results of the stepwise calculations of association	1 Father's occupation	2 Father's vote	3 Own occupation
Step 1.1: Bivariate table	0·35	—	—
1.2: Bivariate table	—	0·48	—
1.3: Bivariate table	—	—	0·48
Step 2: Trivariate table	0·16	0·40	—
Step 3: Four-variate table	0·10	0·34	0·38

Causal interpretation of the statistical components			
Total causal effect (CE: step i for variable *i*)	0·35	0·40	0·38
Direct effect (DE: last step)	0·10	0·34	0·38
Indirect effect (IE: CE − DE)	0·25	0·06	0
Spurious effect (SE: step 1 − CE)	0	0·08	0·10

Further decomposition of indirect effects			
Via variable 2 Father's vote (step 1−step 2)	0·19	0	0
—through the path $1 \rightarrow 2 \rightarrow 4$ (0·19 × (DE/CE for variable 2) = 0·19 × 0·34/0·40)	0·16	0	0
—through the path $1 \rightarrow 2 \rightarrow 3 \rightarrow 4$ (0·19 × (IE/CE for variable 2) = 0·19 × 0·06/0·40)	0·03	0	0
Via variable 3 Own occupation (step 2−step 3)	0·06	0·06	0

— indicates that the variable is not included in this step of analysis.
0 indicates that the variable according to the model cannot have the kind of effect in question (whereas 0·00 would mean that an effect in the empirical analysis turns out to be zero).

effect, are found as *differences* between results from Table 5.2. The *indirect effect* as the difference between the total causal effect and the direct effect, and the *spurious effect* as the difference between the bivariate association and the total causal effect.

From the results we conclude that the three variables have approximately the same causal impact on the probability that a respondent will vote for the socialists. For father's occupation, the major part of the effect is an indirect one, while father's vote and own occupation have primarily or wholly a direct effect on own vote. One implication of this pattern is that if we restricted ourselves to analysing the four-variable table, which only will indicate the strength of the direct effects, we would not have captured the full extent of the causal importance of father's occupation for own vote.

The bottom section of Table 5.3 shows how it is possible to obtain a further decomposition of the indirect effect of father's occupation on own vote by establishing through which of the three different paths leading from this variable via one or both of the intervening variables to own vote the influence flows. The component due to the second variable is split into effect flowing directly onwards to own vote and effect flowing via the third variable in proportion as the causal effect of the second variable is divided into direct and indirect effect. The result is that the indirect effect via father's vote as only intervening variable is found to be 0·16, via both intervening variables 0·03 and via own occupation solely 0·06.

The detailed analysis of how the indirect effect flows via different paths between two variables is, however, more conveniently handled by means of the alternative design for causal analyses, the effect transmittance design.

5.2   The Effect Transmittance Design

In this approach we calculate all direct effects in the complete four-variable model. Since father's occupation is assumed to be the only variable influencing father's vote, we find this direct effect by means of a bivariate table where the last variable is the dependent variable (step 1 in Table 5.4). Having had a father who was a worker is found to increase the probability of the father being socialist by 0·47.

In our model two variables are influencing own occupation, making a trivariate table necessary to find these direct effects (step 2). The effect of father's occupation on the probability that the respondent will be a worker turns out to be 0·16, while the effect of father's vote is 0·15.

For the last variable, own vote, we have three causal variables. The four-variable table used to find these direct effects is identical with step 3 in the effect change design. We have now calculated all direct effects, and the results may be entered in the causal diagram (Figure 5.5).

Table 5.4 The Effect Transmittance Design: Steps in the Analysis

Step	1 Father's occupation	2 Father's vote Proportion socialist	3 Own occupation	4 Own vote	Effect of independent variable X_1	X_2	X_3
1	Worker	$\frac{173}{278} = 0.62$			0.47		
	Farmer/white collar	$\frac{52}{343} = 0.15$					

Proportion worker

Step	1 Father's occupation	2 Father's vote	3 Own occupation	4 Own vote	Effect of independent variable X_1	X_2	X_3
2	Worker	Socialist	$\frac{135}{173} = 0.78$				
		Non-socialist	$\frac{66}{105} = 0.63$		0.16	0.15	
	Farmer/white collar	Socialist	$\frac{32}{52} = 0.62$		0.16		
		Non-socialist	$\frac{137}{291} = 0.47$			0.15	

Proportion socialist

			Proportion socialist			
Worker	Socialist	Worker	$\frac{126}{135} = 0.93$			0·38
		White collar	$\frac{21}{38} = 0.55$		0·34	
	Non-socialist	Worker	$\frac{39}{66} = 0.59$	0·09	0·34	
		White collar	$\frac{8}{39} = 0.21$	0·10		0·38
Farmer/ white collar	Socialist	Worker	$\frac{27}{32} = 0.84$	0·10		0·39
		White collar	$\frac{9}{20} = 0.45$	0·10	0·35	
	Non-socialist	Worker	$\frac{67}{137} = 0.49$		0·34	
		White collar	$\frac{17}{154} = 0.11$			0·38

3

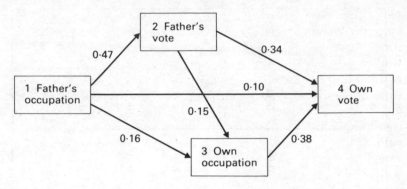

Figure 5.5   *Direct effects in the model for party preference.*

To find the indirect effects of a variable we multiply the direct effects that constitute a path between this variable and the effect variable. Table 5.5 shows a convenient way of presenting the indirect effects of a variable. Adding together the direct and indirect effects of a variable we arrive at its total causal effect. Comparing Tables 5.3 and 5.5 we see that the two designs for decomposing the association between a pair of variables yield identical results.

An intuitive explanation of why we can find an indirect effect by multiplying its constituent direct effects might be the following: if we

Table 5.5   *Calculation of Indirect Effect by Means of Effect Multiplication*

Causal components	Paths X_1 X_2 X_3 X_4	Effect multiplication
1 Father's occupation		
Direct effect	$1 \longrightarrow 4$	0·10
+ Indirect effect	$1 \rightarrow 2 \longrightarrow 4$	$0·47 \times 0·34$ $= 0·16$
+ Indirect effect	$1 \rightarrow 2 \rightarrow 3 \rightarrow 4$	$0·47 \times 0·15 \times 0·38 = 0·03$
+ Indirect effect	$1 \longrightarrow 3 \rightarrow 4$	$0·16 \times 0·38$ $= 0·06$
= Causal effect		0·35
2 Father's vote		
Direct effect	$2 \longrightarrow 4$	0·34
+ Indirect effect	$2 \rightarrow 3 \rightarrow 4$	$0·15 \times 0·38$ $= 0·06$
= Causal effect		0·40
3 Own occupation		
Direct effect	$3 \rightarrow 4$	0·38
= Causal effect		

look at the path from father's occupation via father's vote to own vote, the first direct effect represents the increase in the probability for having a socialist father which follows from the father being a worker rather than a farmer or white collar. How much of this effect is transmitted onwards to own party preference? About one-third, since the direct effect of father's vote on own vote is 0·34. Had this effect instead been zero, nothing of the first effect would have been transmitted, and we would not have had any indirect effect via this path. If it instead had been equal to 1·0, all of the first direct effect would have been brought to bear on own vote.

By multiplying the first direct effect in a path with each of the succeeding ones we find the fraction of the first effect which is transmitted onwards and in the end will affect the last variable in the chain.

To find the components of spurious effect we may multiply the causal effect of the prior variable on each of the variables in the pair we are considering. Father's occupation has a direct effect on father's vote of 0·47, and an effect on own vote directly or indirectly via own occupation of 0·10 + 0·06 = 0·16. The product of these two influences indicates a spurious association between father's and own vote of 0·08. This is identical with the result reached by means of the effect change design. In other cases, however, we may find that the results differ. As will be discussed in Chapter 6, this is due to the fact that the difference in proportions is an asymmetrical measure of association. If we instead rely on the effect change design to establish the size of spurious effects, this problem is avoided.

5.3 The Choice of Design

In Figure 5.6 the scheme for calculation of tables in each of the two designs is recapitulated by means of a six-variable model, the logic being easily extended to any number of variables. The question to be addressed in this section is how to choose between the designs for causal analyses.

Generally, the effect change design is best suited if what we are looking for is a rough picture of how the relationship between two variables may be interpreted causally. No matter how large the number of variables in the model, this can be accomplished by means of a three-step analysis. First, we establish the size of the gross association by means of a bivariate table. Then we find the total causal effect by means of a multivariate table where we control for all prior variables, and by subtracting the causal effect from the gross

Analysis design	Step	Variable 1	Variable 2	Variable 3	Variable 4	Variable 5	Variable 6
Effect change design	1	X					Y
	2	X	X				Y
	3	X	X	X			Y
	4	X	X	X	X		Y
	5	X	X	X	X	X	Y
Effect transmittance design	1	X	Y				
	2	X	X	Y			
	3	X	X	X	Y		
	4	X	X	X	X	Y	
	5	X	X	X	X	X	Y
Gross associations (forms a part of both designs; in the effect change design is step 1.1 already calculated)	1.1	X					Y
	1.2		X				Y
	1.3			X			Y
	1.4				X		Y
	1.5					X	Y
Variable blocs Effect change design for decomposition of associations between variable 3 and 6, with 1–2 and 4–5 as blocs	1			X			Y
	2	X	X	X			Y
	3	X	X	X	X	X	Y

Figure 5.6   *A survey of tables required in each of the causal designs (X: independent variables, Y: dependent variable).*

association we also have the spurious component. Finally, by controlling for both prior and intervening variables we find the direct effect, and subtracting it from the causal effect get the indirect effect. At the bottom of Figure 5.6 this shortcut to a decomposition of the relationship between variables three and six is illustrated.

To arrive at the same results by means of the effect transmittance design would require a lot more tables and extensive calculations to establish the indirect effects. The extra information thus provided may be of great interest to us, however. We get a detailed picture of how much influence flows via each of the indirect paths, and of the strength of each single link in a path. If, for instance, an indirect effect turns out to be weak, or a prior variable produces little spurious association, we may want to know whether this is the result of a single effect being close to zero, or the result of all direct effects involved being of only a modest strength. This information is provided when we apply the effect transmittance design.

The choice between the two designs is, therefore, mainly a

question of what kind of information we want to get out of the analysis. In some cases we may choose to combine them, and use the effect change design to gain a rough impression of the relationships and the effect transmittance design to get at the details. There will be instances, however, where properties of the model or of the data prevent us from using the effect transmittance design. The model may include ambiguous relationships or two-way causation, which we can handle by means of *variable blocs* and the effect change design. And if we want to include variables with more than two values in the analysis, in cases where the *polytomy* is used as a control variable we are also restricted to the effect change design. Finally, as already mentioned, we should use the effect change design to find components of spurious effect. These special situations are discussed in Chapter 6.

Summary

To find the causal components which according to our model make up the association between a pair of variables two different designs for the analysis may be used. In the effect change design we find the gross association by means of a bivariate table. Controlling for prior variables we find the causal effect, and the change relative to the gross association gives the spurious effect. Controlling for all other causal variables establishes the direct effect, and the change relative to the causal effect gives the indirect effect. In the effect transmittance design all direct effects in the model are calculated, and indirect effects found by multiplying the direct effects of each path linking the two variables in question.

The choice of design depends on the kind of information wanted from the analysis. The effect change design easily provides information on the main aspects of the causal interpretation, while the effect transmittance design gives all details on how the various components are produced.

Glossary

EFFECT CHANGE DESIGN: analysis design where causal components are found by studying the changes in the association between two variables resulting from controlling for other variables.
EFFECT TRANSMITTANCE DESIGN: analysis design where causal components are found by multiplying the relevant direct effects.
TOTAL CAUSAL EFFECT: association net of prior variables in the causal model; sum of direct and indirect effect.

Exercises

5.1　Attitude towards Premarital Sex
Below a data matrix from a representative survey of the American population containing the variables age, place of residence, education and attitude towards premarital sex is given (General Social Survey 1975). The frequencies have been somewhat adjusted to remove a modest statistical interaction in the original data.

Construct a causal model for the four variables, and use the data in the matrix to perform an analysis by means of each of the two designs.

Age	Residence	Education	Attitude premarital sex	Frequencies
Older	Rural	High	Positive	10
Older	Rural	High	Negative	12
Older	Rural	Low	Positive	68
Older	Rural	Low	Negative	136
Older	Urban	High	Positive	37
Older	Urban	High	Negative	33
Older	Urban	Low	Positive	91
Older	Urban	Low	Negative	127
Younger	Rural	High	Positive	57
Younger	Rural	High	Negative	25
Younger	Rural	Low	Positive	129
Younger	Rural	Low	Negative	90
Younger	Urban	High	Positive	214
Younger	Urban	High	Negative	63
Younger	Urban	Low	Positive	259
Younger	Urban	Low	Negative	127

Source: Lecture by James A. Davis.

5.2　Promotion Opportunity in the American Army
In Exercise 1.3 a trivariate analysis of the variables education, rank, and satisfaction with promotion opportunities during the Second World War were to be performed for each of the two branches Military Police and Air Corps separately. Suggest a model where branch of service is included as a fourth variable, and perform the analysis using each of the two designs. (*Hint:* consider whether additional information to that given in Exercise 1.3 is needed or not.)

6

Special Problems of Design

So far we have dealt with analyses of the 'neat and clean' kinds of situation where the model is recursive (no reciprocal causation) and the variables all are dichotomies. In this chapter we shall look at how it is possible to handle some of the less straightforward problems we are bound to get into in the analysis of real data.

6.1 Bloc Recursive Models

When we have reciprocal causation or ambiguous relationships between variables in our model, we can still obtain a decomposition of the relationships between other variables of the model. The variables which are ambiguously or reciprocally related are treated as a bloc, the internal relationships of which we make no effort to analyse. In this way we arrive at a model of variables and blocs of variables without reciprocal causation, called a *bloc recursive model*. An example is given in Figure 6.1.

In this six-variable model the first two variables influence each other reciprocally, while variable four and five have an ambiguous relationship. The result is a nonrecursive model, which in the diagram has been turned into a bloc recursive model by joining together each of the two pairs of variables in blocs.

If we want to decompose the association between variable three and six, this may be accomplished by means of the effect change design. Variables within a bloc are entered simultaneously instead of

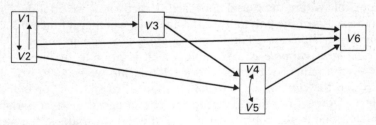

Figure 6.1   *Bloc recursive model.*

one by one in the stepwise calculation of tables. We would thus need the three tables listed at the bottom of Figure 5.6. First, we would find the bivariate association between variable three and six. Next by controlling for the two prior variables simultaneously, and noting the change in association between variable three and six, we would get the component of spurious effect in their relationship, as well as the total causal effect. Finally, a six-variable table where the two intervening variables have been added, gives the direct effect of variable three on variable six, and comparing with the result from the previous table we get the indirect effect via one or the other or both variables in the intervening bloc.

To perform an analysis based on a bloc recursive model we have to make use of the effect change design. For the variables within each bloc, the part of the association with the effect variable due to other variables from the same bloc cannot be given a definite interpretation with regard to how much is indirect and how much spurious effect. These variables will, therefore, have a component of *ambiguous* (or unanalysed) *association* in their relationship with the effect variable.

6.2   Polytomous Variables

There exist many sociological variables which are natural dichotomies. The sex of a person is one example, to vote in an election or abstain is another. More often, however, variables have from three values (for example, marital status: unmarried, married, previously married) up to an infinitely large number (for example, income). Since all such variables can be made dichotomous by grouping together the values into two categories, designs for dichotomies are generally applicable. To group together values gives us a cruder measure for the variable, however, with a loss of information and possibly even a distortion of the results as a consequence.

It would, therefore, be very useful to have a design that allows us to include polytomous variables in the analysis. We shall see that this is possible within the causal approach. Exactly how we do it depends on the status of the polytomy in the analysis, whether it functions as a control variable, an independent variable, or a dependent variable.

A *control variable* is a variable which is prior to or intervening between a pair of variables whose relationship we want to explain. Through the control we find the component of spurious or indirect effect in the association between the causal and the effect variable which is due to the control variable. For control variables, the number of values makes no difference for the analysis. The calculation of net effect and the interpretation of what a change in effect means will be, for instance, exactly the same in a situation with two dichotomous control variables, and a situation with one control variable with four values. In both cases we will have four control groups, for which we find partial effects and calculate a weighted average in order to obtain the net effect.

We can, therefore, use any number of values we want on a control variable, provided we have a sufficiently large number of units for the increased number of control groups. We cannot, however, calculate a single direct effect going into or out from the polytomy, so we cannot use the effect transmittance design to find indirect effect mediated via such a variable, but have to rely on the effect change design.

An *independent variable* is a causal variable whose effect on other variables we want to assess. Where the independent variable is a polytomy, we will have more than two proportions with a certain value on the dependent variable that can be compared in order to calculate a difference in proportions. Given the proportion voting in an election among unmarried, married and previously married, by comparing two at a time we will find three differences in the proportion voting. There does not seem to be any meaningful way to combine these three effects into a single measure for the causal effect of marital status. There exists no metric allowing us to talk about changes in 'maritalness' in general. What we have to consider is change from one specific marital state to another.

We thus cannot avoid dealing with several separate effects, each showing how a substitution of one particular value for another on the causal variable influences the chances of obtaining a certain value on the effect variable.

In a multivariate analysis with a polytomous causal variable we will have to perform several *separate analyses*, one for each pair of values on the polytomy we want to compare, leaving out units with other values on this variable. For instance, when we want to assess the effect of being married rather than previously married on the probability of voting, we would leave aside for the moment unmarried persons. Thus marital status would reduce to a dichotomy, which can be combined with other causal variables in an analysis using the effect change or effect transmittance design. Then we might pick another pair of values, and perform a similar analysis for units which have one of these two values on the polytomy. We would thus end up with several sets of results, one for each pair of values we have chosen to compare.

Finally, the polytomous variable may serve as a *dependent variable* in the analysis, and we want to assess how it is affected by causal variables, by calculating differences in proportions. Since the sum of proportions for all values on the dependent variable always equals 1, the sum of all differences in proportions will equal 0. For a dichotomous dependent variable, this implies that when we have found one difference in proportions to be d, the other will equal $-d$. To report more than one difference would accordingly be super-fluous. With three or more values on the dependent variable, however, the situation is different. By learning how a causal vari-able influences the chances for being married, we would not know its effect on the chances for being previously married, or being unmarried.

Generally, with r values on a variable, we will need $(r - 1)$ differences in proportions to get a complete picture of how it is affected by a causal variable. Each effect measured tells us how the causal variable influences the probability of obtaining a particular value (or set of values) on the effect variable. Each analysis is carried out on all units as an ordinary causal analysis, with the dependent variable successively dichotomised in different ways.

Treating a variable as a polytomy rather than collapsing it into a dichotomy may in some cases have great impact on the results reached in a causal analysis. The analysis of sex, seniority and legislative career in the Norwegian Parliament (Exercise 1.2) pro-vides a vivid illustration.

In the data matrix in Exercise 1.2 all three variables were dichoto-mised. Seniority, however, was at the outset measured as the number of sessions (that is, years) previously attended by a representative, and then collapsed into a dichotomy by grouping together the values 0–3 and 4–30. Rank is based on what leadership positions in Parliament a representative is elected to, dichotomised into one or more *vs* none. We shall now change the two variables into poly-tomies, to give an empirical illustration of the various ways in which such variables may be incorporated in a causal analysis. The low number of units restricts us to a tripartitioning of the variables, with the frequencies given in Table 6.1. (Even so, the number of units is very small in some cells, a problem that will be discussed in Chapter 7.)

For seniority, the distinction is made between having attended 0–3 sessions (less than one electoral period of four sessions), 4–7 sessions, and 8 or more sessions. With regard to rank, the measure-ment is made more refined by distinguishing between politically important positions (high rank), ceremonial positions which wields little power (medium rank), and no position held at all (low rank).

Table 6.1   *Sex, Seniority and Rank for Members of the Norwegian Parliament,*
1973−81 (Skard 1980)

Sex	Seniority (No. of sessions)	Conservative Party Rank in Parliament			Labour Party Rank in Parliament		
		High	Medium	Low	High	Medium	Low
Male	High (8−)	17	1	6	27	5	19
Male	Medium (4−7)	4	1	9	4	5	27
Male	Low (0−3)	0	1	14	0	0	21
Female	High (8−)	1	1	1	4	0	3
Female	Medium (4−7)	1	1	5	3	4	2
Female	Low (0−3)	0	1	6	1	3	10

Table 6.2 shows how we easily find the effect of sex on rank (still dichotomised) when the *control variable* seniority has three values, using the data for the representatives from the Conservative Party. The weighted sum of the three partial effects turns out to be close to zero. Comparing with the results from the analysis with a dichotomised seniority variable in Exercise 1.2 we see that the direct effect of sex on rank has been reduced from 0·12 to a mere 0·03, and the indirect effect correspondingly increased from 0·04 to 0·13. In contrast to the previous findings the conclusion this time is that the difference in legislative career between male and female representatives from the Conservative Party almost entirely is a result of lack of seniority on the part of the women. There are no longer signs of a direct discrimination of female representatives on the basis of their sex.

Why do the results change when the measure for the control variable is made more refined? From Table 6.2 we see that most of the men who have attended four or more sessions actually have reached the highest level of seniority (24 out of 38), while this is the case for a minority of the women (3 out of 10). Thus a high value on the dichotomised seniority variable did not signify the same level of seniority for male and female representatives. This means that the first control for seniority was too crude to remove all of the difference between the sexes, which leads us to underestimate the indirect effect of sex via seniority and correspondingly overestimate the direct effect of sex on rank. By shifting from a dichotomised to a trichotomised seniority variable we avoid this pitfall.

To illustrate the analysis of polytomous *independent variables* we will look at the effect of seniority on rank in Table 6.2. We have three proportions and accordingly three differences in proportions which

Table 6.2 The Effect of Sex on Rank Controlling for Seniority (Trichotomised) among Conservative Representatives

Seniority (No. of sessions)	Male representatives Proportion H + M rank	(N)	Female representatives Proportion H + M rank	(N)	Partial effect of sex	Weights	Weighted effect
High (8–)	0·750	(24)	0·667	(3)	0·083	$\frac{27}{70} = 0·386$	0·03
Medium (4–7)	0·357	(14)	0·286	(7)	0·071	$\frac{21}{70} = 0·300$	0·02
Low (0–3)	0·067	(15)	0·143	(7)	−0·076	$\frac{23}{70} = 0·314$	−0·02

Effect of sex on rank net of seniority: 0·03

may be calculated for both sexes. If we choose to compare the extreme values of high and low seniority, we find a partial effect of 0·683 for the men and 0·524 for the women. To obtain a measure of how a change from low to high seniority controlled for sex affects the probability of acquiring a leadership position we have to weight the two partial effects. In this case we will disregard the representatives with a medium level of seniority, rendering the weights $(24 + 15)/49 = 0·796$ for the men, and $(3 + 7)/49 = 0·204$ for the women, and the net effect $0·683 \times 0·796 + 0·524 \times 0·204 = 0·54 + 0·11 = 0·65$. We would leave the medium seniority representatives out of the analysis also when calculating the bivariate association between seniority and rank, or the effect of sex on seniority and rank, thus rendering the analysis identical to an ordinary causal analysis with dichotomies. We might then proceed to consider other pairs of values on the seniority variable, obtaining a new set of results for each separate analysis.

Finally, we shall look at how the analysis is affected when the *dependent variable*, rank, is turned into a trichotomy. In Table 6.3 the proportions and differences in proportions of Table 6.2 have been split in two, by distinguishing between politically important positions and positions with primarily a ceremonial function. (If the left part of Table 6.3 is placed on top of the right part, we are back to Table 6.2.) Since the control groups are the same for the two tables, the weights will be the same, and they therefore are not shown in Table 6.3.

Table 6.3 gives new and highly interesting insights into the relationship between sex and legislative career for Conservative Members of Parliament. With regard to politically important positions, male representatives are favoured. Controlling for seniority we find a direct effect of sex of 0·18. When we look at ceremonial positions wielding little or no power, however, the pattern is reversed. Here female representatives have a higher probability of being recruited than males on all levels of seniority, resulting in a direct effect of sex of −0·15.

The negligible effect of sex on the probability of obtaining any kind of leadership position found in Table 6.2, turns out to be the result of two opposing tendencies when rank in Parliament is trichotomised in Table 6.3. Thus, while the change from a crude to a more refined measure for the control variable seniority seemed to clear the Conservative Party from charges of a recruitment practice that directly discriminates against female representatives, the introduction of a more subtle measure for rank in Parliament once more

Table 6.3 The Effect of Sex on the Probability of Acquiring High or Medium Rank among Conservative Representatives

Seniority (No. of sessions)	High rank (important positions)				Medium rank (ceremonial positions)			
	Male representatives	Female representatives	Effect of sex	Weighted effect	Male representatives	Female representatives	Effect of sex	Weighted effect
High (8–)	0·708	0·333	0·375	0·14	0·042	0·333	−0·291	−0·11
Medium (4–7)	0·286	0·143	0·143	0·04	0·071	0·143	−0·072	−0·02
Low (0–3)	0·000	0·000	0·000	0·00	0·067	0·143	−0·076	−0·02
Net effect of sex				0·18				−0·15

revealed a pattern that may sustain such accusations. Before drawing any definite conclusions, however, we must consider alternative explanations of the pattern disclosed in Table 6.3. We will return to this topic in Chapter 7.

6.3   The Asymmetry of the Difference in Proportions

In Chapter 5 it was mentioned that multiplying direct effects in order to find the size of spurious components may lead to inaccuracies, making the effect change design preferable for this purpose. We shall now see how the problem with effect multiplication stems from the asymmetric nature of the difference in proportions, and how it is possible to overcome this problem.

To say that a measure of statistical association is asymmetric, means that for a given bivariate frequency distribution its size will depend upon which of the variables is treated as the dependent variable, and which as independent variable. With a symmetrical measure (for instance, gamma or Pearson's r), we need not make any distinction between independent and dependent variables at all. Not so with the difference in proportions, where we have to decide which groups of units to compare (as classified according to one or more independent variables) with regard to what characteristics (values on the dependent variable).

In Table 6.4 fictitious bivariate distribution of 1,000 persons on the variables sex and membership in political parties is used to demonstrate the asymmetry of the difference in proportions. If sex is taken to be the independent variable, and we compare the proportion of party members for men and women, we find a difference of 0·20. If instead the units are split up according to party affiliation, and we compare the proportion of men among members and non-members, the difference in proportions comes out 0·31.

The reason why the association as measured by the difference in proportions turns out to be stronger when party membership is used as the independent variable is that the distribution of units on this variable is more uneven – has a smaller *dispersion* – than the distribution on sex, a 200–800 split as compared to 500–500. The reader may see this by constructing a table with 500 members and 500 non-members and an identical split for men and women. With the same dispersion for the two variables, we will get the same difference in proportions regardless of which way we choose to calculate the proportions.

In a causal analysis it would not have occurred to us to use party

Table 6.4   *The Asymmetry of the Difference in Proportions*

(a) *Bivariate distribution on sex and party membership (absolute frequencies)*

Party membership	Sex		
	Male	Female	Sum
Member	150	50	200
Non-member	350	450	800
Sum	500	500	1,000

(b) *Difference in proportions;*
Sex independent variable

← Difference —			
Proportions →	Male	Female	d
Member	0·30	0·10	0·20
Non-member	0·70	0·90	−0·20
Sum	1·00	1·00	0·00

(c) *Difference in proportions;*
Party Membership independent variable

	— Proportions →		
Difference ↓	Male	Female	Sum
Member	0·75	0·25	1·00
Non-member	0·44	0·56	1·00
d	0·31	−0·31	0·00

membership as independent variable, since being a party member or not, hardly can be expected to influence the sex of a person. Having decided that sex is the causal and party affiliation the effect variable, the assignment of roles as independent and dependent variable follows straight away from the design for causal analyses, and we would use the association of 0·20 to describe the relationship between the two variables. Why, then, concern ourselves with the asymmetry of the difference in proportions and the alternative measure of association of 0·31 at all?

The reason for taking up this question is that it gives the key to an understanding of why the effect transmittance design may yield inaccurate results regarding the size of spurious effects. To illustrate how we must develop our example into a three-variable relationship. In Table 6.5 the variable interest in an election campaign has been added to the previous two, whose relationship is unaltered from that of Table 6.4. Sex and party membership are assumed to influence the probability of taking a high interest in the campaign, and the trivariate table reveals effects of 0·20 and 0·40 respectively. By collapsing the relevant columns we also find the bivariate associations between each of the causal variables and the effect variable.

Table 6.5 *Relationship between Sex, Party Membership and Interest in Election Campaign (Fictitious Data)*

Distributions:	Trivariate				Bivariate		Bivariate		Univariate
Sex	male		female		male	female	—	—	—
Party member	yes	no	yes	no	—	—	yes	no	—
Interest									
High	120	140	30	90	260	120	150	230	380
Low	30	210	20	360	240	380	50	570	620
Sum	150	350	50	450	500	500	200	800	1,000
Proportion H	0·80	0·40	0·60	0·20	0·52	0·24	0·75	0·29	0·38
d_{sex}		0·20	0·20		0·28				
$d_{p.m.}$		0·40		0·40				0·46	

In Figure 6.2 the direct effect of sex on party membership (from Table 6.4), and the direct effects of both these variables on campaign

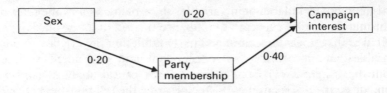

Figure 6.2   *Causal model for sex, party membership and campaign interest.*

interest (from the trivariate section of Table 6.5), have been entered. If we use the effect transmittance design to find the components of the association between sex and interest, we get a direct effect of 0·20 and an indirect effect of 0·20 × 0·40 = 0·08. The sum of components is 0·28, which is exactly equal to the bivariate association found in Table 6.5.

If we then turn our attention to the relationship between party membership and interest, and multiply the direct effects from the prior variable sex in order to find the spurious component, the result is 0·20 × 0·20 = 0·04. Adding the direct effect of 0·40 we arrive at a sum of components of 0·44. Consulting Table 6.5 we see that this falls slightly short of the bivariate association of 0·46. The spurious effect is 0·06, and not 0·04 as we found.

When we use the effect transmittance design to calculate the size of a spurious effect, what we actually do is to proceed as if party membership affected sex, which in turn influences interest in the campaign, and take this 'indirect effect' as the spurious effect we are looking for. If, however, party membership had in fact been the first variable, and the path via sex to interest in fact an indirect effect, the first direct effect from party membership to sex would have been 0·31 instead of 0·20 (Table 6.4(c)).

To find the spurious effect we accordingly ought to multiply the 'reversed' effect between sex and party membership with that of sex on interest. This gives us the desired result: 0·31 × 0·20 = 0·06.

Several conclusions may be drawn from this discussion. First of all, we see that the inaccuracy resulting from using the direct effects of sex in Figure 6.2 to find the spurious effect between party membership and interest in the election campaign is modest. Very often the distribution on the variables in question will be even more similar than in our example, due among other things to a desire on the part of researchers who dichotomise polytomous variables to obtain an even split of the units. With similar dispersions for the causal variables, it will not matter much which way we calculate the effects, and only minor inaccuracies can result from applying the effect transmittance design to calculate spurious effects.

If we have a case of clearly different dispersions for the causal variables, and the effects to be multiplied are strong, the deviation from the correct result may become unacceptably large. One solution, of course, is to use the reversed direct effect as in the above example. It seems more reasonable, however, to follow the rule stated in Chapter 5, that the effect change design should be used to establish the size of spurious components of association. This is particularly to be recommended when the number of prior variables creating such association is two or more, making the job of establishing all the 'paths' connecting the two variables via the prior variables tedious and even complicated.

At the end of this discussion of the consequences of the asymmetrical nature of the difference in proportions for causal decomposition it may be pertinent to mention that a symmetrical measure can be obtained by means of so-called *standardisation*. In regression analyses of metric variables it may be difficult to compare the effects of different independent variables due to differences in the nature of the metrics involved (for example, years of education, number of siblings, income, and so on). Therefore, the ordinary ('raw') regression coefficients are often made comparable by standardising the variables, making one standard deviation the common metric. While the raw regression coefficients like the difference in proportions are asymmetrical, the standardised coefficients are symmetrical. A bivariate association comes out the same no matter which variable is defined as independent and which dependent.

It falls outside the scope of this book to go into the topic of standardised variables, interested readers are referred to textbooks of statistics (see, for instance, Iversen 1979: ch. 4). We shall restrict ourselves to an illustration of how we may calculate *standardised differences in proportions*, which in turn may be used to find spurious components by means of effect multiplication.

A standardised difference in proportions is obtained by multiplying the regular difference with the ratio of the standard deviations for the independent and the dependent variable. The *standard deviation* (sd) is a measure for the dispersion in the distribution on a variable. For a dichotomy, it is defined as the square root of the product of the two proportions divided by the number of units in the sample:

$$sd = \sqrt{P(1-P)/N}$$

The standardised difference in proportions d^* can thus be found by means of the following formula:

$$d^* = d(\text{sd}_I/\text{sd}_D) = d\sqrt{P_I(1-P_I)/P_D(1-P_D)}$$

The symbols P_I and $(1-P_I)$ refer to the proportions in the univariate distribution on the independent variable, which in our example in Table 6.4 with sex as the independent variable are 0·50 for men and 0·50 for women. Likewise P_D and $(1-P_D)$ stand for the proportions in the distribution on the dependent variable, or 0·20 and 0·80 for members and non-members with regard to party affiliation. We thus get the following standardised effect of sex on party membership:

$$d^* = 0·20\sqrt{0·5 \times 0·5/0·2 \times 0·8} = 0·20(0·5/0·4) = 0·25$$

If we instead take Table 6.4(c) where party membership is the independent and sex the dependent variable as the point of departure, the regular difference in proportions is 0·31 instead of 0·20, and the numerator and denominator of the fraction within the square root change place:

$$d^* = 0·31\sqrt{0·2 \times 0·8/0·5 \times 0·5} = 0·31(0·4/0·5) = 0·25$$

The standardised difference in proportions is the same regardless of which way we choose to calculate the proportions and take the difference.

In Table 6.6 all the effects needed for a causal analysis of the relationship between the variables in Table 6.5 have been standardised. Using the standardised effects we may apply the effect transmittance design also when we want to obtain spurious components, without any risk of inaccurate results, as illustrated in Table 6.7.

Since standardised coefficients are commonly utilised in causal analyses by means of regression, it may be useful to be acquainted with this procedure from crosstable analysis. When to use which coefficients is a matter of debate within path analysis (cf. Section 9.1). The pro-standardisation arguments are mostly irrelevant when we are dealing with dichotomies, while the anti-arguments apply. Of particular importance is the straightforward intuitive interpretation of the regular difference in proportions as a difference in probability, which is lost if we choose to standardise.

Table 6.6 The Calculation of Standardised Associations

Independent variable	Dependent variable	Control variable	Difference in proportions d	Standardised association $d^* = d\sqrt{P_I(1 - P_I)/P_D(1 - P_D)}$
Sex	Party membership	—	0·20	$0\cdot20\sqrt{\dfrac{0\cdot50(1 - 0\cdot50)}{0\cdot20(1 - 0\cdot20)}} = 0\cdot25$
Sex	Campaign interest	—	0·28	$0\cdot28\sqrt{\dfrac{0\cdot50(1 - 0\cdot50)}{0\cdot38(1 - 0\cdot38)}} = 0\cdot29$
Party membership	Campaign interest	—	0·46	$0\cdot46\sqrt{\dfrac{0\cdot20(1 - 0\cdot20)}{0\cdot38(1 - 0\cdot38)}} = 0\cdot38$
Sex	Campaign interest	Party membership	0·20	$0\cdot20\sqrt{\dfrac{0\cdot50(1 - 0\cdot50)}{0\cdot38(1 - 0\cdot38)}} = 0\cdot21$
Party membership	Campaign interest	Sex	0·40	$0\cdot40\sqrt{\dfrac{0\cdot20(1 - 0\cdot20)}{0\cdot38(1 - 0\cdot38)}} = 0\cdot33$

Table 6.7   *Decomposition of Standardised Associations by Means of Effect Transmittance Design*

	Sex and interest in campaign	Party membership and interest in campaign
Direct effect	0·21	0·33
Indirect effect	0·25 × 0·33 = 0·08	0
Spurious effect	0	0·25 × 0·21 = 0·05
Sum of components	0·29	0·38
Bivariate association	0·29	0·38

Summary

Non-recursive models can be transformed into bloc recursive models by joining variables with reciprocal or ambiguous relations together in blocs, and analysed by means of the effect change design.

When we wish to include polytomous variables in a causal analysis, the consequences for the design depend upon the status of the polytomy in the analysis. As a control variable the polytomy does not require any special procedures, except for restricting us to apply the effect change design. As an independent variable we have to perform a separate analysis for each pair of values we want to compare, leaving units with other values on the polytomy out of the analysis. A polytomous dependent variable is handled by a series of ordinary analyses with the dependent variable successively dichotomised in different ways.

A bivariate difference in proportions will in general vary in size when we alternate the roles of independent and dependent variable in a table, more so the more dissimilar are the distributions on the two variables. The asymmetrical nature of the difference in proportions may lead to inaccuracies if we use the effect transmittance design to calculate the strength of spurious effects.

Glossary

AMBIGUOUS ASSOCIATION: association between pair of variables whose causal nature cannot be determined on the basis of the model.

ASYMMETRIC MEASURE OF ASSOCIATION: size varies according to which variable is chosen as independent variable.

BLOC OF VARIABLES: set of variables joined together in a causal model, whose internal relationships are not analysed.

BLOC RECURSIVE MODEL: model where the relationships between the blocs are free from reciprocal causation (which may occur within each bloc).

DISPERSION: distribution of units on a variable, varying between all having the same value (minimum *d*) to an even split between the values (maximum dispersion).

POLYTOMOUS VARIABLE/POLYTOMY: variable with three or more values.

STANDARD DEVIATION: measure of dispersion.

STANDARDISED DIFFERENCE IN PROPORTIONS: regular difference in proportions made symmetrical by multiplication with the ratio of the standard deviations for the independent and the dependent variable.

SYMMETRIC MEASURE OF ASSOCIATION: size is invariant of which variable is chosen as independent variable.

TRICHOTOMOUS VARIABLE/TRICHOTOMY: variable with three values.

Exercises

6.1 Bloc Recursive Model for Social Background Variables

In the answer to Exercise 3.2 a recursive model for social background variables influencing political participation is suggested. For some of the variables, reciprocal causation might seem a more realistic assumption than one-way causation.

Where would you suggest that two-way causation may occur? How can the revised model be made recursive by joining variables together in blocs? For which causal variables does the bloc recursive model imply a component of ambiguous association in the relationship with political participation?

6.2 The Implications of Assuming Reciprocal Causation

In Exercise 5.1 a recursive model with the four variables in the order of age, residence, education and attitude to premarital sex may seem the natural choice on which to base the analysis. While place of residence may be assumed to influence the probability of acquiring a higher education, influence flowing in the opposite direction is also conceivable, as a result of geographical mobility related to occupational career patterns which differ according to education.

How will the assumption of reciprocal instead of one-way causation between place of residence and education affect the causal interpretation of the relationships between the variables in Exercise 5.1?

6.3 Sex and Legislative Career for Labour Representatives

In Table 6.1 the trivariate frequencies for sex, seniority and rank for Labour Party members of the Norwegian Parliament in 1973–81 are given. Perform an analysis with seniority and rank trichotomised. Compared with the results of the analysis in Exercise 1.2 using dichotomous variables, what is the effect of changing to more refined measures?

6.4   The Asymmetry of the Difference in Proportions

Select one or more of the earlier examples of trivariate causal analyses (for example, status, record and sentence in Chapter 1, sex, occupation and income in Exercise 1.1, or sex, seniority and rank in Exercise 1.2), and check whether the distributions on the two causal variables are sufficiently dissimilar to make their bivariate association differ, depending upon which variable we choose as independent variable.

7

Interpreting the Results

Up to now the findings from our causal analyses have been given straightforward interpretations. Without reservations, a gross association has been explained as the result of direct, indirect and spurious effects. Now it is high time to stress that any such explanation of a statistical relationship, no matter how plausible it may seem, need not be the right one. If the model is adequate in the sense that it has captured the main features of the social phenomena we are studying, and if the data are valid in the sense that they truly reflect these phenomena, then the interpretation will be a sound one. However, these are big ifs, as will be discussed in this chapter.

7.1 Methodological and Substantive Interpretations

Textbooks on methodology tell us how we ought to go about collecting, processing and analysing data in order to avoid the possibility that the final results will give a misleading picture of the social realities we want to portray. By using a random sampling procedure we avoid running the risk that systematic sampling errors will produce statistical association between variables in our material; by means of reliability tests we may be able to rule out the possibility that random measurement errors are the source of the patterns observed in our data; and so on.

We may call all interpretations which explain the outcome of our analysis as a consequence of how the investigation was carried out *methodological interpretations*. Instead of reflecting social realities, a certain pattern is explained as an 'artefact', a result of how the variables were defined, how the sample was drawn, how the data were analysed, or some other characteristic of the investigation. While a comprehensive treatment of this important subject falls outside the scope of this book, in this chapter we will look at some of the main forms of methodological interpretations. The aim is to alert the reader to the importance of taking such explanations into account when the results of a study are discussed.

A researcher will make every effort to disconfirm all methodological interpretations of his/her results which at the outset might seem plausible, thus making substantive interpretations more probable. A *substantive interpretation* is one which explains the patterns found in the data as a result of actual social processes. The influence relations depicted in the causal model need not be the source of these patterns, however, quite different causal mechanisms may actually have produced the associations found between the variables. At the end of this chapter the main kinds of alternative substantive interpretations, that is, causal models where the direction of influence between variables of the original model has been changed, or new variables have been added, will be discussed.

7.2   Sampling Errors

Whenever we analyse data from a sample instead of the entire population of units, the possibility exists that the results reflect peculiarities in the composition of the sample rather than true characteristics of the population. If we have used a random sampling procedure, the interpretation that the effects found in the analysis are caused by systematic sampling errors, which may have large and unpredictable impact on the results, can be ruled out. By following the procedures of probability sampling, we are even in a position to test whether it is likely that random sampling errors may have produced effects of the magnitude we have found in the sample if there in fact are no such effects in the population.

A proper treatment of this topic must be referred to statistics texts (see Blalock 1972, or Iversen 1979), but a brief illustration of how we can assess what impact random sampling errors may be expected to have on the the results of our analysis will be given. In order to calculate a confidence interval for an effect from the sample we start by finding the variance of each partial effect, which equals the sum of the variances for the two proportions from which it is calculated. When $d = P_1 - P_0$, the variance of d is defined as

$$\mathrm{var}(d) = \mathrm{var}(P_1) + \mathrm{var}(P_0)$$
$$= P_1(1-P_1)/n_1 + P_0(1-P_0)/n_0$$

where n_1 (or n_0) is the number of units in the group for which P is calculated, that is, the number of units with the value 1 or 0 respectively on the independent variable. When d is a bivariate difference in proportions, the above formula is all we need to find the variance. When d is one of several partial effects used to obtain the weighted net effect (D), we obtain the variance for D by multiplying the variance of each partial effect by the square of its weight, and sum for all partials (Davis 1975: 128).

$$\text{var}(D) = w_1^2 \times \text{var}(d_1) + w_2^2 \times \text{var}(d_2) + \cdots$$
$$= \Sigma(w_i^2 \times \text{var}(d_i))$$

As an empirical illustration, we may calculate the variance of the effect of status on sentence controlled for record (Table 1.7). We will assume the 216 cases of convicted larcenists to constitute a simple random sample from a larger population, and use the above formulae to assess how far a sample result may reasonably be expected to deviate from the true population figure.

We start by computing the variance of each of the two partial effects, using the information from Table 1.7 on P and n. (Strictly speaking the proportions in the formula refer to the population figures, but when they are unknown to us, we use the sample results instead.)

$$\text{var}(-0.18) = 0.63(1-0.63)/40 + 0.81(1-0.81)/117$$
$$= 0.00583 + 0.00132 = 0.00715$$
$$\text{var}(-0.41) = 0.08(1-0.08)/24 + 0.49(1-0.49)/35$$
$$= 0.00307 + 0.00714 = 0.01021$$

Then we multiply the variances for the partials with the squared weights and sum to get the variance of the weighted overall effect:

$$\text{var}(-0.24) = 0.73^2(0.00715) + 0.27^2(0.01021)$$
$$= 0.00381 + 0.00074 = 0.00455$$

A *confidence interval* is an interval around a sample result that we may expect will include the true population value. With a 95 per cent confidence interval, we mean an interval which is sufficiently large that in a long series of samples 95 per cent will give results which include the population value in the interval. To obtain a 95 per cent confidence interval for the effect of status on sentence we calculate the standard deviation (which is the square root of the variance), and multiply with the factor 1·96:

$$-0.24 \pm 1.96\sqrt{0.00455} = -0.24 \pm 1.96 \times 0.067 = -0.24 \pm 0.13$$

This result tells us that if the effect of status on sentence controlled for record of −0·24 stems from a simple random sample, the true value for the entire population probably lies somewhere between −0·11 and −0·37. The possibility that status actually has no effect on sentence in the population, but that random sampling errors have produced the sample result of −0·24, can accordingly be discarded as highly unlikely. We may feel confident that high status, in fact, does reduce the probability for obtaining a severe sentence within the population.

With more complex sampling designs, the above formulae must be modified. Cluster sampling does, for instance, increase the margin for random errors compared with simple random samples of the same size. As a rule-of-thumb, it has been suggested to increase the confidence intervals with a factor 1·5 (Davis 1975: 128–9). If the effect of −0·24 had come from a cluster sample, we accordingly would have a 95 per cent confidence interval of −0·24 ± 0·20. Even in this case the interpretation that the negative effect of status on sentence may be a result of random sampling error can be dismissed as unlikely.

7.3   Measurement Errors

The possible impact on the results of random measurement errors may be assessed through reliability tests. One way to get a rough impression of the importance of this methodological interpretation in situations where we lack reliability scores, is to look at how the results would be influenced if we change the value of one unit on the dependent variable in the group where the impact of such a change will be greatest, that is, the smallest group. With a group of ten units, to change value for one would change the proportion and the difference in proportions involving this group by 0·1. This means that one such error of measurement would be sufficient to explain effects between 0·1 and −0·1.

As the number of units increases so will, of course, the incidence of measurement errors. So long as they are random, however, we may assume that they will cancel each other out in the long run. It, therefore, still makes sense to look at the impact of a change in value for 1 unit, which with 100 units is reduced to 0·01 and with a 1,000 units to a mere 0·001 for the effects involving this group.

In the table for status, record and sentence (Table 1.4) the smallest group contains 24 units. A change in value from lenient to severe sentence for 1 unit from this group would increase the proportion severe by $1 \cdot 0/24 = 0 \cdot 04$, thus reducing the effect of status among first-offenders to $-0 \cdot 37$. If we make a similar change among high-status recidivists ($1 \cdot 0/40 = 0 \cdot 03$), the effect of status goes down to $-0 \cdot 15$ within this control group. Judging from these results random measurement errors do not seem a very likely explanation of the negative effects of status on sentence.

While the development of random sampling procedures has made it fairly simple to avoid the danger of systematic sampling errors, the problem of systematic measurement errors is still a serious one in social research. Often referred to as lack of *validity* of the measures used to represent the variables of the causal model in the empirical analysis, this shortcoming may influence the results very strongly. As an illustration, we shall look at a case of a researcher analysing data from a nation other than his own, suggesting that lack of familiarity with a social system is one possible source of systematic measurement errors.

The case in hand is a study of difference between male and female candidates in the chances of being elected Members of Parliament in Denmark and Norway (Foverskov 1978). The Danish political scientist found that in the elections he analysed, male candidates had an election rate $0 \cdot 06$ above that of the female candidates in Norway. Does this mean that the voters prefer male candidates?

At this point it is vital to be aware that in Norway parliamentary elections take place within multimember constituencies, ranging in size from four to fifteen in the number of representatives elected. The seats are distributed between the five to ten competing party lists in proportion to the number of votes received. Each list contains a number of candidates equal to the number of seats plus six. In contrast to several other electoral systems with multimember constituencies, the voters cannot influence the ranking of the candidates made by a party. If the list obtains one seat, the candidate ranked number one gets it, a second seat goes to candidate number two, and so on.

This arrangement suggests one important intervening variable between sex and election success for candidates, their position on the party list. Are female candidates less likely to be elected simply because they occupy lower positions on the lists than their male competitors? To find out the researcher controlled for list position by comparing candidates occupying the top three positions and candidates in lower positions separately. Instead of disappearing, however, the control for list position actually rendered the effect of sex on election success slightly stronger.

Before drawing the conclusion that Norwegian voters shun the lists featuring women in high positions, a closer look at the measure for list position is in order (the other two variables, male/female and elected/not elected, hardly pose any measurement problem). The purpose of controlling for list position is to make sure that the men and women we compare with regard to election success had the same chances for being elected in the outset. Anyone familiar with Norwegian elections would know, however, that this is not attained by classifying the top three positions as high regardless of which party list they belong to, and likewise positions from number four and down as low for all party lists. If you were a candidate from a major party in a large constituency, you actually may be ranked four, five, or even six and still be confident of being elected, since the list normally wins that many seats. On the other hand, being second or even first candidate on a list for a minor party in a small constituency means that you are practically without any hope of being elected, since the list cannot be expected to obtain even one seat.

To treat all party lists as equal when defining list position, therefore, results in a systematic measurement error. Some candidates for large parties are classified as occupying low positions while they in fact have a very favourable position, and some candidates for small parties with virtually no chances for being elected are classified as having a high position. A more valid measure for list position would be to classify the places on a list on the basis of the number of seats obtained by the list in the preceding election, since the changes from one election to the next usually are modest (to use predictions based on the polls for party preference would be another possibility). In Figure 7.1 the results of an analysis of a more recent election (Hellevik 1979) using both measures for list position are displayed.

The difference is striking. Using a measure for the intervening variable which has low validity as one would expect lowers the effect of list position on election success. The systematic measurement errors will necessarily lower the proportion of candidates being elected within the high position category (due to top three candidates from minor parties), while at the same time increasing the proportion elected from the low position category (candidates ranked 4, 5, etc. from major parties). The result is a lower difference in proportions for the effect of list position on election success.

It also turns out that reduced validity lowers the association between sex and list position. This means that the female candidates must have had a disproportionate large share of the 'worthless' top three positions, while male candidates have been overrepresented in

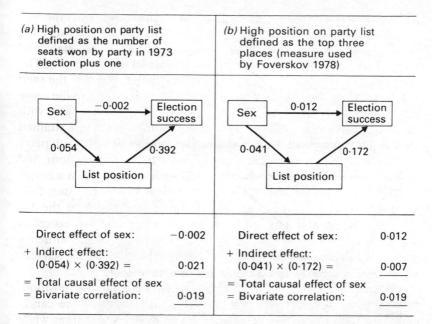

Figure 7.1 *The effect of sex on election success for the 1977 election to the Norwegian Parliament, controlling for two different measures for list position.*

the positions from four to six or seven on major party lists with a seat in Parliament within reach.

Underestimating the real strength of both direct effects in the path leading from sex through list position to election success means ending up with too weak an indirect effect via this path. And the direct effect of sex on election success comes out too strong, since the control for list position fails to remove the full impact of the intervening variable on the relationship. The causal analysis with a more valid measure for list position leads to a conclusion which departs from the original one. Anyone concerned with increasing the proportion of seats in Parliament held by women, instead of blaming the voters ought to direct their attention to the nomination process when the parties compose the list of candidates. The effect of sex on the election rate is totally an indirect effect due to differences in list position. (Readers thinking that too much fuss is being made over such a small effect, may consider the fact that since so few are elected, only 0·055 of the male and 0·036 of the female candidates, the difference in the election rate has the consequence of reducing *(a)* Seniority dichotomised 0–3/4– sessions; rank no position/any position

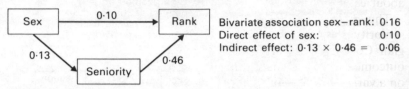

Bivariate association sex–rank: 0·16
Direct effect of sex: 0·10
Indirect effect: 0·13 × 0·46 =   0·06

(b) Seniority dichotomised 0–7/8– sessions; rank as under *(a)*

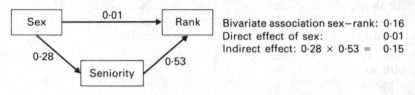

Bivariate association sex–rank: 0·16
Direct effect of sex: 0·01
Indirect effect: 0·28 × 0·53 =   0·15

(c) Seniority as under *(b)*; rank dichotomised no or ceremonial
position/politically important position

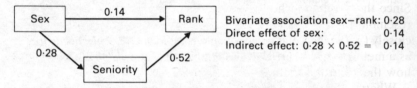

Bivariate association sex–rank: 0·28
Direct effect of sex: 0·14
Indirect effect: 0·28 × 0·52 =   0·14

Figure 7.2   *Impact of changes in dichotomisation on the decomposition of*
the association between sex and rank for Conservative
representatives (data from Table 6.1).

the women's share from one-third of the candidates to one-quarter of
the representatives.)

7.4 Categorisation Effects

As demonstrated in Section 6.2, polytomous variables may be
included in a causal analysis. A polytomy means a more complex
design and an increase in the number of effect measures in the results
(when used as independent or dependent variable), and entails
spreading the units on more groups, thus lowering the basis for each
proportion (when used as independent or control variable). It will,
therefore, always be tempting and sometimes necessay to work with
dichotomies. Collapsing a variable into a more crude measure may
have dramatic consequences for the results, however. If the number
of categories used when collapsing a variable, or where the cuts are

made, influences the results reached in the analysis, we may talk about categorisation effects.

The analysis in Section 6.2 of the relationship between sex, seniority and legislative career for representatives from the Norwegian Conservative Party provided a striking example of how the outcome of a causal analysis may be affected when we use two values on a variable instead of three. In Figure 7.2 the changes in the causal decomposition of the association between sex and rank in Parliament produced by changes in the way seniority and rank are dichotomised are shown. (To avoid confusion among readers with a memory alert enough to recall that the effects computed in Exercise 1.2 differ slightly from those in Figure 7.2(a) it should be mentioned that a more complex weight has been used than the one we have worked with so far, anticipating the discussion of weights in Chapter 8.)

Moving the cut on the seniority variable upwards from 3–4 to 7–8 sessions attended increases the effect of sex on seniority, as well as the effect of seniority on rank. The consequence is a stronger indirect effect, while the direct effect of sex on rank virtually disappears. Since the results reached with the dichotomisation of Figure 7.2(b) resemble those we got with a trichotomised seniority variable quite closely (Table 6.2), the outcome of Figure 7.2(a) must be interpreted as a methodological artefact, an effect of an unfortunate choice as to how the control variable was dichotomised.

When the cut on the dependent variable is changed from analysing how the probability of acquiring any kind of leadership position is affected by sex and seniority to looking only at positions with a potential for wielding political power, we, first of all, note that the bivariate association between sex and rank is increased. Men are more favoured with regard to the important positions than with regard to positions in general. Secondly, we see that in this case sex has a direct effect of equal importance as the indirect effect (Figure 7.2(c)).

If we want to collapse a polytomous variable in a causal analysis, we ought to test whether different solutions with regard to the number of categories and where the cuts are made influence the outcome of the analysis. Otherwise, we cannot be certain that our results are not a reflection of categorisation effects rather than characteristics of the social phenomenon we study.

7.5 Alternative Substantive Interpretations

If we feel confident that methodological interpretations of the results of a causal analysis can be dismissed as unlikely, the question of whether other causal mechanisms rather than the one depicted in our model may explain the observed relationships remains. Assumptions made with regard to the sign or strength of effects between variables of the model may be proven wrong by the outcome of the analysis. The assumptions with regard to which variables to include and how to order them will not be tested, however. The question of alternative substantive interpretations to the original model asks whether models with changes in the direction of influence between variables, or with new variables added, may be envisaged.

Our ability to come up with reasonable alternative models will, of course, depend upon our theoretical imagination and knowledge of the social phenomena under study. The causal approach helps us by providing the general structure of alternative interpretations, directing us to look for causal influences which conceivably might flow in the opposite direction, and prior variables affecting causal as well as effect variables of our model. It is our job, however, to come up with the concrete proposals.

As an illustration of such an effort, we may consider the interpretation of results from a survey showing the political activity to be higher among married than unmarried men, while for women the proportion active was highest among the unmarried (Halsaa Albrektsen 1977; the results are given in Exercise 7.3). The author suggests one way of explaining this pattern, that marriage constitutes a resource for politically active men, while it hampers the activity of women, who have to cater to their husband's needs as well as their own. This explanation is portrayed in Figure 7.3 with separate models for men and women, since the effect of marriage on political activity is assumed to differ according to sex (a case of statistical interaction).

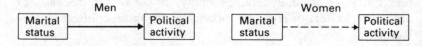

Figure 7.3   *Original model explaining the association between marital status and political activity.*

What about alternative substantive interpretations? First, we consider the possibility of a change in the causal ordering. May political activity affect the probability of getting (or staying) married, rather than the other way round, as assumed in Figure 7.4? Such a causal mechanism cannot be discarded as totally implausible. Politically active women may see marriage as a threat to their career, or perhaps

Figure 7.4 *Alternative model with changed causal direction.*

be considered less attractive as partners by some men. A man who wants to make a political career will see the need for a supporting wife, and so on.

With regard to additional variables, we will primarily be concerned with prior variables. In some cases the distinction between direct and indirect effect may be of crucial importance, as for instance in the analysis of whether there is any direct discrimination of women in the recruitment to leadership positions within a political assembly. In most cases, however, the distinction between on the one hand causal effect, be it direct or indirect, and on the other spurious effect, is the important one. So also with the case at hand. Although it is possible to envisage several intervening variables between marital status and political activity, our primary interest will be whether there may exist prior variables rendering the association between the original pair wholly or partly spurious.

There are a lot of variables known to influence political activity (cf. Exercise 3.2), but in order to create spurious effect they must also influence marital status. Furthermore, the two effects from the prior variable must have the same sign for men (in order to account for the positive association between marital status and political activity), and opposite signs for the women (so as to cause negative association).

These requirements certainly reduce the number of potential candidates, but one possible prior variable with such effects may be age. For men, we would assume that becoming of age increases the chances of being married as well as being politically active. For women, we might postulate a similar positive effect of age on marital status, but a negative effect with regard to political activity, arguing that the new wave of feminism has made the younger generation more active than older women, thus offsetting the difference created by the tendency for a person to become more involved in politics as she grows older (Figure 7.5).

Perhaps the most plausible model would be one combining the assumptions of the first three, saying that age causes some spurious effect between the original two variables, at the same time as marital status has some effect on political activity, and there also is a certain effect in the opposite direction (Figure 7.6).

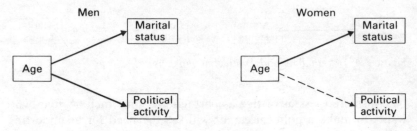

Figure 7.5   *Alternative model with prior variable.*

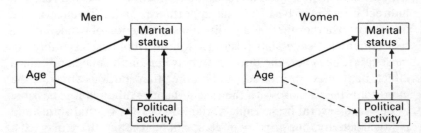

Figure 7.6   *Alternative model combining the assumptions of the prior three models.*

The task now is to come up with empirical grounds for choosing one of the models at the expense of the others. Ideally, a researcher will think through the alternative ways of explaining an expected finding before collecting the data, in order to make sure that the study design makes testing of the competing models possible. If the causal ordering or the variables is not evident, this entails collecting data from at least two different points in time. With regard to the relationship between marital status and political participation, we need to know how active a person was at an early age, to see if differences in activity level is associated with differences in the probability of entering into marriage. A measure of activity at a later stage will then tell us if an eventual marriage has been followed by a change in political participation. Such data may be provided by means of recall questions, or by repeated interviews with the same respondents (panel design), but as discussed in methodology texts both approaches may give rise to methodological interpretations.

Ideas about sources of spurious effect may be tested by controlling for the prior variables in question, provided that they are included in the data matrix, and the number of units is sufficiently high to permit the multivariate analysis required by the expanded model. The last provision poses a problem for the case at hand, since the number of unmarried men or women in the study is too low to allow further splits according to age. Had the need for such a control been foreseen when the study was planned, a sampling design giving unmarried persons a disproportionately large share might have been contemplated (in which case the weights would have to be based on the composition of the population rather than the sample).

When we are stuck with a data-set which does not permit strict empirical testing of the alternative models, we have to rely on our best judgement of what seems reasonable, supplemented with relevant results from other studies. In the presentation of the results the uncertainties attached to the interpretation must be stressed.

Summary

When we perform a causal analysis, we assume that the observed associations result from the social processes portrayed in our model. This interpretation is not the only one conceivable, however. The way in which the data have been selected, collected and analysed may have influenced the results, making methodological explanations a possibility which has to be considered. Or social processes different from the one postulated in the model may produce the same pattern of associations, thus giving rise to alternative substantive interpretations of the results.

Some main forms of methodological interpretations are systematic and random sampling errors, systematic and random measurement errors, and categorisation effects. Social science methodology suggests how best we may conduct an investigation so as to reduce the danger of getting results which reflect characteristics of the research process rather than of social reality.

Alternative substantive interpretations have two main forms, postulating either a change of causal direction or the addition of new variables in relation to the original model.

Glossary

CATEGORISATION EFFECT: change in results as consequence of collapsing values on variable into broader categories.

CONFIDENCE INTERVAL: interval around sample result which with a specified probability may be expected to contain the true population figure.

MEASUREMENT ERROR: difference between value assigned to units and their true value on a variable.

METHODOLOGICAL INTERPRETATION: explanation of results as a consequence of characteristics of the investigation.
RELIABILITY: degree to which data are free of random measurement errors.
SAMPLING ERROR: difference between results from a sample and those which would have been obtained from the entire population.
SUBSTANTIVE INTERPRETATION: explanation of results as a reflection of social processes.
VALIDITY: degree of correspondance between the theoretical meaning of a variable in the causal model and the measure used for the variable in the empirical analysis.

Exercises

7.1 Direct Wage Discrimination against Women?

In Exercise 1.1 the analysis showed a direct effect of sex on the chances of receiving a high income of 0·45 when controlled for occupation. One straightforward interpretation of this result is that it reflects a practice of paying women less than men for the same kind of work. Suggest other possible explanations.

7.2 Effect of Sex a Result of Measurement Errors?

Consider whether random measurement errors may be a likely explanation of the result reported in Table 6.3 that male representatives from the Conservative Party have a higher likelihood of obtaining important leadership positions than female representatives in the Norwegian national assembly.

7.3 Effect of Marital Status on Political Activity a Result of Sampling Errors?

The results of the survey discussed in Section 7.5 gave the following proportions for a high level of political activity (with bases in parentheses): married men 0·29 (337); unmarried men 0·13 (48); married women 0·11 (335); unmarried women 0·22 (27), deleting the figures for the very small groups of previously married (Halsaa Albrektsen 1977: 174). Assuming that the sample used is a simple random sample, is it likely that the positive effect of marriage on political activity among men is a result of random sampling errors? What about the negative effect of marriage among women?

7.4 Age as a Source of Spurious Effect between Marital Status and Political Activity

Due to the low number of unmarried women (see Exercise 7.3), a control for age as proposed in Section 7.5 is not carried out by the researcher. Another table in the book (Halsaa Albrektsen 1977: 176), gives the following proportions politically active with four age categories: men (from youngest to oldest) 18, 21, 33 and 25; women 8, 10, 9 and 19. Do these results make the explanation of the association between marital status and political activity as spurious effect due to the age variable more or less likely?

7.5 Interpret Results of Own Analysis

In Exercise 1.4 you were asked to perform a causal analysis of a table of your own choosing. Discuss possible methodological interpretations of the results you reached, and consider whether alternative substantive models seem plausible. How would you go about testing the competing explanations of your results?

8

The Analysis of Interaction-Ridden Data

Up to now we have not paid much attention to statistical interaction. A reader may have been left with the impression that varying partial effects merely represent a computational nuisance, requiring us to go through the weighting procedure in order to obtain the net effect. There is more to the problem of interaction, however, as will be discussed in this chapter.

First of all, we will often encounter an approach to the analysis of interaction-ridden data quite different from the causal decomposition of associations by means of weighted average effects we have been performing. Focusing on the variation in the proportions of a multivariate table, separate measures for interaction effects are calculated. We shall look at one such scheme for prediction analysis, which decomposes proportions instead of differences in proportions.

Returning to the causal approach we shall see that several different weighting schemes have been proposed over the years. A comparison of the proposals reveals that a more accurate decomposition of associations is obtained by using a more complex weight than the one we have relied on so far.

The rationale for weighting given in this book has been that the partial effects from some control groups will have greater impact on the overall effect than others due to differences in the number of units involved. Most discussions of weighting, however, are carried out with reference to variations in our confidence in each partial effect as an estimate of a common population effect, assuming the differences between the partial effects to be merely a result of random errors in sampling or measurement.

In fact, it is often claimed that causal decomposition presupposes interaction-free data, that significantly different partial effects make the results of a causal analysis inaccurate or even meaningless. Arguments and counterarguments in this debate are presented, giving readers a chance to judge for themselves.

The position taken in this book is that causal decomposition is both feasible and meaningful even with interaction-ridden data. But although the weighted average effects permit us to decompose associations without taking interaction explicitly into account, its occurrence will have implications for a causal analysis. Interaction will in various ways affect our interpretation of the results of the analysis. In some cases it may even lead to a change in design, to a comparative causal analysis allowing variations of particular interest in the effect of a variable to be emphasised.

8.1   Decomposing Proportions: Prediction Analysis

A survey of quantitative empirical analyses will reveal that by no means all of them have the kinds of question we have been asking – 'why are X and Y related', 'can Z explain the association between X and Y' – as their point of departure. Instead we find that the interest is centred on the variation in the proportion of units with a high value on the dependent variable between groups with different combinations of values on the independent variables.

The reason for such an interest may be a desire to be able to predict whether a unit will have a high value on the dependent variable or not. If, by means of the independent variables, we manage to sort the units into groups where either all or none have a high value on the dependent variable, that is, proportions of either $1 \cdot 0$ or $0 \cdot 0$, such predictions could be made with absolute certainty on the basis of knowledge of which values a unit has on the independent variables.

In practice the goal of complete certainty in the predictions will seldom be reached. Instead the proportions will lie somewhere between the extremes of $0 \cdot 0$ and $1 \cdot 0$, indicating the probability for a high value on the dependent variable for each particular group. We shall call an analysis which aims at describing the variation in this probability as a function of the independent variables a *prediction analysis*. Instead of decomposing a difference in proportions into causal components, as in a causal analysis, a prediction analysis decomposes proportions into variable effects and interaction effects.

In situations with interaction-free data the same effect measures can be used for both purposes. To illustrate this we may use data from Exercise 1.1 (Table 8.1). A proportion is designated by the values of the two independent variables (P_{11} accordingly is the proportion with a high income among men in white-collar occupations, P_{10} the proportion for the group with a high value on sex and a low value on occupation, and so on). The two partial effects for sex $d_{.1}$ and $d_{.0}$, where the position of the dot indicates that these are the

Table 8.1 *Prediction Analysis with Interaction-Free Data: Decomposing the Proportion of High-Income Earners (Exercise 1.1)*

Occupation	Sex		Difference
	1 Male	0 Female	
1 White collar	P_{11} 0·76	P_{01} 0·31	$d_{.1}$ 0·45
0 Blue collar	P_{10} 0·56	P_{00} 0·11	$d_{.0}$ 0·45
Difference	$d_{1.}$ 0·20	$d_{0.}$ 0·20	

Occupation	Sex		Difference
	1 Male	0 Female	
1 White collar	$P_{11} = C + E_1 + E_2$ $= 0·11 + 0·45 + 0·20 = 0·76$	$P_{01} = C + E_2$ $= 0·11 + 0·20 = 0·31$	$d_{.1}$ 0·45
0 Blue collar	$P_{10} = C + E_1$ $= 0·11 + 0·45 = 0·56$	$P_{00} = C$ $= 0·11$	$d_{.0}$ 0·45
Difference	$E_1 = d_{.1} = d_{.0} = 0·45; \quad E_2 = d_{1.} = d_{0.} = 0·20$ $C = P_{00} = 0·11$		

effects of the first variable, and the numbers refer to the value kept constant on the control variable occupation) are identical. Correspondingly, the partial effects of occupation on income are the same for men and women. The result is a net effect of sex on income of 0·45, and of occupation on income of 0·20.

We expect other variables than sex and occupation to affect the probability for a high income. Assuming that these variables are unrelated to our two independent variables their contribution will be the same for all four groups. Among female blue-collar workers, neither sex nor occupation have a high value. The proportion of 0·11 high-income earners in this group P_{00} may be regarded as the *constant* impact from other unrelated variables. By adding the effect of sex to this constant we arrive at the proportion among *male* blue-collar workers ($P_{10} = 0·11 + 0·45 = 0·56$). For female *white-collar workers*, occupation has taken on its high value, while sex remains 'low'. We, therefore, find the proportion with a high income by adding the effect of occupation to the constant ($P_{01}=0·11+0·20= 0·31$). Among *white-collar men*, both independent variables contribute to the probability for a high income ($P_{11} = 0·11 + 0·45 + 0·20 = 0·76$).

It has thus been demonstrated that by means of the constant and the effect of the two variables we are able to reproduce the four proportions of the multivariate table. In Exercise 1.1 we used the same variable effects to measure direct effects in our causal analysis. With interaction-free data, the identical partial effects give us a measure for the net effect of a variable which may be used to decompose the proportions of a dependent variable as well as its association with the independent variables. With interaction-ridden data, however, the same effect measure can no longer serve both purposes. To demonstrate this we shall use the data analysed in Chapter 1 on social status, criminal record and sentence.

Table 8.2 shows the proportion receiving a severe sentence for each of the four groups, and the differences in proportions giving the partial effects. In Chapter 1 we calculated weighted averages of the two dissimilar partial effects of each independent variable (Table 1.7). The result was an overall effect of −0·24 for status (which we may refer to as D_1, to distinguish it from the effect we later shall calculate for prediction purposes E_1), and of 0·39 for record (D_2).

If we now proceed as in the previous example (Table 8.1), taking P_{00} as the constant C, and adding D_1 for groups where the status is high, and D_2 for those with a criminal record, we soon discover that our predictions are going astray. The proportion severely sentenced

Table 8.2 Prediction Analysis with Interaction-Ridden Data: Decomposing the Proportion Severely Sentenced (Table 1.5)

Criminal record	Social status		Difference
	1 High	0 Low	
1 Criminal	P_{11} 0.63	P_{01} 0.81	$d_{.1}$ −0.18
0 Clean	P_{10} 0.08	P_{00} 0.49	$d_{.0}$ −0.41
Difference	$d_{1.}$ 0.55	$d_{0.}$ 0.32	

Decomposition:

	Social status	
	1 High	0 Low
	$P_{11} = C + E_1 + E_2 + I_{12}$ $= 0.37 - 0.30 + 0.44 + 0.12$ $= 0.63$	$P_{01} = C + E_2$ $= 0.37 + 0.44$ $= 0.81$
	$P_{10} = C + E_1$ $= 0.37 - 0.30$ $= 0.07$	$P_{00} = C + I_{12}$ $= 0.37 + 0.12$ $= 0.49$

$$E_1 = \tfrac{1}{2}(d_{.1} + d_{.0}) = \tfrac{1}{2}(-0.18 - 0.41) = -0.30$$
$$E_2 = \tfrac{1}{2}(d_{1.} + d_{0.}) = \tfrac{1}{2}(0.55 + 0.32) = 0.44$$
$$I_{12} = \tfrac{1}{2}(d_{1.} - d_{0.}) = \tfrac{1}{2}(0.55 - 0.32) = 0.12$$
$$C = P_{00} - I_{12} = 0.49 - 0.12 = 0.37$$

predicted for *high-status* first-offenders is $C + D_1 = 0.49 - 0.24 = 0.25$, far from the actual proportion P_{10} of 0.08. For low-status *recidivists*, the prediction is $C + D_2 = 0.49 + 0.39 = 0.88$, which deviates from the correct figure of 0.81 (P_{01}). For the last group, we come close $(C + D_1 + D_2 = 0.49 - 0.24 + 0.39 = 0.64$, as compared to P_{11} of $0.63)$. But on the whole the precision of our predictions of the proportion receiving a severe sentence is far from impressive when we use the weighted average effects from our causal analysis.

The source of our problems is the interaction. When the effect of a variable changes as we move from one control group to another, it is impossible to reproduce the four proportions by means of two variable effects and a constant, in addition we need a measure for the interaction effect. Table 8.2 shows one way of doing this, following a scheme proposed by Coleman (1964).

As the effect E of a variable we take the unweighted average of its two partial effects. The interaction between the two independent variables in their effect on the dependent variable is measured as the distance between this midpoint and the partial effects, or in other words, as one-half of the distance between them $(I_{12} = \frac{1}{2}(d_{.1} - d_{.0}) = \frac{1}{2}(d_{1.} - d_{0.})$, the result is the same whichever set of partials we use). We thus find the prediction effect of status to be -0.30, telling us that compared to a low-status group with the same criminal record, a high-status group on the average has a proportion with a severe sentence which is 0.30 lower. A criminal record leads us to expect an increase in the proportion severely sentenced of 0.44. The interaction effect of 0.12 tells us that for groups where the independent variables have consonant value combinations (11 or 00), there will be an increase in the expected proportion of this magnitude.

This time we cannot take P_{00} as a measure for the constant, since there is an interaction effect present in this group. By subtracting the interaction effect from the proportion we obtain the size of the constant: $C = P_{00} - I_{12} = 0.49 - 0.12 = 0.37$. (Any other group might have been chosen to find C, by subtracting the relevant effects from the proportion found in the group.)

By means of the four effects $(C, E_1, E_2,$ and $I_{12})$ we as Table 8.2 shows are able to reproduce all four proportions accurately (disregarding a rounding error for P_{10}). It has thus been demonstrated that with interaction-ridden data we cannot use the effects from a causal analysis to decompose a multivariate set of proportions, to accomplish this we need effect measures which take the variation in partial effects into account.

Just as the causal effects are unsuited for prediction purposes, however, the effects of our prediction analysis cannot be used when we are seeking a causal decomposition of bivariate differences in proportions. Causal diagrams are sometimes used to display the results of prediction analyses, with interaction effects indicated by drawing arrows from the control variables on to the effect which it affects (Knoke and Burke 1980: 47). In Figure 8.1 the results from Table 8.2 are presented in this way, with the bivariate association between status and record added.

Is it possible to utilise the information on interaction in Figure 8.1 to obtain a causal decomposition of the association between status or record and sentence? So far, no one has come up with a practical suggestion as to how this may be done. If we cannot incorporate the interaction effect in the causal decomposition, a possibility might be to disregard it and just use the variable effects. This, however, as will be shown later in this chapter when alternative weighting schemes are discussed, leads to inaccuracies in the decomposition of associations.

In a situation with interaction we thus have to ask ourselves whether we are interested in analysing the proportions of the multivariate table or in explaining why pairs of variables are related. The way we proceed to find the statistical effects will depend on the purpose of the analysis. Weighted averages of the partial effects permit us to decompose associations in a causal analysis, while unweighted averages supplemented with interaction effects make it possible to predict the proportion with a high value on the dependent variable for each combination of values on the independent variables. The important thing is to avoid applying statistical measures which are inappropriate for the aim of our analysis.

In a prediction analysis we need not concern ourselves with the

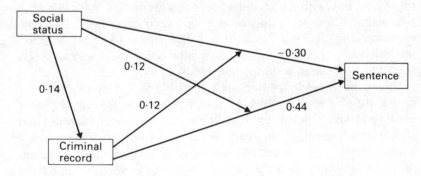

Figure 8.1   *Graphical presentation of results of prediction analysis (Table 8.2).*

Table 8.3 The Effect of Father's Occupation, Father's Vote, and Own Occupation on Own Vote (Valen and Katz 1964: 177)

X_1 Father's occupation	X_2 Father's vote	X_3 Own occupation	X_4 Own vote Proportion socialist	Partial effects of variable: X_1	X_2	X_3
1 Worker	1 Socialist	1 Worker	P_{111} 0·90			$d_{11.}$ 0·24
		0 White collar	P_{110} 0·66		$d_{1.1}$ 0·28	
	0 Non-socialist	1 Worker	P_{101} 0·62	$d_{.11}$ −0·04	$d_{1.0}$ 0·48	$d_{10.}$ 0·44
		0 White collar	P_{100} 0·18	$d_{.10}$ 0·40		
0 Farmer/ white collar	1 Socialist	1 Worker	P_{011} 0·94	$d_{.01}$ 0·14	$d_{0.1}$ 0·46	$d_{01.}$ 0·68
		0 White collar	P_{010} 0·26	$d_{.00}$ 0·07	$d_{0.0}$ 0·15	
	0 Non-socialist	1 Worker	P_{001} 0·48			$d_{00.}$ 0·37
		0 White collar	P_{000} 0·11			

relationship between the independent variables (for example, the effect of status on record in Figure 8.1), since indirect or spurious effects are irrelevant for an analysis of the variation in the proportions of a multivariate table. In order to obtain an accurate decomposition of these proportions, however, it is not enough to work with one direct effect for each independent variable as we do in a causal analysis, an additional interaction effect is required. This distinguishing characteristic becomes more pronounced as the number of variables rises. To illustrate the increasing complexity of the interaction effects we shall take a brief look at a four variable prediction analyses.

Table 8.3 gives the actual proportions from the study of how the tendency to vote socialist depends on father's occupation, father's vote and own occupation. The data were used in a modified interaction-free version to illustrate analysis designs in Chapter 5 (Table 5.1). The real data are far from interaction-free, as the varying partial effects of each variable indicate.

Table 8.4 shows how to find the prediction effect of the three

Table 8.4   *The Calculation of Variable and Interaction Effects (from Table 8.3)*

Variable effects:

$$E_1 = \tfrac{1}{4}(d_{.11} + d_{.10} + d_{.01} + d_{.00})$$
$$= \tfrac{1}{4}(-0\cdot04 + 0\cdot40 + 0\cdot14 + 0\cdot07) = 0\cdot14$$

$$E_2 = \tfrac{1}{4}(d_{1.1} + d_{1.0} + d_{0.1} + d_{0.0})$$
$$= \tfrac{1}{4}(0\cdot28 + 0\cdot48 + 0\cdot46 + 0\cdot15) = 0\cdot34$$

$$E_3 = \tfrac{1}{4}(d_{11.} + d_{10.} + d_{01.} + d_{00.})$$
$$= \tfrac{1}{4}(0\cdot24 + 0\cdot44 + 0\cdot68 + 0\cdot37) = 0\cdot43$$

Interaction effects:

$$I_{12} = \tfrac{1}{4}((d_{.11} + d_{.10}) - (d_{.01} + d_{.00}))$$
$$= \tfrac{1}{4}((-0\cdot04 + 0\cdot40) - (0\cdot14 + 0\cdot07)) = 0\cdot04$$

$$I_{13} = \tfrac{1}{4}((d_{.11} + d_{.01}) - (d_{.10} + d_{.00}))$$
$$= \tfrac{1}{4}((-0\cdot04 + 0\cdot14) - (0\cdot40 + 0\cdot07)) = -0\cdot09$$

$$I_{23} = \tfrac{1}{4}((d_{1.1} + d_{0.1}) - (d_{1.0} + d_{0.0}))$$
$$= \tfrac{1}{4}((0\cdot28 + 0\cdot46) - (0\cdot48 + 0\cdot15)) = 0\cdot03$$

$$I_{123} = \tfrac{1}{4}((d_{.11} - d_{.10}) - (d_{.01} - d_{.00}))$$
$$= \tfrac{1}{4}((-0\cdot04 - 0\cdot40) - (0\cdot14 - 0\cdot07)) = -0\cdot13$$

independent variables, by taking the unweighted average of the partial effects. Then pairwise interaction effects are computed from the partial effects of one of the variables in the pair, adding the two partials where the other variable has its high value, and subtracting the two where the value is low. All three pairwise interactions (often called *first-order interactions*) are small, the strongest being the one between X_1 and X_3 (father's occupation and own occupation). The interaction effect of -0.09 indicates a tendency for the partial effects of either variable to be on the average somewhat stronger in control groups where the other variable has its low value.

Finally, we have the possibility that all three independent variables may interact in their effect on own vote. This *second-order interaction* is computed by taking the difference between each of the two partial effects we summed to find a first-order interaction, and then the difference between these differences (compare the way I_{123} is computed in Table 8.4 with the computation of I_{12}). A negative second-order interaction tells us that the effect of anyone of the three independent variables is stronger when the other two variables have dissonant value combinations (10 or 01) than when the combination is consonant (11 or 00).

For two of the variables, father's occupation and own occupation, the value combinations have an interesting substantive meaning, in relation to intergenerational social mobility. Dissonant values mean that the children have been socially mobile compared to their fathers, while consonant values indicate occupational stability across generations. One theoretically interesting interpretation of the second-order interaction of -0.13 accordingly is that social mobility enhances the effect of the party preference of the father on the party chosen by his offspring.

Figure 8.2 shows how the results of the prediction analysis may be displayed graphically. Since an interaction effect is symmetric for the independent variables involved, curves connecting the relevant effects are used instead of arrows as in Figure 8.1. In this way we avoid unnecessary cluttering, and make it easier to incorporate higher-order interactions.

Finally, Table 8.5 gives the decomposition of the eight proportions of Table 8.3 by means of our three variable effects, four interaction effects and the constant (found by subtracting the relevant effects from whichever proportion we choose). Except for a rounding error for P_{000}, all proportions are accurately reproduced.

It would not be surprising if this rather brief exposition of a four-variable prediction analysis leaves the reader confused as to how

Table 8.5 Decomposition of the Proportions of Table 8.3

$$P_{ijk} = C + E_1 + E_2 + E_3 + I_{12} + I_{13} + I_{23} + I_{123}$$

1 Father's occupation	2 Father's vote	3 Own occupation	4 Own vote socialist	P_{ijk}	Constant $= C$	Variable effects E_1	E_2	E_3	I_{12}	Interaction effects I_{13}	I_{23}	I_{123}
1 Worker	1 Socialist	1 Worker	0·90	P_{111}	= 0·14	+0·14	+0·34	+0·43	+0·04	−0·09	+0·03	−0·13
		0 White collar	0·66	P_{110}	= 0·14	+0·14	+0·34		+0·04			
	0 Non-socialist	1 Worker	0·62	P_{101}	= 0·14	+0·14		+0·43		−0·09		
		0 White collar	0·18	P_{100}	= 0·14	+0·14					+0·03	−0·13
0 Farmer/white collar	1 Socialist	1 Worker	0·94	P_{011}	= 0·14		+0·34	+0·43			+0·03	
		0 White collar	0·26	P_{010}	= 0·14		+0·34			−0·09		−0·13
	0 Non-socialist	1 Worker	0·48	P_{001}	= 0·14			+0·43				−0·13
		0 White collar	0·11	P_{000}	= 0·14				+0·04	−0·09	+0·03	

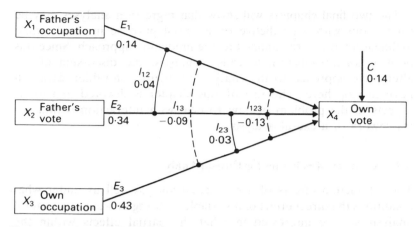

Figure 8.2   *Prediction effects on own vote (from Table 8.4)*

the interaction terms are computed, in which groups they take effect and how they are to be interpreted. Try then to imagine an analysis with five variables, presenting us with the possibility of having to cope with 11 interaction effects (6 first-order, 4 second-order and 1 third-order interaction). Or a six-variable analysis, with 26 different interaction effects, one of them involving five independent variables! The challenge would not so much be on the computational side, however tedious the calculations, but on our ability to digest the information contained in the results, growing in amount and complexity at a rate which soon exceeds the limits of our comprehension.

A prediction analyst, therefore, will always hope that at least some of the interaction effects will turn out to be insignificant. By deleting them we obtain a simplification in the sense that the set of proportions may be reproduced by means of a number of effects smaller than the number of proportions. As we shall see in Chapter 10, an appealing property of loglinear analysis is its efficiency when it comes to detecting the most parsimonious way of describing a multivariate table, by systematically testing out the consequences for the accuracy of our predictions of deleting interaction or variable effects.

The complexities of multivariate prediction analysis also serve to set off an advantage of the causal approach, its guarantee for simple and intelligible results. It does not matter if we have four, five, six, or even more variables in our model, we can always decompose a bivariate association into components which we interpret as direct, indirect, or spurious effect (given a recursive model and a sufficient number of units for the analysis).

Table 8.6 shows how this is done for the effect of status on sentence controlled for record.

To find the standardised proportion severely sentenced among high-status defendants the two proportions from the trivariate table involving high-status defendants are used. A weighted average of the two proportions is obtained by using the share of all units having the relevant value on the control variable as weight. The same set of weights are then used to find the standardised proportion from the two trivariate proportions for low-status defendants. The difference between the two proportions -0.24 can be interpreted as the association between status and sentence we would have in a population where status and record are made unrelated, other factors remaining as before.

The effect of status on sentence net of record found by means of test factor standardisation is the same as we obtained in Chapter 1 (Table 1.7) by weighting the two partial effects of status. This is no coincidence. In both cases the relative size of the control groups is used as weighting. It should be easy to see that whether we weight the proportions and then take the difference, or find the differences in proportions first and then weight, the result must come out the same. Test factor standardisation has thus been shown to be equivalent to the control-group-size-weights used so far in this book. We prefer the latter procedure, since it is an advantage that the partial effects are calculated, and since the relationship to other crosstabular techniques is more easily seen.

Rosenberg's proposal can hardly be said to have found widespread application, but at least it has received some attention in discussions of the analysis of non-metric data (see Reynolds 1977; Little and Pullum 1979; Gilbert 1981). In recent years the causal approach to crosstabular analysis has been revived through the work of Jim Davis, who in several articles (1975, 1976, 1978, 1980) has outlined a scheme called d-*systems* (*d* as in difference). In *d*-systems causal decomposition is combined with predictions, in particular of the overall proportion with a high value on the dependent variable. At first sight this double purpose of the analysis may make it appear a bit confusing, since more information than required in an ordinary causal analysis has to be included (in addition, a special flow graph terminology is used). For the prediction part to work, the data must be interaction-free, or close to it.

Figure 8.3 has been designed to give an impression of the special features of a *d*-systems analysis, using the interaction-free data from Exercise 1.1. The diagram includes the usual direct effects from an

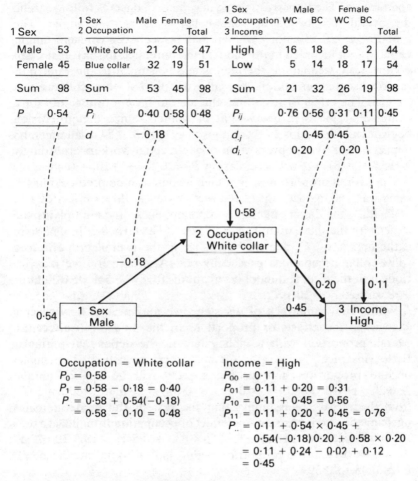

Figure 8.3 *An Example of a d-Systems Analysis (Data from Exercise 1.1)*

effect transmittance causal analysis, found as differences in proportions from the bivariate and trivariate tables above the diagram in Figure 8.3. What is new is the figure giving the proportion with a high value on each variable, for the second and third variable the conditional proportion where the prior variables have their low value.

The calculations beneath the diagram in Figure 8.3 show how the six pieces of information from the diagram may be used to find the conditional proportions and the overall proportions for occupation and income. The underlying logic may be explained as follows, using the overall proportion of white-collar workers as example. The proportion of 0·58 among women may be seen as a constant due to variables not included in the model (and unrelated to sex). If sex had no effect on occupation, the men would be similar to the women as regards occupation, and the overall proportion of white-collars equal to 0·58. The effect of sex shows the men to have a probability for a white-collar job 0·18 below that of women. Since the proportion being men is 0·54, this effect applies to a share of 0·54 of all units. Its impact on the overall proportion of white-collar workers accordingly is $0·54(-0·18) = -0·10$, rendering $P_{..} = 0·58 - 0·10 = 0·48$.

The overall proportion with a high income can be predicted in the same way, taking account of indirect as well as direct effect of sex, and adding the direct effect of occupation, each time multiplying the effect with the share of units it applies to. (The term $0·54(-0·18)0·20$ is the impact on $P_{..}$ due to the change in the overall proportion in white-collar occupations caused by sex. Alternatively, we may include it in the direct effect of occupation: $(0·58 + 0·54(-0·18)0·20 = 0·48 \times 0·20 = 0·10$.)

Within the framework of d-systems we may predict how specific changes in the effects or proportions of the model will affect the overall proportion with a high value on the dependent variable. If, for instance, the proportion men goes down 0·20, the impact on the proportion high-income earners will be $(-0·20)0·45 + (-0·20) (-0·18)0·20 = -0·09 + 0·01 = -0·08$, reducing $P_{..}$ from 0·45 to 0·37 (assuming that the rest of the model remains unchanged). An increase in the effect of occupation from 0·20 to 0·50 will in itself lead to a change of $0·58 \times 0·30 + 0·54(-0·18)0·30 = 0·17 - 0·03 = 0·14$ in the proportion with a high income, increasing $P_{..}$ from 0·45 to 0·59.

Just as predictions of the conditional proportions of a multivariate table by means of causal effects become inaccurate when there is interaction present in the data, predicting the overall proportion also requires interaction-free data. If, for instance, we use the d-systems prediction scheme on the data for status, record and sentence analysed in Chapter 1, the predicted proportion severely sentenced is 0·70, while the actual proportion is 0·64.

When it comes to calculating an overall effect from a set of dissimilar partial differences in proportions, Davis uses another weighting formula than the one we have applied, which as we saw corresponded to test factor standardisation. In d-systems the weight used to obtain a weighted average effect is the *inverse of the variance* of each partial effect. The overall effect of variable X_1 on X_3 in a trivariate analysis thus becomes:

$$D_1 = \sum \left(\frac{c_{.i}}{\sum c_{.i}} \, d_{.i} \right), \quad \text{where} \quad c_{.i} = \frac{1}{\text{var}(d_{.i})}$$

$$= \frac{1}{\text{var}(P_{1i}) + \text{var}(P_{0i})}$$

$$= \frac{1}{P_{1i}(1-P_{1i})/n_{1i.} + P_{0i}(1-P_{0i})/n_{0i.}}$$

$$= \frac{n_{1i.} \times n_{0i.}}{n_{1i.}(P_{0i})(1-P_{0i}) + n_{0i}(P_{1i})(1-P_{1i})}$$

In Table 8.7 the actual calculations are performed for the effect of status on sentence, with the result of an overall effect of -0.275.

In the formula for c the terms $P(1 - P)$ characterise the conditional distributions on the dependent variable X_3 (if the proportions were those of the population, they constitute the conditional population variances for X_3). With Ps ranging from 0.3 to 0.7, the variances will be highly similar (vary between the maximum of 0.25 and 0.21), and they may be deleted from the weighting formula with only minor changes in the weights as a consequence.

Such a weighting formula has been proposed by Richard P. Boyle (1966). He argued that the sample proportions for small groups due to random errors may come out too close to the extremes of 0.0 or 1.0. This means a lowering of the variance, and according to the weighting formula an increase in the weight given to differences based on these proportions at the expense of differences between proportions located around 0.5.

Boyle's proposal gives the following formula for the overall effect of X_1 on X_3 (keeping in mind that $n_{1i.} + n_{0i.} = n_{.i.}$):

$$D_1 = \sum \left(\frac{a_{.i}}{\sum a_{.i}} \, d_{.i} \right), \quad \text{where} \quad a_{.i} = \frac{n_{1i.} \times n_{0i.}}{n_{.i.}}$$

Using Boyle's weighting scheme we arrive at an effect of status on sentence net of record equal to -0.257 (Table 8.7).

Just as the difference between the two formulae above is that the conditional population variances of the dependent variable are

Table 8.7   The Overall Effect of Status on Sentence Computed by Means of Three Different Weighting Schemes

X_1: Social status	X_2: Criminal record	X_3 Severity of sentence 1 Severe	X_3 Severity of sentence 0 Lenient	Sum	Proportion severe	Partial effects X_1	Partial effects X_2
1 High	1 Yes	n_{111} 25	n_{110} 15	$n_{11.}$ 40	P_{11} 0·625		$d_{1.}$ 0·542
	0 No	n_{101} 2	n_{100} 22	$n_{10.}$ 24	P_{10} 0·083	$d_{.1}$ −0·187	
0 Low	1 Yes	n_{011} 95	n_{010} 22	$n_{01.}$ 117	P_{01} 0·812		$d_{0.}$ 0·326
	0 No	n_{001} 17	n_{000} 18	$n_{00.}$ 35	P_{00} 0·486	$d_{.0}$ −0·403	

Relative size of control group

$w_{.i} = n_{.i}/n;$ $w_{.0} = 59/216 = 0.273;$ $w_{.1} = 157/216 = 0.727$

$D_1 = 0.273(-0.403) + 0.727(-0.187) = -0.110 - 0.136 = -0.246$

Relative size of control group and variance of independent variable

$w_{.i} = a_{.i}/\Sigma a_{.i};$ $a_{.i} = n_{1i.}n_{0i.}/n_{.i.}$

$a_{.0} = 24 \times 35/59 = 14.24;$ $a_{.1} = 40 \times 117/157 = 29.81$

$w_{.0} = 14.24/(14.24 + 29.81) = 0.323;$ $w_{.1} = 28.81/(14.24 + 28.81) = 0.677$

$D_1 = 0.323(-0.403) + 0.677(-0.187) = -0.130 - 0.127 = -0.257$

Inverse of variance of conditional effect

$w_{.i} = c_{.i}/\Sigma c_{.i};$ $c_{.i} = n_{1i.}n_{0i.}/(n_{1i.}P_{0i}(1 - P_{0i}) + n_{0i.}P_{1i.}(1 - P_{1i}))$

$c_{.0} = 24 \times 35/(24 \times 0.486(1 - 0.486) + 35 \times 0.083(1 - 0.083)) = 97.01$

$c_{.1} = 40 \times 117/(40 \times 0.812(1 - 0.812) + 117 \times 0.625(1 - 0.625)) = 139.58$

$w_{.0} = 97.01/(97.01 + 139.58) = 0.410;$ $w_{.1} = 139.58/(97.01 + 139.58) = 0.590$

$D_1 = 0.410(-0.403) + 0.590(-0.187) = -0.165 - 0.110 = -0.275$

included in the first but not in the second, it can be shown that by deleting the conditional population variances for the independent variable X_1, we simplify the second formula to our previous weighting formula based on the relative size of the control groups. If the proportion with a high value on the independent variable within a control group is P, then the population variance is $P(1 - P)$, which can be expressed as $(n_{1i.}/n_{.i.}) \times (n_{0i.}/n_{.i.})$ when the control variable X_2 has the value i. Multiplying the variance with the relative size of the control group $n_{.i.}/n$ we arrive at the weighting factor a_i:

$$\frac{n_{.i.}}{n} \times \frac{n_{1i.}\, n_{0i.}}{n_{.i.}^{\,2}} = \frac{1}{n}\frac{n_{1i.}\, n_{0i.}}{n_{.i.}} \rightarrow \frac{n_{1i.}\, n_{0i.}}{n_{.i.}} = a_{.i}$$

(The constant $1/n$ can be deleted from the formula, since being the same for all partial effects, it cannot influence their relative weight.)

When we use the least complex of the three weights (and carry out the calculations with three decimal digits), the result as shown in Table 8.7 is an effect of status on sentence of -0.246.

Our empirical illustration of the use of the three different weighting schemes shows the resulting direct effect of status on sentence to vary between -0.246 and -0.275 depending on which weights are chosen. For those who are not particularly fascinated by the details of the calculations, there is no reason to spend much time brooding over Table 8.7. The important thing, of course, is which weighting formula is best suited for the purpose of causal decomposition, which is discussed in the next section.

8.3   When, Why, and How to Weight

Our discussion so far implies that the need for weighting arises in situations with interaction, becoming more urgent the stronger the interaction. When the partial effects are identical, weighting is superfluous (if $d_{.1} = d_{.0} = d$, then $D_1 = w_{.1}d_{.1} + w_{.0}d_{.0} = (w_{.1} + w_{.0})d = d$, since the sum of weights equals 1). With highly similar partial effects, the choice of weights will not matter much for the resulting average, and we may as well use the simple unweighted average. As the partial effects grow more dissimilar the choice of weights becomes crucial for the outcome of the analysis.

So much for the question of *when* to weight. As regards *why*, the answer suggested earlier in this book has been that some partial effects contribute more to the overall difference in proportions than others. In Chapter 2 causal effect was defined as the change in the probability for a high value on the effect variable resulting from a substitution of units with dissimilar values on the causal variable. Interaction implies that the effect of a substitution varies depending upon the value kept constant on the control variable(s). In our reappearing example, switching from a low-status defendant to a high-status defendant affects the probability for receiving a severe sentence stronger among first-time offenders than among recidivists. The purpose of the weighting of partial effects is to give more prominence to 'typical' than to 'rare' substitutions when we calculate the summary measure for overall effect net of influence from the control variables.

It would intuitively seem obvious that the incidence of various kinds of substitutions is affected by the size of control groups. This is the rationale for using the size-weights instead of the unweighted average (that is, equal weights), thus making the contribution from each partial effect to the overall effect proportionate to the relative share of all units for which it applies. As we saw in Chapter 1 (Table 1.6), taking account of the relative size of control groups is sufficient to obtain an accurate causal decomposition when the causal variables are unrelated.

The implication of related causal variables is that their distribution within each control group will vary. The proportion of high-status defendants is, for instance, larger among those with a clean record than among the recidivists. We will now argue that the distribution on a causal variable within each control group will affect the causal importance of the partial effects, and thus ought to be incorporated in the weighting formula.

Consider a hypothetical example with two control groups of 100 defendants each, where the distribution on high *vs* low status is 50–50 in the first and 5–95 in the second control group. It may here seem reasonable that the partial effect of status on sentence from the first, evenly divided, control group will have greater impact on the overall difference between high-status and low-status defendants than the partial effect from the second group, containing so few with a high status. Substitutions can be seen as comparisons between pairs of defendants which differ with regard to status. The more evenly divided the control group, the larger the share of pairs where the units have dissimilar status of all possible pairs that can be formed.

By including the variance of the independent variable along with the relative size of the control group in the weighting formula we increase the importance of evenly divided control groups for the weighted measure of overall effect. It can be shown that the weights proposed by Boyle can be interpreted as the probability that a pair of units with dissimilar values on the causal variable will come from a particular control group, when we use a two-stage sampling scheme where first a control group and then a pair of units are randomly selected (Hellevik 1983). These 'substitution probability weights' (Boyle's weights) seem to capture the typicality of the different substitutions better than the simpler control-group-size-weights.

In the inverse of the variance weights used by Davis still another aspect of the multivariate distribution is taken into consideration. The implication of including the $P(1-P)$ term for the proportions of the dependent variable in the weighting formula is to increase the importance of partial differences between proportions lying near the extremes of 0.0 or 1.0, at the expense of partial differences between proportions located closer to 0.5. Other things being equal, a partial effect of 0.20 based on the proportions 0.10 and 0.30 will carry more weight than a similar partial effect for the proportions 0.40 and 0.60.

As long as bivariate differences in proportions are considered the same regardless of where the proportions are located on the scale from 0.0 to 1.0, including this aspect in the weighting formula leads to inaccuracies in the causal decomposition of associations. While the relative-size-of-control-groups-weights suffer from a failure to take account of a factor relevant for the causal importance of a partial effect, the problem with the inverse-of-the-variance-weights is the opposite, an irrelevant factor is included.

The difference in proportions is sometimes criticised for not taking the location of effects into consideration, and measures such as those of loglinear analysis, which as demonstrated in Chapter 10 increase as we move from proportions around 0.5 towards 0.0 or 1.0, recommended instead. When analysing the change in a proportion over time, for example, in the socialist share of the votes, it seems reasonable to assume that it may take more to get a certain increment when starting out from a low level, or that it will be difficult to increase a proportion which lies close to the ceiling of 1.0. The point is, however, that in this case the latter proportion will be causally dependent upon the proportion prior in time. The proportions we are comparing in our crosstabulations are independent of each other, the level of one proportion in the table in no way restricts the expected range of another. This would seem to make consideration of the level of proportions when we take their difference less relevant.

For those readers who find the above reasoning obscure, and rather have a preference for 'the test of the pudding is in the eating' – approach, Figure 8.4 puts the various weighting schemes to the test of

Weighting scheme	Paths and direct effects	Components
(a) Unweighted average (Coleman 1964)	Status $\xrightarrow{-0.295}$ Sentence Status $\xrightarrow{-0.145}$ Record $\xrightarrow{0.434}$ Sentence	Direct: −0·295 Indirect: −0·063 Sum −0·358 Deviation 0·043
(b) Relative size of control group/test factor standardisation (Rosenberg 1962)	Status $\xrightarrow{-0.246}$ Sentence Status $\xrightarrow{-0.145}$ Record $\xrightarrow{0.390}$ Sentence	Direct: −0·246 Indirect: −0·057 Sum −0·303 Deviation −0·012
(c) Relative size of control group and variance of independent variable (Boyle 1966)	Status $\xrightarrow{-0.257}$ Sentence Status $\xrightarrow{-0.145}$ Record $\xrightarrow{0.403}$ Sentence	Direct: −0·257 Indirect: −0·058 Sum −0·315 Deviation 0·000
(d) Inverse of variance of partial effect (Davis 1975)	Status $\xrightarrow{-0.275}$ Sentence Status $\xrightarrow{-0.145}$ Record $\xrightarrow{0.431}$ Sentence	Direct: −0·275 Indirect: −0·062 Sum −0·337 Deviation 0·022

Figure 8.4   Decomposing the association between status and sentence of −0·315 by means of different weighting schemes (based on Table 8.7).

decomposing the association between social status and sentence. The direct effect of status is taken from Table 8.7, and the direct effect of record on sentence has in the same way been calculated by means of the various weighting formulae. The effect of status on record is the same for all schemes, since being a bivariate association there is no weighting involved.

We see that the only weights giving a completely accurate decomposition of the association of −0·315 are the ones proposed by Boyle. The size-weights come closest, while the equal weights (unweighted average) are most off target.

For three variables Boyle (1966) was able to prove that his weights gave a result identical to the unstandardised regression coefficient for binary variables (dichotomies coded 0 and 1), a point we will return to in Chapter 9 on regression analysis. We can thus refer to the 'theorem of path analysis' (Duncan 1966) to sustain that Boyle's weights are guaranteed to give perfect decomposition for three-variable models.

The conclusion for the question of *how* to weight is thus that the scheme proposed by Boyle is the optimum one. But the two other schemes have their attractions as well. When calculating the weighted average by hand, the simple size-weights have a clear advantage. If the distributions on the causal variable are not too dissimilar for the control groups, the impact on the average effect of deleting their variances from the weights will be negligible, and more so the smaller the interaction.

In a larger causal analysis weighting by hand becomes tedious, and the question is what standard program packages are available. Though simple enough to construct, for lack of demand programs applying Boyle's weights are not generally accessible as of now. One exception is the program NONCAN in the package DDPP developed at the University of Oslo, which performs a complete causal analysis once a model is specified for a set of variables (see p. 203–4). In the interactive version of SPSS, called SCSS, there is in the subprogram Crosstabs a routine CATFIT which performs d-systems analyses, applying the inverse of the variance weights. Once again, we may reason that the 'harm' done by including the variances for the dependent variable in the weighting formula will be minor if the proportions are reasonably similar and the interaction not extremely strong.

Boyle thought that the equivalence between his weighted average of differences in proportions and the regression coefficient was generally valid, but as we shall see in Chapter 9, the two effect measures may give dissimilar results when the number of independent variables exceeds two, in which case only the regression coefficients will yield a completely accurate decomposition of associations. In most cases, however, the results reached by means of Boyle's weights will be highly accurate. If we apply these weights to obtain the direct effects of the three variables affecting party preference in Table 8.3 (using three decimals and *ns* found in the table p. 204), the result is identical to the regression coefficient for two of the variables, and deviates with the minuscule fraction of 0·003 for the last one, which hardly affects the decomposition at all.

Having answered the questions of when, why and how to weight in order to obtain an accurate decomposition of the association between a pair of variables, it should be made clear that most discussions of weighting schemes are carried out from a quite different perspective. When Boyle (1966) or Davis (1975) present their schemes, or when test factor standardisation is discussed (Kalton 1968; Reynolds 1977; Little and Pullum 1979), it is claimed that weighting presupposes interaction-free data. Taken literally, as when it is said that standardisation is appropriate only when the choice of weights do not influence the result (Little and Pullum 1979: 475), this position makes little sense, since a technique whose use is restricted to situations where it is of no consequence can hardly be of interest.

A more reasonable interpretation is that weighting is recommended when the interaction is small enough to be caused by random measurement and sampling errors, for the purpose of estimating the common population effect assumed to underlie the varying partial effects. The rationale for weighting thus is to make the impact of each partial effect proportionate to the confidence we have in it as an estimate of the population effect.

While the answers to the why and when questions thus are quite different from those of the causal approach, the how answer comes out more or less the same. The inverse of the variance are the optimum weights for estimating a common population effect, but the 'approximate solution' obtained by treating the conditional variances of the dependent variable as equal, so that they may be deleted from the weighting formula (as in Boyle's weights), 'will in general be satisfactory, and on occasion may even be preferable' (Kalton 1968: 125).

While thus there would be no serious objections to using Boyle's weights to obtain an average of partial effects which do not deviate significantly from each other, averaging highly dissimilar partial effects would seem to go contrary to traditional views on weighting. This issue is dealt with in the next section.

8.4   Objections to Averaging Significantly Dissimilar Partial Effects

In order to be able to decompose associations we have calculated weighted averages of partial effects also in situations where the interaction may be assumed to reflect real variations in the effect of a variable between control groups. Anyone performing causal analyses ought to consider the objections raised against such a procedure, which now will be presented and countered.

Weighted effects give inaccurate or even 'impossible' predictions of proportions. With interaction-ridden data, weighted averages as we have seen cannot reproduce the proportions of a multivariate table accurately. When adding together the weighted effects, we even risk getting a sum of effects lying below $0 \cdot 0$ (that is, is negative) or above $1 \cdot 0$, which is an impossible result in the sense that proportions are restricted to range between the extremes of $0 \cdot 0$ and $1 \cdot 0$.

This objection reflects a failure to distinguish between the different purposes of causal and prediction analyses. It is misplaced when the aim of the analysis is to obtain an accurate decomposition of associations, rather than proportions.

Using a weighted average of varying partial effects means throwing away information. It is true that the direct effects entered in a causal diagram will not in themselves tell us whether they are based on similar or highly different partial effects. While this may be seen as 'throwing away information' on interaction (Reynolds 1977: 96), the point is that this information is not required in order to obtain an accurate causal decomposition of associations. All forms of statistical analysis reach their goal of simplifying the overwhelming amounts of information in the data matrix by disregarding all details which are not essential for the purpose of the analysis.

Even if a causal decomposition can be accomplished by means of weighted average effects without taking interaction explicitly into account, however, its occurrence has important implications for a causal analysis. By inspecting the partial effects used to obtain the overall effect we learn whether interaction is present or not. Section 8.5 discusses how the occurrence of interaction may influence the design and interpretation of results in a causal analysis.

Averaging dissimilar partial effects is substantively meaningless. Even if we obtain an accurate causal decomposition of associations by means of the weighted average of varying partial effects, this average effect does not make sense substantively, one argument goes. Dissimilar partial effects indicate that different causal mechanisms are at work, averaging them is like mixing apples and oranges in primary school arithmetic.

This objection is a serious one, and will in some cases force us to adopt a comparative analysis design where the dissimilar causal processes are studied separately, as will be discussed in the next section. In other cases we may feel, however, that the varying partial effects reflect differences in degree rather than differences in the kind of causal influence at work. To stay with the apples and oranges metaphor we may find it reasonable to assume that we have a case of apples of differing sizes, rather than a mixture of fruits. In this situation the weighted average seems like a sensible measure for what effect the varying partials add up to.

The crucial question to ask is whether a particular bivariate association is of interest in itself, or whether it appears to be a mixture of unrelated social processes, on which it makes little sense to elaborate. If we, for instance, find the question of how the bivariate association between sex and legislative career (Exercise 1.2) can be explained an interesting one, it would seem odd to claim that a causal analysis is meaningful only for the Labour Party, where the partial effects of sex on rank came out identical when controlled for seniority, and not for the Conservative Party, where the partial effects turned out to differ. In both cases part of the association between sex and rank according to the model is a result of differences in seniority between male and female representatives. The weighting procedure helps us assess how large a part, what indirect effect flows via seniority, also for the Conservative Party.

We thus conclude that contrary to traditional opinions about averaging significantly different partial effects, causal analysis of interaction-ridden data is both feasible and meaningful. We now turn to the question of how interaction may affect the execution of a causal analysis.

8.5   Implications of Interaction for Causal Analyses

When interpreting the results of a causal analysis, interaction means that the overall effects are dependent not only on the strength of each partial effect, but also on the particular composition of the population under investigation, with regard to the multivariate distribution on the independent variables. If the composition is changed, the weights will change too, and this in turn may affect the weighted average even if all partial effects remain constant. This means that the overall effects cannot be presented as general 'causal laws', but as effects restricted in time and space to the particular population which is being analysed.

Correspondingly, if the direct effect of a variable turns out to vary between populations, or over time within the same population, in a situation with interaction this may be explained in two quite different ways. Imagine that a new study shows an increasing direct effect of social status on sentence, controlled for record, within the Norwegian court districts of the former study. The reason for this might be an increased impact of status in each individual case, manifesting itself in higher partial effects within the new than in the old data-set. But the source of the change in overall effect might also be a change in the composition of the population of defendants, resulting in an increase in the weight assigned to the strong partial effect from the control group of first-offenders. Or the explanation may turn out to be a difference in both aspects between the two data-sets we are comparing.

This distinction can be shown to be fruitful in the analysis of a variety of social phenomena (Stinchcombe 1968: 60–79, gives some interesting examples under the heading of demographic explanations).

The occurrence of interaction may also provide us with clues when we are searching for a deeper understanding of the causal processes underlying the statistical relationships we are studying. Our analyses of the relation between status, record and sentence, or between father's occupation, father's vote, own occupation and own vote, are superficial in the sense that very little is said about the concrete mechanisms underlying the effects we are measuring. The arrows in a diagram may be seen as a kind of shorthand for the complex social phenomena the model seeks to portray. For the purpose of gaining a deeper understanding of the processes at work, the decomposition of statistical associations represents a first step. The results indicate which effects are important and which may be safely ignored, that is, where we ought to start digging in order to uncover the nature of the causal mechanisms producing association between our variables.

In this context information on interaction is useful. The variation between control groups in the effect of a variable may provide clues in our search for a better understanding of the nature of the influence relation.

Take as an example the effect we have assumed the social status of a defendant to have on his chances of being sentenced to imprisonment. What concrete mechanisms can produce such an effect? The analysis told us that the effect of status was markedly stronger among first-offenders than among the recidivists. What does this variation in effect signify?

One possible mechanism working in favour of high-status defendants would be a tendency for the judges to have more understanding and sympathy for persons with a social background similar to their own than for persons where the social distance is great. Another mechanism that may favour high-status defendants is the considerations of the judges with regard to the possibility for criminal conduct in the future, and how it will be influenced by a jail sentence. Here a high-status person will be able to argue that he has a steady job, good family relations and other social advantages when it comes to steering clear of criminal behaviour, while on the other hand a jail sentence will be more detrimental for him socially.

The variation in the effect of social status may be interpreted as an indication of the importance of the last mechanism. While there is no obvious reason for the social prejudice mechanism to be more decisive for defendants with a clean record than for recidivists, it is easily seen that the advantages of a high status when appealing for another chance will be drastically reduced as the number of previous convictions increases.

The above discussion is just a brief illustration of how we may try to make use of information on interaction when we are striving to gain a deeper understanding of the nature of the causal processes at work. In future research one may then test the validity of these ideas by trying to obtain measures for the new aspects of the situation deemed to influence the outcome of the causal process.

Finally, we shall turn our attention to situations where interaction makes a *comparative analysis design* appropriate. Crosscultural research may provide an illustration. Surveys are usually restricted to one particular nation, but sometimes researchers try to collect comparable survey data from several nations. In the analysis of these data-sets we hardly ever see that they are joined together to one large data-base which is analysed without taking nationality into account. Instead parallel analyses are carried out, showing the relationships between a set of variables for each nation separately. The probable reason for this is that the researchers consider the nations to be too different to make the bivariate associations obtained by pooling the data-sets of much interest. Instead the emphasis is on studying variations in the relationship between variables from one nation to another.

If the analysis is carried out on the basis of a causal model, the variable nationality will not enter into the model. We may call this variable, which is used to separate the units for the parallel analyses, the *comparative variable*. If the results turn out to vary between the nations, we have a case of interaction between the comparative variable and the independent variables of the causal model.

The fruitfulness of this approach is, of course, not restricted to crossnational comparisons. In Section 7.5 we discussed how to interpret the association between marital status and political activity. Since the assumed causal influences were supposed to be markedly different (of opposite signs) for men and women, separate models were presented with sex as the comparative variable. Or to take another example, in our previous analyses of sex differences in legislative career (Exercise 1.2 and Section 6.2) there are several reasons for treating the party variable as a comparative variable rather than including it in the causal model alongside sex, seniority and rank.

First of all, we have a theoretical argument springing from our knowledge of the social system under analysis. In the Norwegian Parliament the process of selecting representatives to leadership positions takes place within each party separately. The question of which positions a party is entitled to is decided through negotiations between the parties, but the actual recruitment of individuals does not take place on the level of the assembly as a whole, but on the party level. Just as for the nationality variable, therefore, we have a case of independent causal processes taking place within each subsystem, with a possibility for quite different patterns of relationships between the variables.

The analysis of the data in Exercise 1.2, in fact, revealed a quite different pattern for the Labour Party and the Conservative Party, with a direct effect of sex on rank in favour of female representatives in the former party and in favour of men in the latter. If we had decided to analyse the relationship between sex, seniority and rank for all representatives taken together, the difference in the impact of sex on the legislative career within the two parties would have passed unnoticed. What if we instead had included party as a fourth variable in the causal model?

As Exercise 8.5 will give you the chance to try out for yourself, the effect of sex on rank turns out to be negative, the pattern from the larger of the two parties, the Labour Party, dominates. The example manifests two characteristics which may serve as empirical criteria for when we ought to consider a comparative analysis. First of all, when we inspect the partial effects to look for interaction, it turns out that among Labour Party representatives, both partial effects of sex on rank are strongly negative, that is, clearly in favour of the women. Among Conservative representatives, we find a strong positive and a weak negative effect, indicating an overall effect in favour of the men. In situations where the partial effects vary so markedly, and especially where they are of opposite signs, separate analyses are in order, to avoid the clear differences in the influence patterns going unnoticed.

Secondly, it turns out that the party variable is hardly related to the other three variables of the model at all. This means that it does not create any spurious or indirect effect between them, and can thus be taken out of the model without affecting the decomposition of association between the remaining three variables. In cases where we use a variable which is strongly related to the other variables of the model as a comparative variable this is done at the expense of losing the information on how this variable affects the others and their relationships. With the party variable, no such loss is incurred. When we are studying the importance of sex for legislative career, party is of interest only as a comparative variable.

Summary

In situations with interaction between the independent variables one may wish to perform a prediction analysis where the proportion of units which have a certain value on the dependent variable is predicted by means of variable and interaction effects. In order to obtain a causal decomposition of gross associations we make use of weighted averages of the partial effects to assess the overall effect net of the control variables. A weighting formula where the distribution on the causal variable is included along with the size of the control group guarantees an accurate decomposition of gross associations for all three variable models, and a close fit for most others.

Even if the weighting procedure permits us to ignore a possible interaction when we are decomposing associations, the occurrence of interaction should also be taken into account in a causal analysis. The pattern of variation in the partial effects may provide clues for our efforts to obtain a deeper understanding of the nature of the social mechanisms underlying the observed statistical relationships. Comparative analyses of interaction-ridden data ought to be considered, especially in situations where separate causal processes are at work, and where partial effects have opposite sign.

Glossary

COMPARATIVE ANALYSIS: analyses using the same model on separate sets of units.

COMPARATIVE VARIABLE: variable used to separate units for comparative analyses.

CONSTANT: effect assumed to be caused by variables not included in the analysis, of the same magnitude for all groups.

FIRST-ORDER INTERACTION: interaction involving two independent variables.

INTERACTION EFFECT: difference between partial effects.

PREDICTION ANALYSIS: analysis decomposing multivariate proportions into variable effects, interaction effect(s) and constant, which can be used to predict the proportion with a certain value on the dependent variable for any combination of values on the independent variables.

PREDICTION EFFECT: unweighted average of partial effects of a variable used in prediction analyses.
SECOND-ORDER INTERACTION: interaction involving three independent variables.
VARIANCE: measure of dispersion.

Exercises

8.1 Sex and Legislative Career: a Prediction Analysis
Use the data in Exercise 1.2 to perform a prediction analysis of the relationship between sex, seniority and rank for representatives of the Conservative Party. Show how the multivariate proportions can be reproduced by adding together variable and interaction effects, and that the results cannot be used to obtain an accurate decomposition of the relationship between status and rank in Parliament.

8.2 Sex and Legislative Career: a d-Systems Analysis
The data for the Labour Party (Exercise 1.2) are nearly interaction-free, and can thus be analysed by means of the d-systems technique allowing us to predict the overall proportion of representatives with a high rank in Parliament on the basis of direct effects and the relevant proportions. Perform the analysis.

8.3 Predicting the Proportion Socialists: a Four-Variate d-Systems Analysis
For those seeking greater challenges, the interaction-free data in Chapter 5 permits a four-variate analysis on which we may base predictions of the overall proportion of socialists (Table 5.4 gives all effects and proportions – except for X_1 – required).

How will the proportion of socialists be influenced if we assume that the proportion of fathers who are workers has an increase of 0·15, at the same time as the effect of own occupation declines from 0·38 to 0·18?

8.4 Sex and Legislative Career: the Choice of Weights for Causal Decomposition
How well do the results reached by means of the simple size-weights in Exercise 1.2 do when it comes to decomposing the gross association between sex and rank for Conservative representatives? How are the results for the direct effects of sex and seniority on rank influenced when we change to the more complex weights proposed by Boyle (1966)?

8.5 *Comparative Analysis or Ordinary Design?*

Use the data in Exercise 1.2 to perform a four-variate causal analysis by including party in the model (*suggestion:* enter the party variable between sex and seniority). Compare the results with those reached when each party was analysed separately by means of the three-variable model. Which approach do you find best suited for the empirical problem at hand?

9

Regression Analysis

Readers familiar with path analysis will have noticed that the causal models we have used to represent our ideas about the relations of influence between the variables are the same as those of the path analytic approach. So, too, with the effect change or effect transmittance analysis designs defining which statistical relationships we need to study in order to find the components in the association between a pair of variables. Only in the last stage of the analysis, the calculation of effects, do the two approaches differ. We have worked with differences in proportions from contingency tables, while path analysis makes use of regression analysis to establish the size of causal effects.

Regression analysis is ordinarily performed on *metric variables*. Income is one such variable, measured in for instance thousands of dollars, pounds, or a comparable metric. To characterise what is the typical income for our material we may calculate the *mean* income by summing the values for all units and dividing by the number of units. A regression coefficient expresses the expected difference in mean value on the dependent variable for units which are one unit of measurement apart on an independent variable, for instance, the expected difference in mean income for persons who are one year apart in school attendance.

For non-metric variables, we cannot calculate a mean value on the dependent variable, nor measure distance along the independent variable. It does not make much sense to ask what is the expected difference in average marital status for individuals who are one unit of nationality apart.

By assigning the values 0 and 1 to a dichotomous variable, however, it is possible to get around this problem. In *binary regression analysis* the coefficient expresses the expected difference in the *probability for a high value* on the dependent variable, instead of distance along this variable, for units with a high value compared to those with a low value on the independent variable. Even polytomous non-metric variables may be analysed in this way, by creating a set of binary variables (so-called *dummy variables*) to represent their values (see Nie *et al.* 1975: 373–83).

While the assumptions and procedures of ordinary least-squares regression analysis of metric variables at first may appear complex and hard to understand, we shall see that binary regression coefficients can be found quite easily by means of contingency tables. They, in fact, turn out to be identical to our old acquaintance, the difference in proportions, and can be given a straightforward interpretation accordingly.

In a regression analysis interaction is captured by creating new interaction variables as products of independent variables. A *saturated regression equation* includes all possible interaction variables which may be formed by the independent variables and is guaranteed to reproduce the set of proportions of the multivariate table accurately. The variable and interaction effects will differ from those of a Coleman prediction analysis of the same data, for reasons which will be made clear.

Since interaction in a regression analysis is measured as the effect of a variable, it is possible to incorporate interaction in a causal analysis by including the interaction variable(s) in the causal model. While interaction effects thus may be part of the causal decomposition of the association between a pair of variables, we shall see that such an approach runs into several difficulties. By using an *unsaturated regression equation* where the interaction variables are left out effects identical (for three-variable analyses) or highly similar (for most analyses involving four or more variables) to those reached by means of Boyle's weights for differences in proportions will result. An interesting aspect of the way interaction is handled in a regression analysis is the new perspective which is provided on the implications of leaving the interaction out of a decomposition analysis.

9.1 Binary Regression Analysis

Just as we have been analysing the variation in the proportions of a dependent variable, regression analyses are concerned with means. For a 0–1 variable, however, the proportion with a high value turns out to be the same as the mean. When we add together the values for all units in order to obtain the mean, the n_0 units with the value zero contribute nothing to the sum, while the result for the n_1 units with the value 1 equals their number: n_1. Dividing by the total number of units $(n_0 + n_1)$ we have the mean, which as we see is nothing but the proportion: $n_1/(n_0 + n_1) = P$.

For the convicted larcenists in Table 1.1, the proportion receiving a severe sentence is 0·64. Since the variable sentence does not take on other values than 1 (severe) or 0 (lenient), it may seem odd to call the in-between figure of 0·64 a 'mean'. Instead we will refer to it as a *probability*, the long-run proportion of times that a randomly selected defendant has received a severe sentence.

When we introduce a 0–1 independent variable, for example, record with values criminal (1) and clean (0), the regression coefficient for the effect of record on sentence is defined as the expected difference in the 'mean' sentence for defendants which are 'one unit' of record apart or, in the terms of binary regression analysis, the difference in the probability for a severe sentence for recidivists as compared to first-time offenders. With proportions of 0·76 and 0·32 (Table 1.3), we find the regression coefficient as the difference of 0·44. The bivariate regression coefficient for binary variables is thus the same as the difference in proportions, and can be given the same interpretation.

Bivariate regression analyses are often presented by means of a diagram with the independent variable along a horizontal axis and the dependent variable along the vertical axis, as in Figure 9.1 for our example. The regression equation defines X_2 (the proportion with a high value on the dependent variable sentence) as a linear function of a constant term b_0 and the coefficient b_1 for the effect of the independent variable X_1 (record) times the value of X_1:

$$X_2 \ (= P) = b_0 + b_1 X_1$$

The *constant* b_0 may like the C term in a Coleman analysis be interpreted as the constant effect of variables not included in the regression equation. It is found as the mean of X_2 when X_1 is zero, or in other words, as the proportion P_0, which in our example equals 0·24. In the diagram it is represented by the distance from the origo to the intercept between the regression line and the axis for the dependent variable.

The *regression line* is the line connecting the two means (proportions). The *regression coefficient* b_1 is represented by the slope of the regression line, showing the rate of the increase in the dependent variable to the increase in the independent variable. When record changes value from 0 to 1, the proportion severely sentenced is predicted to increase from 0·24 (b_0) to 0·68 ($b_0 + b_1$).

When the independent variable has just two values, we will always be able to draw a straight line connecting the two means for the

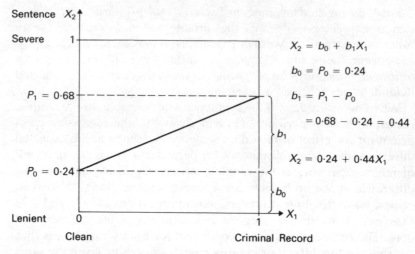

Figure 9.1   *Bivariate binary regression analysis (data from Table 1.3).*

dependent variable. With three or more values, the curve connecting the means will seldom be a straight line. In a regression analysis one will usually fit a straight line which has the property of minimising the squared deviations of the means from the regression line (ordinary least-squares regression). From this criterion the formula for b_1 is derived as the covariance between X_1 and X_2 divided by the variance of X_1. In a binary regression analysis the line between the two means satisfies the least-squares criterion, and we find b_1 simply as the difference in proportions from a bivariate contingency table without having to worry about variance and covariance.

The regression coefficients we have been discussing are called *unstandardised* (or 'raw') *coefficients*. They may be standardised in the same way as shown for differences in proportions in Section 6.3. The effects reported in path analyses often are *standardised regression coefficients*. When variables with dissimilar metrics are included in the analysis (for example, thousands of pounds, years at school, number of siblings, and so on), standardisation has the advantage of making the coefficients comparable since all effects are measured in terms of the common metric standard deviations. This problem does not arise with binary variables.

The main argument against standardisation, that differences in the distribution on a variable will influence its standardised effect when we compare across populations (Asher 1976: 47–8), is relevant also for binary variables. Another factor tipping the scales in favour of the unstandardised coefficient is its equivalence with the familiar difference in proportions, facilitating an intuitive understanding of the results.

Turning from bivariate to multivariate analyses the equivalence between the results reached in a binary regression analysis and a contingency table analysis holds as long as the data are interaction-free. The effects of father's occupation, father's vote and own occupation on the probability for voting socialist in the four-variable analysis in Chapter 5 are, for instance, identical to the regression coefficients we would get if we had a computer do a regression analysis of the data. When interaction occurs, however, this in a regression analysis is handled in ways different from the crosstabulation approaches we have considered so far. As for these approaches, we have to distinguish between the purpose of predicting multivariate proportions and the purpose of decomposing bivariate associations when we discuss the implications of interaction for regression analysis.

9.2 Prediction Analysis by Means of Binary Regression

To predict proportions by means of regression coefficients we use the same set of effects as in a Coleman prediction analysis (Section 8.1). However, the definitions of the constant, the variable effects and the interaction effect(s) are different, rendering corresponding effects dissimilar in size for the two schemes.

A saturated regression equation predicts a multivariate set of proportions by means of a number of regression coefficients equal to the number of proportions. For the trivariate Table 8.2 with status and record as independent variables and sentence as the dependent variable, we get the following saturated equation:

$$P_{ij} = b_0 + b_1X_1 + b_2X_2 + b_{12}X_1X_2$$

where P_{ij} is the proportion severely sentenced for defendants with value i on X_1 (status) and value j on X_2 (record). The variable defined as the product of the two independent variables X_1X_2 is called an *interaction variable*. It will have the value 1 when both independent variables equal 1, while all other value combinations (10, 01, or 00) render the product equal to 0.

When both X_1 and X_2 have the value 0, the regression equation for the corresponding proportion becomes:

$$P_{00} = b_0 + b_1 \times 0 + b_2 \times 0 + b_{12} \times 0 = b_0$$

The constant b_0 accordingly is defined as the proportion for the group where both independent variables equal 0:

$$b_0 = P_{00} = 0 \cdot 49 (P_{00} \text{ from Table 8.2})$$

By means of the regression equations for the other proportions we find the rest of the regression coefficients:

$$P_{10} = b_0 + b_1 \times 1 + b_2 \times 0 + b_{12} \times 0 = b_0 + b_1$$
$$b_1 = P_{10} - b_0 = P_{10} - P_{00} = d_{.0} = -0 \cdot 41$$
$$P_{01} = b_0 + b_1 \times 0 + b_2 \times 1 + b_{12} \times 0 = b_0 + b_2$$
$$b_2 = P_{01} - b_0 = P_{01} - P_{00} = d_{0.} = 0 \cdot 32$$

In words: the regression coefficient for the effect of a variable is the same as the partial difference in proportions when the control variable has its low value. This has the important implication that if we reorder the values on the control variable (change 0 to 1 and vice versa), the other partial effect will be selected as the regression coefficient. Should we, for instance, decide to let a clean record be coded 1 and a criminal record 0, the partial effect $d_{.0}$ for status would change from $-0 \cdot 41$ to $-0 \cdot 18$, which then would constitute the regression coefficient b_1.

In the Coleman scheme a reordering of the values on the control variable will not influence the effect of an independent variable, since the effect is measured as an average of the partial effects. Comparing b_1 and b_2 with the corresponding effects E_1 and E_2 in Table 8.2 b_1 is smaller than E_1, while b_2 is larger than E_2, due to the fact that for status the strongest partial effect is defined as b_1, while for record the weakest of the two partial effects has been selected as b_2. As long as the ordering of the values on the control variable may be a rather arbitrary decision, it would seem misleading to call b_1 the 'main effect' of variable X_1, suggesting that the d_0 partial effect somehow is more basic than the other partial effect(s). For the same reason it would be incorrect to infer from the fact that b_1 is larger than b_2 that status (X_1) has a greater impact than record (X_2) on the probability of receiving a severe sentence.

Finally, the coefficient for the interaction variable is found as the difference between P_{11} and the three effects already established:

$$P_{11} = b_0 + b_1 \times 1 + b_2 \times 1 + b_{12} \times 1 = b_0 + b_1 + b_2 + b_{12}$$

$$b_{12} = P_{11} - b_0 - b_1 - b_2 = P_{11} - P_{00} - (P_{10} - P_{00}) - (P_{01} - P_{00})$$
$$= (P_{11} - P_{01}) - (P_{10} - P_{00}) = d_{.1} - d_{.0} = 0.23$$
$$= (P_{11} - P_{10}) - (P_{01} - P_{00}) = d_{1.} - d_{0.} = 0.23$$

The interaction effect measures the change in the effect of an independent variable as the value of the control variable changes from 0 to 1, and can be found by taking the difference between the partial effects of either of the two independent variables. It is twice the size of the Coleman I_{12} effect from Table 8.2, which measures the distance from the midway average effect to the partial effects.

Entering the results for the four regression coefficients in the equation we are able to predict all four proportions of Table 8.2 accurately by entering the relevant values for X_1 and X_2 in the equation:

$$P_{ij} = 0.49 - 0.41X_1 + 0.32X_2 + 0.23X_1X_2$$

We have now seen how it is possible to decompose a multivariate set of proportions into variable and interaction effects by means of binary regression analysis, using the same kinds of effects as in a Coleman analysis, but with a dissimilar definition of how to obtain the effects from the partial differences in proportions. The regression approach may have an advantage in that it may be easier to see for what value combinations of the independent variables the interaction effects occur, and how they are to be interpreted. Table 9.1 gives the reader a chance to try this out, by presenting the results of a four-variable binary regression analysis of the same data analysed by means of the Coleman scheme in Tables 8.3 and 8.4.

To save space the interaction variables are referred to as X_{12} instead of X_1X_2, X_{123} instead of $X_1X_2X_3$, and so on. The effect of a variable is found as its partial effect when both control variables have the value 0, its interaction with a second variable as the change in the partial effect of the first variable when the value of the second variable changes from 0 to 1, the third variable remaining equal to 0. To find the second-order interaction involving all three independent variables we look at the change in the interaction between the first two variables as the third changes value from 0 to 1.

If the partial effects of each variable are of the same size, the interaction coefficients will come out equal to zero. In this case the results of the regression analysis will be identical to those reached with the Coleman scheme or any of the schemes based on weighted differences in proportions. In this case the same variable effects can

Table 9.1 A Saturated Regression Analysis of the Tendency to Vote Socialist (Data from Table 8.3)

X_1	X_2	X_3	X_{12}	X_{13}	X_{23}	X_{123}	Proportion socialist $P_{ijk}(X_4=1)$	$= b_0$	$+ b_1X_1$	$+ b_2X_2$	$+ b_3X_3$	$+ b_{12}X_{12}$	$+ b_{13}X_{13}$	$+ b_{23}X_{23}$	$+ b_{123}X_{123}$
									$+0.07$	$+0.15$	$+0.37$	$+0.33$	$+0.07$	$+0.31$	-0.51
1	1	1	1	1	1	1	P_{111} 0.90	$=0.11$	$+0.07$	$+0.15$	$+0.37$	$+0.33$	$+0.07$	$+0.31$	-0.51
1	1	0	1	0	0	0	P_{110} 0.66	$=0.11$	$+0.07$	$+0.15$		$+0.33$			
1	0	1	0	1	0	0	P_{101} 0.62	$=0.11$	$+0.07$		$+0.37$		$+0.07$		
1	0	0	0	0	0	0	P_{100} 0.18	$=0.11$	$+0.07$						
0	1	1	0	0	1	0	P_{011} 0.94	$=0.11$		$+0.15$	$+0.37$			$+0.31$	
0	1	0	0	0	0	0	P_{010} 0.26	$=0.11$		$+0.15$					
0	0	1	0	0	0	0	P_{001} 0.48	$=0.11$			$+0.37$				
0	0	0	0	0	0	0	P_{000} 0.11	$=0.11$							

$b_0 = P_{000} = 0.11$

$b_1 = P_{100} - P_{000} = d_{.00} = 0.07$

$b_2 = P_{010} - P_{000} = d_{0.0} = 0.15$

$b_3 = P_{001} - P_{000} = d_{00.} = 0.37$

$b_{12} = (P_{110} - P_{010}) - (P_{100} - P_{000}) = d_{.10} - d_{.00} = 0.40 - 0.07 = 0.33$

$b_{13} = (P_{101} - P_{001}) - (P_{100} - P_{000}) = d_{.01} - d_{.00} = 0.14 - 0.07 = 0.07$

$b_{23} = (P_{011} - P_{001}) - (P_{010} - P_{000}) = d_{0.1} - d_{0.0} = 0.46 - 0.15 = 0.31$

$b_{123} = \{(P_{111} - P_{011}) - (P_{101} - P_{001})\} - \{(P_{110} - P_{010}) - (P_{100} - P_{000})\}$
$= (d_{.11} - d_{.01}) - (d_{.10} - d_{.00}) = (-0.04 - 0.14) - (0.40 - 0.07) = -0.51$

$P_{ijk} = 0.11 + 0.07X_1 + 0.15X_2 + 0.37X_3 + 0.33X_{12} + 0.07X_{13} + 0.31X_{23} - 0.51X_{123}$

serve the double purpose of predicting multivariate proportions as well as decomposing bivariate associations. The occurrence of interaction made it necessary to choose between measures of prediction effect and measures of causal effect when working with difference in proportions schemes. Having looked at how prediction analysis is handled by means of binary regression, we now turn to the question of how to perform a causal analysis of interaction-ridden data within this approach.

9.3 Causal Analysis by Means of Binary Regression

In Section 8.1 we were unable to incorporate the interaction effects from a Coleman analysis in the causal decomposition of associations. In a regression analysis this may seem less of a problem, since the interaction effects are measured as effects of variables created for this purpose, which then may be included in the causal model. This solution is suggested in discussions of how to deal with interaction in path analyses (Boyle 1966: 849; Blalock 1971: 178–86). However, it is hard to find examples where this advice is followed in actual analyses, and if we try, we run into several problems.

Figure 9.2 presents the results of one such effort with regard to the relationship between status, record and sentence. When setting up the model, we confront the first problem, how to interpret causally the relationship between the two independent variables and the interaction variable defined by them. The solution chosen in Figure 9.1, for reasons which will be revealed later, is to consider the interaction variable as intervening between status and record on the one hand, and sentence on the other.

The causal effects on sentence entered in the diagram are coefficients from a saturated regression analysis with status and record as independent variables (for the sake of accuracy, three decimals are used, as in Table 8.7). The effect of status on record is a bivariate regression coefficient (equal to the difference in proportions). Measuring the two remaining effects, those of status and record on the interaction variable, is more of a problem. There certainly is interaction in the effect of X_1 and X_2 on the probability for a high value on X_{12} (the partial effect being $1 \cdot 0$ when the control variable has the value 1, and $0 \cdot 0$ when the value is 0). At the same time a saturated analysis is meaningless, since this would involve X_{12} as both independent and dependent variable. The effects given in the diagram are, therefore, unsaturated regression coefficients, to be explained later in this section.

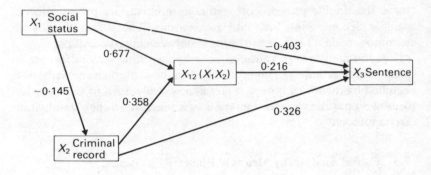

Decomposition of bivariate association of -0.315 between status and sentence
(a) for complete model   (b) for model omitting X_{12}

Direct effect:	-0.403	Direct effect:	-0.403
Indirect effect:			$+\ \underline{0.146}$
$0.677 \times 0.216 =$	0.146		$=\ -0.257$
$(-0.145)0.358 \times 0.216 =$	-0.011	Indirect effect:	-0.011
$(-0.145)0.326 =$	$\underline{-0.047}$		$+\ \underline{-0.047}$
	0.088		$=\ -0.058$
Sum $DE + IE$	-0.315	Sum $DE + IE$	-0.315

Figure 9.2   *Causal model including interaction variable with regression coefficients (data from Table 8.7)*

As shown beneath the diagram, we obtain a completely accurate decomposition of the association between status and sentence by means of the regression coefficients including the interaction effect. The result is a direct effect of -0.403, and a sum of indirect effects via record, the interaction variable, or both, of 0.088. The bivariate association of -0.315 is thus a result of direct and indirect effects working in opposite directions, the former being the stronger of the two causal influences.

Even if these comments on the analysis results seem reasonable enough, a property of saturated regression coefficients mentioned in the preceding section put their meaningfulness in serious doubt. If we choose to reorder the values on the variable record, the direct effect of status will change from -0.403 to -0.187 (the other partial effect). Since the bivariate association will remain -0.315, we without any further calculations of effects can infer that the sum of indirect effects this time will be $-0.315-(-0.187) = -0.128$. In other words, the outcome of the causal decomposition of the association between status and sentence depends on how we more or less arbitrarily choose to assign the values 0 and 1 to the categories of the third variable record, a result that would lead one to question the usefulness of including interaction variables in a causal model.

If we delete the interaction variable from the model, the indirect effect which originally flowed from status via X_{12} to sentence will become fused with the original direct effect of status on sentence to form the new direct effect in the simplified model. The result is a direct effect of status on sentence of $-0.403 + 0.677 \times 0.216 = -0.403 + 0.146 = -0.257$. Reordering the values on the control variable record does not influence the direct effect of status calculated in this way: $-0.187 + 0.323(-0.216) = -0.187 - 0.070 = -0.257$ (in this case the effect of status on X_{12} equals $1.000 - 0.677 = 0.323$, while the effect of X_{12} on sentence changes sign).

By deleting the interaction variable from the causal model we obtain a decomposition of the association between status and sentence of -0.257 as a direct effect, and -0.058 as an indirect effect via record, which is not affected by the way we choose to order the values on the record variable. The direct effect from the regression equation where the interaction term has been deleted is called an *unsaturated regression coefficient*. The relationship between b_1 from the saturated regression equation and b_1' from the unsaturated equation is given by the formula:

$$b_1' = b_1 + b_{1-12}' b_{12}$$

where b_{1-12}' is the effect of X_1 on X_{12} in a regression analysis including X_2 as independent variable. The term $b_{1-12}' b_{12}$, which constitutes the deviation between the saturated and the unsaturated coefficient, is sometimes referred to as the 'specification error', resulting from applying an equation without the interaction variable when there is interaction present in the data. Comparing with Figure 9.2 we see that the 'error' term is identical to the indirect effect of X_1 on X_3 via X_{12}. In the unsaturated coefficient b_1' this indirect effect is combined with the direct effect of the complete model (b_1) to the direct effect of X_1 in a model where X_{12} has been left out.

In a causal analysis it will always be possible to insert a large number of intervening variables between any pair of variables in the model, splitting the original direct effect between them into components of direct and indirect effect. In most cases the theoretically important distinction will be between causal and spurious effect, with the detailed analysis of the composition of the causal effect being of less interest. To leave out an intervening variable under such circumstances would hardly be considered an 'error', but rather a legitimate and even desirable step in order to obtain a simpler model. In a causal perspective there is thus nothing inherently wrong in leaving out an intervening interaction variable. By doing it we not only obtain a simpler model, but also a decomposition which no longer is influenced by the ordering of values on control variables, and still is completely accurate.

The attractions of the simpler model without interaction variables are better appreciated as the number of variables in an analysis increases. With three independent variables, as in the example with father's occupation, father's vote and own occupation influencing own vote, to include interaction variables in the causal model would mean an addition of five new variables (one for interaction in the effect of X_1 and X_2 on X_3, and the four interaction effects on X_4 given in Table 9.1), if none could be deleted as insignificant. To give an impression of how the interaction variables will mess up the original four-variable model, Figure 9.3 presents the results of the saturated regression analysis from Table 9.1, with the effects of the independent variables on the interaction variables added (to avoid a complete cluttering of the diagram the relationships between the three

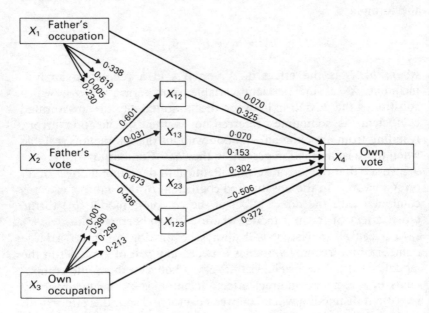

Figure 9.3   *Causal model including interaction effects for three independent variables (effects on X_4 from Table 9.1).*

independent variables, including the interaction variable involved, have been left out).

A common feature of path analyses is that interaction either is not mentioned at all, or is assumed to be absent in the data. One reason may be that it takes an extra effort – the creation of interaction variables to be added to the regression equation – to detect whether the data are interaction-free or not. Another reason may be the increased complexity of the causal models incurred by trying to incorporate the interaction variables. The conclusion of our discussion is that the common practice of performing path analyses by means of unsaturated regression coefficients, albeit sternly criticised by methodologists, is the appropriate way of dealing with interaction within the framework of causal decomposition of associations. As will be discussed in the final section of this chapter, such a solution is comparable to the use of weighted averages of differences in proportions advocated in Chapter 8.

The objections against the use of weighted average effects discussed in Section 8.3 are also raised against the use of unsaturated regression coefficients. Once more, we will argue that inaccurate predictions of multivariate proportions, or predictions falling outside the interval 0–1, is not a problem as long as the purpose of the analysis is causal decomposition of associations.

One drawback of the unsaturated regression coefficients as compared to the saturated ones, is that they do not lend themselves so easily to computation by hand. The saturated coefficients are quickly obtained from the differences in proportions of a multivariate contingency table. There exist formulae which enable us to calculate an unsaturated coefficient from bivariate regression coefficients (or differences in proportions). Below, it is shown how b'_1 for the effect of status on sentence can be calculated (Table 8.7 has the data needed to find the bivariate associations):

$$b'_1 = \frac{b_{1-3} - b_{1-2}b_{2-3}}{1 - b_{1-2}b_{2-1}} = \frac{-0.315 - (-0.145)0.442}{1 - (-0.145)(-0.152)} = -0.257$$

where b_{i-j} means the effect of variable i on variable j.

The formula, derived from the assumptions of ordinary least-squares regression, is hard to make sense of intuitively. As the number of variables in the regression equation increases the formula becomes complex and calculation by hand tedious. To analyse large models by means of unsaturated regression coefficients access to a computer is a necessity.

9.4   Unsaturated Regression Coefficients and Weighted Differences in Proportions

The unsaturated regression coefficient for the effect of status on sentence calculated in the preceding section was -0.257. This is exactly the same result as obtained in Table 8.7 for the average of the partial differences in proportions when using the weights proposed by Boyle. The identity of the effects is no coincidence, as mentioned in Chapter 8 it is possible to give algebraic proof that the measures are equivalent for trivariate analyses (Boyle 1966).

To see the correspondence between the weighted average of partial differences in proportions and the unsaturated regression coefficient it may be useful to define both measures as functions of either saturated regression coefficients or partial ds. The formula for b_1' was given in the preceding section. We obtain comparable formulae for D_1 by rearranging the terms of the original form:

$$b_1' = b_1 + b_{1-12}' b_{12} = d_{.0} + b_{1-12}'(d_{.1} - d_{.0})$$
$$D_1 = w_{.0}d_{.0} + w_{.1}d_{.1} = (1 - w_{.1})d_{.0} + w_{.1}d_{.1}$$
$$= d_{.0} + w_{.1}(d_{.1} - d_{.0}) = b_1 + w_{.1}b_{12}$$

The only difference between the two formulae is that the effect of X_1 on the interaction variable (b_{1-12}') in the regression formula is replaced by the weight $w_{.1}$ in the formula for the weighted average of differences in proportions. For the case of two independent variables, it can be shown that $w_{.1}$ will always be identical to b_{1-12}'. In our empirical example both equal 0.677 (see Table 8.7 and Figure 9.2).

With three independent variables, we get four interaction effects in the formula for b_1':

$$b_1' = b_1 + b_{1-12}' b_{12} + b_{1-13}' b_{13} + b_{1-23}' b_{23} + b_{1-123}' b_{123}$$

The formula tells us that the unsaturated coefficient will deviate from the saturated coefficient more the stronger X_1 is related to the interaction variables X_1X_2, X_1X_3, X_2X_3, and $X_1X_2X_3$, and the stronger these variables are related to the dependent variable X_4.

If we try to rewrite this formula by replacing the saturated coefficients for effects on X_4 with partial differences in proportions, we discover that the b_{23} effect cannot be expressed by means of the partial effects of X_1. Correspondingly, if we transform the formula for D_1 to contain regression coefficients, the interaction effect b_{23} will be missing. This tells us that the weighted average of partial differences in proportions will deviate from the corresponding un-saturated regression coefficient in cases where the independent variable is related to interaction variables involving only other independent variables. Ordinarily this association will be slight (cf. the results entered in Figure 9.3), and if in addition the interaction effect is moderate, the term $b'_{1-23}b_{23}$ will be very small and the divergence between b'_1 and D_1 negligible or equal to zero.

It was the identical results in empirical analyses using the two techniques that convinced Boyle that the identity between the measures which he had been able to prove for two independent variables had general validity (Boyle 1966). When three or more independent variables are highly related, and the interaction effects very strong, however, the weighted average may differ markedly from the regression coefficient. Whenever this is the case, only the regression coefficients will give a completely accurate decomposition of bivariate associations.

The guarantee for a perfect decomposition would seem to be a strong argument in favour of using binary regression analysis in causal analyses of non-metric variables rather than the contingency table approach outlined in this book. Another advantage is the easy access to regression programs in computer packages (their signi-ficance tests will not be appropriate, however; cf. Goodman 1973; Amundsen 1974).

Without a computer, formulae based on bivariate associations may be used, like the one below for the effect of X_2 on X_4 controlled for X_1 and X_3:

$$b'_2 = \frac{(b_{3-1}b_{2-3} - b_{2-1})b_{1-4} - (b_{2-3} - b_{1-3}b_{2-1})b_{3-4} + (1 - b_{1-3}b_{3-1})b_{2-4}}{(b_{3-1}b_{2-3} - b_{2-1})b_{1-2} - (b_{2-3} - b_{1-3}b_{2-1})b_{3-2} + (1 - b_{1-3}b_{3-1})}$$

Having spent some time pondering the rationale behind such a formula, the attractions of the more simple and intuitively under-standable crosstabulation approach will be evident. Another advan-tage of working with contingency tables is that the amount and nature of the interaction is easily established by inspecting the set of partial differences in proportions, it does not take the extra effort of creating interaction variables and carrying out a new analysis by means of a saturated regression equation.

When there is interaction, even the proportions of the multivariate table will be of interest, to see what pattern lies behind the varying partial effects. If, for instance, we find that the effect of sex on political participation is smaller among the unmarried than among the married, we might like to know whether this difference between the partial effects is due to an increase in the level of participation of women when we shift from the married to the unmarried, or rather a comparable decrease for the men, or some other pattern, which a look at the proportions of the contingency table will immediately reveal.

When using a regression program to obtain the causal effects of non-metric variables, it would, therefore, seem advisable to combine this with a contingency table analysis, to get information on the partial effects and the multivariate proportions.

Summary

In path analyses effects are measured by means of regression coefficients. By giving dichotomous variables the values 0 and 1 regression analysis may be performed also with non-metric data. In the bivariate case a binary regression coefficient is identical to the difference in proportions, and can likewise be interpreted as the effect of the independent variable on the probability for a high value on the dependent variable.

By means of a saturated regression equation the multivariate set of proportions can always be accurately predicted. The coefficients for variable effects equal the partial difference in proportions when the control variables have their low value. The coefficients for the interaction variables, defined as the product of independent variables, equal the change in the partial effects as the relevant control variables change from a low to a high value.

Even if it is possible to include the interaction variables in the causal decomposition of associations, several reasons can be given for deleting the interaction variables from the regression equation when the analysis has a causal purpose. The resulting unsaturated regression coefficients are identical to Boyle's weighted average of partial differences in proportions for trivariate analyses, and will usually come quite close with four or more variables.

Glossary

BINARY REGRESSION ANALYSIS: regression analysis with dichotomous variables coded 0 or 1.
INTERACTION VARIABLE: variable formed by multiplying two or more independent variables.
MEAN (arithmetic *m*): measure of central tendency found as sum of values

on a variable for a set of units divided by the number of units, which for a dichotomy coded 0 or 1 equals the proportion with value 1.

SATURATED REGRESSION COEFFICIENT: coefficient from a saturated regression equation.

SATURATED REGRESSION EQUATION: equation including all interaction variables that can be formed from the independent variables of the equation.

STANDARDISED REGRESSION COEFFICIENT: coefficient measuring effect in terms of standard deviations for the variables involved.

UNSATURATED REGRESSION COEFFICIENT: coefficient from equation without interaction variables.

UNSATURATED REGRESSION EQUATION: equation where one or more of the variables from the saturated equation has been deleted.

UNSTANDARDISED REGRESSION COEFFICIENT: coefficient measuring effect in terms of the original metric of the variables involved.

Exercises

9.1 A Regression Analysis of the Effect of Sex and Seniority on Legislative Career

Use the data in Exercise 1.2 to perform a saturated regression analysis of the effect of sex and seniority on rank in Parliament for members of the Conservative Party. Compare the results with those obtained by means of the Coleman prediction scheme in Exercise 8.1.

Find the unsaturated regression coefficients for the effects of sex and seniority on their interaction variable (use the formula given on p. 167, and alter the variables referred to in the indexes, substituting the independent variable for 1, the dependent variable (X_1X_2) for 3 and the control variable for 2). Carry out a causal decomposition analysis for a model including the interaction variable. Check if the results are influenced by a reordering of values on the control variable as discussed in the text.

Calculate the direct effects of sex and seniority on rank in a simplified model, where the interaction variable has been deleted, by summing direct and indirect effects of the original model. Compare the results with those obtained in Exercise 8.4 by means of the weighted average proposed by Boyle (1966).

10

Loglinear Analysis

The approach to contingency table analysis presented in this book can be seen as an elaboration of traditional percentage table analysis, building on the causal tradition founded by Lazarsfeld and represented today first and foremost by Jim Davis. It utilises the same designs for analysis as those developed within path analysis, the major new addition to the set of statistical tools for social research of the 1960s. As shown in Chapter 9, there is even a close relationship between the weighted difference in proportions and the regression coefficient used in path analyses.

The 1970s have seen the advent of a new approach to contingency table analysis. Loglinear analysis cannot yet be said to have attained a widespread application in social research. Compared to percentage table analysis it appears complicated and hard to make sense of intuitively, a problem not alleviated by a lack of more informal introductory texts until recently (Knoke and Burke 1980; Gilbert 1981).

The purpose of including a chapter on loglinear analysis in this book is to point out some important similarities and dissimilarities as compared to the techniques presented so far. While it is, of course, impossible to do justice to the loglinear approach within the limits of one short chapter, it is hoped that the discussion will elucidate some of the aspects which are important when we are considering which scheme of analysis to apply to a specific research problem.

Loglinear analyses deal with relationships between categoric variables, just as in the difference in proportions and binary regression techniques we have discussed so far. In the same way as the constant, variable effects and interaction effects from the Coleman scheme or saturated regression analysis can be used to predict a multivariate set of proportions, the effects of a loglinear analysis can be used to predict the *frequencies* of the multivariate table. Predicting frequencies instead of proportions implies, first of all, that the variables are treated symmetrically, in contrast to selecting one as a dependent variable. Secondly, the number of effect measures needed is doubled, since the number of frequencies will be twice the number of proportions in a multivariate table.

The general loglinear model has two equivalent mathematical forms. In the *multiplicative form* the frequencies are predicted as a function of the product of effects called tau (τ). In the *linear logarithmic form* (which has given the approach its name) the natural logarithm of the frequency is predicted as an additive function of the natural logarithms of the taus, called lambdas (λ) in the loglinear terminology. Since these effect measures are essential for an understanding of the loglinear approach, we will take a closer look at how they are derived in the next section. Starting with the bivariate case we shall see how tau and lambda are calculated from odds and odds ratios, the loglinear parallel to proportions and differences in proportions.

In Section 10.2 the multivariate situation is discussed. It turns out that the relationship between partial effects, overall effect and interaction in a loglinear analysis is the same as in Coleman's scheme for differences in proportions.

A main concern in loglinear analyses is the search for simpler models which may explain the frequencies in the multivariate table. A saturated model contains all possible effects (equal in number to the number of frequencies), and will always reproduce the frequencies with complete accuracy. By deleting effects we get simpler unsaturated models, which are used to generate expected frequencies. A comparison of the actual frequencies and the expected frequencies predicted by the unsaturated model is made in order to decide whether the difference is small enough to be considered a result of random factors, in which case the actual frequencies are represented in a more parsimonious way by the simpler rather than by the saturated model. The loglinear technique includes statistical tests of whether the discrepancy between predicted and actual frequencies is significant or not, and guidelines for how to search for the simplest possible model with a satisfactory fit to the data. The procedure is illustrated in Section 10.3.

The implications of the characteristics of a loglinear analysis for the choice of approach when confronting a particular research problem are discussed in the final section of the chapter.

10.1 The Effect Measures of Loglinear Analysis

An alienating aspect of loglinear analysis when first encountered is the multitude of new names and Greek letters for various statistical measures. The loglinear analogue to a proportion characterising the distribution on a variable within a group is the *odds*, which is defined as the ratio between the number of units with a high value and the number with a low value on the variable ($O = n_1/n_0$, while $P = n_1/n$). The proportion indicates the probability that a unit randomly selected from the group will have a high value on the variable, the odds the ratio between the probabilities for a high *vs* a low value.

In Table 10.1 proportions and odds are calculated for a set of groups. When the proportions with a high value on X lies below 0·5, the odds for a high value is less than 1. As the proportion increases so do the odds that a randomly selected unit will have a high value. The odds of 3 (group C) tells us that a high value is three times as likely as a low value (corresponding to a proportion of 0·75, saying that three out of four units have a high value).

Up to now we have compared groups by taking the difference in proportions, which is 0·10 for all adjacent pairs of groups in Table 10.1, indicating the increase in the probability for a high value on X as we move from group J to I, or I to H, and so on. The loglinear comparison is in terms of *odds ratios*, that is, the ratio between the odds for the two groups. When the odds for a high value on X is 0·18 for group I and 0·05 for group J, we get an odds ratio of 3·6 (or more accurately of $(15/85)/(5/95) = 3·35$ as shown in the table), saying that the odds in favour of a high value is more than three times greater in group I than in group J.

The *tau* used in the multiplicative version of the loglinear model is found as the fourth root of the odds ratio (when the latter is calculated from four frequencies). The *lambda* from the loglinear version is defined as the natural logarithm of tau (which is the same as one-fourth of the logarithm of the odds ratio). When the two groups being compared have the same distribution on X, the odds will be identical, and the odds ratio 1. In this case we get a tau of 1, and a lambda equal to 0. When the odds are greater in the first than in the second group (as for A in relation to B in the table), the odds ratio and tau will be greater than 1, and lambda positive. If the difference goes in the opposite direction (as if we take group B in relation to A), the odds ratio and tau will be less than 1, and lambda negative.

The difference in proportions is 0 when the two groups which are compared have the same distribution on X, and varies between -1 and 1 when the distributions differ. To gain an impression of how this measure of effect compares to effect as defined in a loglinear analysis lambda is the most useful of the various equivalent loglinear measures. As Table 10.1 shows, the difference in proportions and lambda

Table 10.1 A Comparison of the Difference in Proportions and Loglinear Effect Measures

Group:		A	B	C	D	E	F	G	H	I	J
Distribution on variable X	$X=1: n_1$	95	85	75	65	55	45	35	25	15	5
within group K	$X=0: n_0$	5	15	25	35	45	55	65	75	85	95
Sum	$n.$	100	100	100	100	100	100	100	100	100	100
Proportion	$P_K = n_1/n.$	0·95	0·85	0·75	0·65	0·55	0·45	0·35	0·25	0·15	0·05
Difference in proportions	$d = P_K - P_L$	0·10	0·10	0·10	0·10	0·10	0·10	0·10	0·10	0·10	
Odds	$O_K = n_1/n_0$	19·0	5·67	3·00	1·86	1·22	0·82	0·54	0·33	0·18	0·05
Odds ratio	$OR = O_K/O_L$	3·35	1·89	1·62	1·52	1·49	1·52	1·62	1·89	3·35	
Tau	$\tau = OR^{1/4}$	1·35	1·17	1·13	1·11	1·10	1·11	1·13	1·17	1·35	
Lambda	$\lambda = \ln(\tau) = \tfrac{1}{4}\ln(OR)$	0·30	0·16	0·12	0·10	0·10	0·10	0·12	0·16	0·30	

actually have the same size when we compare groups where the proportions lie within the range 0·65–0·35 (D–G). Just as we may find the difference in proportions for non-adjacent groups by adding the set of ds which lie between them (for instance, for group D as compared to G: $d = 0·10 + 0·10 + 0·10 = 0·30$), we may add together lambdas to find the difference for any pair of groups. The difference between groups D and G as measured by lambda also is 0·30.

While the difference in proportions for adjacent groups is the same for the entire spectrum of distributions in the table, lambda increases when the distribution on X becomes less even. Comparing groups A and B, or I and J, where nearly all, or hardly any, units have a high value on X, lambda is 0·30 and the difference in proportions still just 0·10.

What do we learn from the comparison of d and lambda? First of all, that lambda will be either identical to or larger than d, depending upon the range of the proportions. For the proportions 0·65–0·35 (D–G), d and lambda are both 0·30, while 0·75–0·25 (C–H) give a slight difference ($d = 0·50$, $\lambda = 0·54$). Extremely high or low proportions result in a substantial difference, as when we compare groups A and J. The difference in proportions is $0·95 - 0·05 = 0·90$, while lambda takes on the value of 1·46. The latter result teaches us a second lesson, that unlike the difference in proportions, the range of lambda is not restricted.

While our discussion so far has been limited to the bivariate case (assuming that we compare groups defined according to value on a second variable with regard to their distribution on X), Table 10.1 also highlights another important difference between the two approaches to contingency table analysis, that they may disagree on whether there is *interaction* present in the data or not.

For the pair of groups E–F, d as well as lambda equals 0·10, for the pair A–B, d still is 0·10 while lambda is 0·30. These two set of effects from the four groups might constitute the partial associations for two variables controlling for a third variable. According to the difference in proportions, which is identical for the two pairs of groups, the data are interaction-free. When we measure instead association by means of lambda, the partial effect for the A–B pair is much stronger than the effect for the E–F pair, and varying effect between control groups indicates that the data are interaction-ridden.

In the same way we might construe an example where the partial lambdas come out identical, while the differences in proportions vary. Take the two pairs of groups A–B and D–G, which both have lambdas of 0·30, while the difference in proportions is 0·10 for the first pair and 0·30 for the second. The conclusion with regard to interaction is that if the distribution on X lies within the range where d and lambda are approximately the same for the groups to be compared, the measure of interaction also will come out more or less the same (the next section will show how interaction is measured in a loglinear analysis). If one or more of the groups have proportions outside this range, the interaction effects of a loglinear analysis can be either stronger or weaker than those of a difference in proportions analysis.

One important consideration when deciding whether to choose the loglinear or the traditional difference in proportions approach to the analysis of a particular set of data, will accordingly be which definition of effect one feels is most meaningful in relation to the substantive problem at hand. This problem was briefly touched upon in Section 8.3, in relation to the choice of weighting scheme. If we find it reasonable to assume that it 'takes more' to get a difference of 0·10 between proportions which lie close to one of the extremes of 0·0 or 1·0 than between proportions in the range from 0·35 to 0·65, this will be reflected in the lambda of a loglinear analysis. A case in hand might be if the proportions in Table 10.1 represented the illiteracy rate of a population at different points in time. To increase the level of literacy will be hard when starting out from a low level, and also when the level has become so high as to leave little room for any increase.

If the pairs of groups in Table 10.1 instead represent men and women at different levels of political interest, and the proportions the voting turnout, it may seem more reasonable to regard the difference between the proportions of, for example, 0·15 and 0·05 to indicate the same effect of sex on voting as the difference between 0·55 and 0·45 or between 0·75 and 0·65. In this case the difference in proportions would give results in accordance with our substantive understanding of effect, and lambda would not.

10.2 Partial Effects, Overall Effect and Interaction

To illustrate a multivariate loglinear analysis we shall once more return to the table for social status, criminal record and severity of sentence. In Table 10.2 the odds for a severe over a lenient sentence are calculated for all four combinations of status and record, with results varying from more than four to one for low-status recidivists to a mere 0·09 for high-status first-offenders.

Table 10.2 Partial Effects, Overall Effect and Interaction in a Trivariate Loglinear Analysis

X_1 Social status	X_2 Criminal record	X_3 Sentence 1 Severe	0 Lenient	Odds X_3: $O_{ij.} = n_{ij1}/n_{ij0}$	Partial Odds Ratio X_2X_3: $OR_{i..} = O_{i1.}/O_{i0.}$
1 High	1 Criminal	n_{111} 25	n_{110} 15	$\dfrac{n_{111}}{n_{110}} = \dfrac{25}{15} = 1.67$	$\dfrac{n_{111}}{n_{110}} = \dfrac{n_{111}n_{100}}{n_{110}n_{101}} = \dfrac{1.67}{0.09} = 18.56$
	0 Clean	n_{101} 2	n_{100} 22	$\dfrac{n_{101}}{n_{100}} = \dfrac{2}{22} = 0.09$	$\dfrac{n_{101}}{n_{100}}$
0 Low	1 Criminal	n_{011} 95	n_{010} 22	$\dfrac{n_{011}}{n_{010}} = \dfrac{95}{22} = 4.32$	$\dfrac{n_{011}}{n_{010}} = \dfrac{n_{011}n_{000}}{n_{010}n_{001}} = \dfrac{4.32}{0.94} = 4.60$
	0 Clean	n_{001} 17	n_{000} 18	$\dfrac{n_{001}}{n_{000}} = \dfrac{17}{18} = 0.94$	$\dfrac{n_{001}}{n_{000}}$

Overall Odds Ratio X_2X_3: $(OR_{1..})(OR_{0..}) = \dfrac{n_{111}n_{100}}{n_{110}n_{101}} \times \dfrac{n_{011}n_{000}}{n_{010}n_{001}} = 18.56 \times 4.60 = 85.38$

Interaction $X_1X_2X_3$: $OR_{1..}/OR_{0..} = \dfrac{n_{111}n_{100}}{n_{110}n_{101}} \Big/ \dfrac{n_{011}n_{000}}{n_{010}n_{001}} = 18.56/4.60 = 4.03$

By taking the ratio of the odds for high-status defendants with a criminal *vs* a clean record we obtain the *partial odds ratio* for record and sentence (or to use the common term, the conditional odds ratio for the two variables) among high-status defendants. Since the odds for a severe sentence are much greater with a criminal than with a clean record, the partial odds ratio is high: 18·56. Among low-status defendants the ratio of the odds is smaller: 4·60.

We thus have two dissimilar partial odds ratios, each characterising the relationship between record and sentence controlled for status. To obtain a measure for the *overall association* between record and sentence we multiply the two partial effects. To measure how much they differ, that is, the degree of *interaction*, we take the ratio of the odds ratios. The result is an overall odds ratio for record and sentence of 85·38 and an interaction between all three variables of 4·03.

The meaning of these figures may be easier to grasp if we express them as lambdas instead of odds ratios. To obtain the lambda corresponding to a partial odds ratio of 18·56 we take the natural logarithm and divide by four (since there are four frequencies involved): $\frac{1}{4} \ln(18·56) = \frac{1}{4}(2·92) = 0·73$. The lambda for the association between record and sentence among low-status defendants is found as $\frac{1}{4} \ln (4·60) = \frac{1}{4}(1·53) = 0·38$.

Having established the partial lambdas, we find the overall association as their average: $\frac{1}{2}(0·73 + 0·38) = 0·555$. This is the same as we get if we take the natural logarithm of the overall odds ratio and divide by eight (since it is based on eight frequencies): $\frac{1}{8} \ln(85·56) = \frac{1}{8}(4·45) = 0·556$. The interaction correspondingly equals the difference between the overall and the partial lambdas, that is, half the distance between the partials: $\frac{1}{2}(0·73 - 0·38) = 0·175$ (which is the same as one-eighth of the natural logarithm of the ratio of the partial odds ratios of 4·03).

What has thus been shown is that the way we calculate overall association and interaction in a loglinear analysis (in its logarithmic form) is equivalent to the procedures used in the Coleman scheme for calculating variable effect and interaction from a set of partial differences in proportions. The nature of the effect measures differ, but the analysis design is the same. The purpose of the analysis is also the same, even if one technique is concerned with predicting proportions and the other deals with frequencies.

(There is one version of the loglinear approach, called *logit analysis*, where one variable is treated as dependent, and its odds, or their logs, predicted instead of frequencies, making the parallel to the Coleman scheme even more striking. In a logit analysis the effects corresponding to lambdas are called betas, and have exactly twice the size of the lambdas. When you analyse the odds as if they were frequencies, the natural logarithm of the overall and interaction effects in Table 10.2 should be divided by four instead of eight, resulting in new effects – betas – two times the size of the old ones – the lambdas.)

Table 10.3 shows an easy way of obtaining the lambdas if you are to perform the computations yourself. (There exist several standard computer programs that will do the job, with the ECTA-program perhaps being the best known, see Gilbert 1981: 122–4.) We may need eight effect measures in order to reproduce the eight frequencies of Table 10.2 accurately. The one missing from the table is the loglinear equivalent to the *constant* of the Coleman scheme (which equals the eighth root of the product of all frequencies in the multiplicative form – that is, the geometric mean – corresponding to one-eighth of the sum of all logs in the loglinear form).

Of the seven lambdas in Table 10.3, three are *one-variable effects*, characterising the distribution on a single variable while controlling for the other two. We find it by summing the logs of frequencies where the variable has a high value, subtracting the logs where the value is low, and divide the result by eight. Notice that a one-variable lambda may well be different from the lambda for the univariate distribution of this variable (in Table 10.3 the lambda for the distribution on sentence is -0.06, due to the extremely low number of severely sentenced high-status first-offenders, while the lambda for the univariate distribution on sentence – 139 severe and 77 lenient – is $\frac{1}{2}(\ln(139) - \ln(77)) = 0.30$).

The *two-variable effects* likewise show the association for a pair of variables controlling for the third, and are found by adding together the logs of frequencies where the two variables have consonant values (11 or 00), and subtracting the logs for dissonant value combinations (10 or 01). The effects may differ from the bivariate association of the pair of variables. We thus cannot use the X_1X_2 effect from Table 10.3 if we want to enter the lambdas in a causal diagram, since the effect of status (X_1) on record (X_2) according to our causal model should not be controlled for the effect variable sentence (X_3).

The *three-variable effect* corresponds to what we are used to call interaction, and is found by adding the logs of frequencies where the value combination for all three variables contains an even number of low values (none or two zeros), and subtracting the logs for combinations where the number is uneven (one or three zeros).

Readers feeling slightly dizzy after this race through the set of

Table 10.3 The Calculus of Lambda (Λ) from the Logs of the Multivariate Frequencies (from Table 10.2)

Variables X_1 X_2 X_3	n_{ijk}	$\ln(n_{ijk})$	Sign of $\ln(n_{ijk})$ when calculating effect measure for:						
			X_1	X_2	X_3	X_1X_2	X_1X_3	X_2X_3	$X_1X_2X_3$
1 1 1	25	3·219	+	+	+	+	+	+	+
1 1 0	15	2·708	+	+	−	+	−	−	−
1 0 1	2	0·693	+	−	+	−	+	−	−
1 0 0	22	3·091	+	−	−	−	−	+	+
0 1 1	95	4·554	−	+	+	−	−	+	−
0 1 0	22	3·091	−	+	−	−	+	−	+
0 0 1	17	2·833	−	−	+	+	−	−	+
0 0 0	18	2·890	−	−	−	+	+	+	−
Sum of $\ln(n_{ijk})$ =			−3·657	4·065	−0·481	0·221	−3·293	4·429	1·389
Lambda = 1/8 Sum =			−0·457	0·508	−0·060	0·028	−0·412	0·554	0·174

loglinear effect measures with Greek names and unfamiliar definitions, will be glad to hear that we will stop at this point, without
saying more about eta, theta, omega, or phi. Those wanting to make
their acquaintance, or seeking a more thorough understanding of the
measures we have briefly discussed, will find that the book by Knoke
and Burke (1980) is a good place to start.

We shall now turn to what many will experience as a more
attractive side of loglinear analysis, the effective way in which
complex models may be simplified and tested against the data.

10.3   Non-Saturated Models and Model-Testing

The model for the relationship between status, record and sentence
analysed in the preceding section, including all possible effects, is a
saturated loglinear model. Since the number of effects equals the
number of frequencies they are used to predict, we have not obtained
a simplification of the original data, just another way of representing
them. In a loglinear analysis the goal of a more parsimonious
description of the multivariate frequencies is reached through systematically testing how well simpler *non-saturated models* are able to
predict the frequencies.

In the standard notation for loglinear models the saturated three-
variable model is designated $\{X_1X_2X_3\}$, which implies that this and
all lower-order (two-variable and one-variable) effects are present.
Loglinear model-testing most commonly assumes a *hierarchical structure*, meaning that when a certain effect is included in the model, all
lower-order effects which can be formed for the variables involved
will also be included. We thus cannot delete a two-variable effect
while keeping the three-variable effect in the model, and so on.

With four or more variables, the number of non-saturated models
that can be formed is large, even with the restriction of a hierarchical
structure. Various strategies for how quickly to find the simplest
model with a satisfactory fit to the data are discussed, as for instance
whether one should start with the simplest model and add lower-
order effects until the predicted frequencies approximate the actual
ones, or start with the saturated model and delete higher-order
effects until the predicted frequencies deviate too much from the
data. Even a three-variable table gives rise to nineteen different
hierarchical models (Gilbert 1981: 59 has the complete list). In this
case, however, the problem of finding the best model to describe the
data is fairly simple.

In order to obtain a simpler model than the saturated $\{X_1X_2X_3\}$

model, the three-variable effect has to be set equal to zero (when expressed as lambda). This gives us the non-saturated model containing all two-variable effects: $\{X_1X_2\}\{X_1X_3\}\{X_2X_3\}$. Looking at the results for the saturated model (Table 10.3) we notice that lambda for X_1X_2 is very small, indicating that this effect may be left out without harming our ability to predict the frequencies much. The suggested model thus is $\{X_1X_3\}\{X_2X_3\}$, in other words, that we assume status and sentence to be associated, and likewise for record and sentence. Table 10.3 also shows the one-variable effect for X_3 to be small, but since X_3 is included in the higher-order effects of the model, the lambda for X_3 cannot be set equal to zero.

In Table 10.4 the actual trivariate distribution for status, record and sentence, as well as the possible bivariate and univariate distributions that may be formed, are shown. The implications of assuming the model $\{X_1X_3\}\{X_2X_3\}$ is that these bivariate associations and their lower-order relatives $\{X_1\}$, $\{X_2\}$ and $\{X_3\}$ are to be the same for the modelled frequencies (those predicted under the model) as they are for the actual data.

The easiest, and for more complex problems the only, way of obtaining the frequencies predicted by an unsaturated model is to ask the computer to produce them. Beneath the actual data in Table 10.4 the trivariate expected frequencies generated by the ECTA-program are listed. They depart somewhat from the observed frequencies, and so does the bivariate association between X_1 and X_2. The two other bivariate distributions, and the three univariate ones, are as we see identical for the modelled and the actual data, as required by the model.

Since we are working with such a simple model, it is possible to show how the computer arrives at the expected frequencies under the model, which is the story told in the lower part of Table 10.4. We start out by making the (obviously poor) guess that all trivariate frequencies equal 1, obtain the bivariate distribution for X_1X_3 resulting from this guess, and take the ratio of the actual bivariate frequencies over the ones we guessed. By multiplying the trivariate frequencies of guess 1 with this ratio we arrive at the second guess, which starts to look a little more like the actual data. This time we compute the bivariate distribution for the other pair of variables specified by the model, X_2 and X_3. Once more, we take the ratio of observed over guessed frequencies, and correct the frequencies from the second guess by multiplying with the new ratio. When we return to the bivariate relation between X_1 and X_3, we see that guess 3 gives results identical to the observed frequencies. We have thus arrived at

Table 10.4 Obtaining Expected Frequencies under an Unsaturated Model (Actual Data from Table 10.2)

Three-way table {X1X2X3}:

X1	X2	X3=1	X3=0
1	1	25	15
1	0	2	22
0	1	95	22
0	0	17	18

{X1X2} table:

X1	X2=1	X2=0
1	40	24
0	117	35

{X1X3} table:

X1	X3=1	X3=0
1	27	37
0	112	40

{X2X3} table:

X2	X3=1	X3=0
1	120	37
0	19	40

One-way margins:

X1		X2		X3	
1	64	1	157	1	139
0	152	0	59	0	77

Expected frequencies under the model $\{X_1X_3\}\{X_2X_3\}$

$X_1X_2X_3$		X_1X_2		X_1X_3		X_2X_3	
23·31	17·78	41·09	22·91	27·00	37·00	120·00	37·00
3·69	19·22	115·91	36·09	112·00	40·00	19·00	40·00
96·69	19·22						
15·31	20·78						

X_1		X_2		X_3	
	64·00		157·00		139·00
	152·00		59·00		77·00

Iterative proportionate scaling to obtain expected frequencies under the model $\{X_1X_3\}\{X_2X_3\}$

Guess 1 at a solution:

```
        X1  X3            Data/Guess 1
1 1
1 1
1 1     2   2             27/2 = 13·5    37/2 = 18·5
1 1     2   2             112/2 = 56·0   40/2 = 20·0
```

Guess 2 at a solution:

```
1 × 13·5 = 13·5    1 × 18·5 = 18·5          X2    X3
1 × 13·5 = 13·5    1 × 18·5 = 18·5
1 × 56·0 = 56·0    1 × 20·0 = 20·0          69·5  38·5
1 × 56·0 = 56·0    1 × 20·0 = 20·0          69·5  38·5
                                            69·5  38·5
                                            69·5  38·5
```

Data/Guess 2:

```
120/69·5 = 1·727    37/38·5 = 0·961
19/69·5 = 0·273     40/38·5 = 1·039
```

Guess 3 at a solution:

```
13·5 × 1·727 = 23·31    18·5 × 0·961 = 17·78          X1    X3
13·5 × 0·273 = 3·69     18·5 × 1·039 = 19·22
56·0 × 1·727 = 96·69    20·0 × 0·961 = 19·22          27·00  37·00
56·0 × 0·273 = 15·31    20·0 × 1·039 = 20·78          112·00 40·00
```

Data/Guess 3:

```
27/27 = 1·00      37/37 = 1·00
120/120 = 1·00    40/40 = 1·00
```

a set of trivariate frequencies which satisfies the requirement that the bivariate associations specified by the model are the same for the modelled as for the actual data.

The next step in the analysis is to test the degree of fit between the observed trivariate frequencies and those expected under the model. The ECTA-program reports chi-square as well as the related likelihood-ratio statistic, and the degrees of freedom (which is the same as the number of effects set equal to zero in the model). The program even saves us the trouble of looking up in a statistical table the distribution of chi-square, by giving the probability that the observed frequencies could have been generated by a model with the relationships between the variables we have specified.

When the discrepancy between the actual data and the predicted trivariate frequencies is small, as in our example, the probability will be high: 0·24. We thus have little reason to reject the model $\{X_1X_3\}\{X_2X_3\}$ as an inadequate representation of the data. Also the model with all three two-variable effects may have generated the observed frequencies (but the probability is lower: 0·09), while all other unsaturated models give predictions so far from the observed frequencies that their likelihood of producing such frequencies is less than 0·000.

In the usual chi-square test of independence between a pair of variables the researcher will hope for a large value for chi-square, so that the null-hypothesis of no association may be rejected. When testing a loglinear model, however, where some associations have been set equal to zero, we will be looking for a small chi-square, allowing us to accept the model.

We thus reach the conclusion that the trivariate distribution on status, record and sentence may be adequately described by a model where the three-variable association and one of the two-variable associations are assumed to be absent. If we calculate the lambdas for the modelled frequencies (Table 10.5), we see that the $X_1X_2X_3$ and the X_1X_2 effects actually do come out equal to zero, while the remaining effects have been slightly altered as compared to the results from the saturated model (Table 10.3).

Once again, we have to refer to the textbooks on loglinear analysis (Knoke and Burke 1980; Gilbert 1981) for a more thorough discussion of the selection and testing of loglinear models. The brief illustration of the method in this section is hopefully sufficient to demonstrate its potential utility when we are looking for simple ways of describing a multivariate data-set.

Table 10.5 *Effects under the Unsaturated Model* {X₁X₃}{X₂X₃}

Variables X_1 X_2 X_3	n_{ijk}	$\ln(n_{ijk})$	Sign of $\ln(n_{ijk})$ when calculating effect measure for: X_1	X_2	X_3	X_1X_2	X_1X_3	X_2X_3	$X_1X_2X_3$
1 1 1	23·31	3·149	+	+	+	+	+	+	+
1 1 0	17·78	2·878	+	+	−	+	−	−	−
1 0 1	3·69	1·306	+	−	+	−	+	−	−
1 0 0	19·22	2·956	+	−	−	−	−	+	+
0 1 1	96·69	4·572	−	+	+	−	−	+	−
0 1 0	19·22	2·956	−	+	−	−	+	−	+
0 0 1	15·31	2·729	−	−	+	+	−	−	+
0 0 0	20·78	3·034	−	−	−	+	+	+	−
Sum of $\ln(n_{ijk})$ =			−3·002	3·530	−0·068	0·000	−2·690	3·842	0·000
Lambda = 1/8 Sum =			−0·375	0·441	−0·009	0·000	−0·336	0·480	0·000

10.4 The Choice of Approach to the Analysis of Contingency Tables

The purpose of this chapter has been to provide readers with little or no prior knowledge of loglinear analysis with an impression of how this approach in some ways is similar to, and in some ways different from, the various schemes for analysing contingency tables by means of differences in proportions discussed in earlier chapters, as a basis for judging which technique should be applied to solve a particular research problem. Comments by the most ardent proponents of the loglinear approach may sometimes leave the impression that they see no question of choice, the new technique in their view has made earlier approaches to contingency tables obsolete and merely of historical interest. This is hardly the natural conclusion to reach from the comparison of the two traditions made in this chapter.

First of all, it should be clear that the loglinear approach belongs to the prediction analysis category, along with the Coleman scheme and saturated binary regression analysis. It aims at predicting a multivariate distribution, and makes use of interaction effects in order to increase the accuracy of the predicted results when necessary. It thus confronts the same problems as the Coleman scheme when it comes to decomposing associations with interaction effects present. Even when we use the loglinear effects from the model where the interaction effect has been set to zero, we do not obtain an accurate decomposition of the bivariate lambda for X_1X_3 or X_2X_3. The effect measures of a loglinear analysis simply do not seem to be suited for decomposing associations, regardless of whether the data are interaction-ridden or not.

Despite some claims to the contrary (Goodman 1973; Dessens and Janscn 1978), it seems to be generally accepted that loglinear analysis is unsuited for causal decomposition (Davis and Schooler 1974; Reynolds 1977; Fienberg 1977). This is also the view of the introductory texts we have referred to (Knoke and Burke 1980; Gilbert 1981), where causal models are used as a device for displaying the results of a loglinear analysis, with no pretensions that a causal decomposition is possible. For this purpose, we have to use the weighted difference in proportions approach or unsaturated binary regression analysis.

The question of when to use loglinear analysis is thus first of all a question of the comparative advantages of the various approaches to prediction analysis. Here the computer programs which generate expected frequencies for the unsaturated models we specify, test if the fit to the observed frequencies is satisfactory and calculate the variable effects under the model we choose to represent the data, would appear to be a great asset of the loglinear approach. The variable effects in the form of lambdas will, as we have seen, be of the same magnitude as the differences in proportions from a Coleman anaiysis when the proportions fall within the range $0.25-0.75$, which may be helpful to keep in mind when interpreting the results of a loglinear analysis.

The question of whether to choose a causal approach or a prediction approach, depends on the purpose of the analysis, whether we want to explain why a pair of variables are related or describe a multivariate distribution. To some it may be confusing that the term model is used for the relationships we specify between the variables in a causal analysis as well as a loglinear analysis, leading them to believe that the two techniques are more similar than is the case. We will, therefore, end the discussion with a few remarks on the difference between a causal and a loglinear model.

A loglinear model is a specification of which effects are necessary to reproduce a multivariate set of frequencies with a reasonable accuracy. The statistical analysis of the degree of fit between observed and modelled frequencies will enable us to decide whether to accept or reject the model as a satisfactory representation of the multivariate distribution. Sometimes models in a loglinear analysis are specified on the basis of theoretical reasoning or references to characteristics of the subject of the study. Very often, however, no prior justification for preferring a certain model is given. Instead a model is selected by systematically testing one's way through the set of possible models for the variables involved. The very efficiency of this process of trial and error in a loglinear analysis may constitute a danger that atheoretical analyses without substantively interesting comments to the results are carried out.

A causal model may also contain assumptions for which the statistical analysis will decide whether they were correct or not, when it has been made specific by assuming that one or more effects are positive, negative, or absent (cf. Section 3.3). But in addition it will always contain assumptions of a substantive nature, which the statistical analysis in itself cannot test. These concern the time ordering of the variables, and the relationship between variables included in the model and those left outside. Since they cannot be justified by the results of the statistical analysis, but rather constitute the foundation on which this analysis rests, the researcher is forced to rely on theoretical arguments or substantive references to convince his audience that the assumptions are reasonable.

While the existence of assumptions which are not tested in the statistical analysis may induce scepticism about the utility of causal models in some, a positive aspect of this situation is the incentive to exploit one's substantive knowledge of the social phenomenon under study and one's ability to deduce relevant consequences from existing theories.

Summary

There are several versions of loglinear analysis, which are used to predict frequencies, their logs, or odds (the ratio between two frequencies) or their logs. The effects of the logarithmic form of loglinear analysis, called lambda, will give results similar to the difference in proportions when the proportions vary within the range 0·25 to 0·75. With more extreme proportions, the lambdas for variable effects will be larger than the difference in proportions, while interaction effects may come out larger as well as smaller.

The way overall association or interaction is calculated from a set of partial lambdas in a loglinear analysis is exactly the same as in a Coleman analysis of differences in proportions. Compared to other prediction analysis techniques, loglinear analysis has an advantage in the facilities for testing the ability of simpler models where effects from the saturated model have been deleted to account for the observed frequencies. As for the other prediction techniques, loglinear analysis is not suited for the purpose of causal decomposition of the association between a pair of variables.

Glossary

BETA (β): the logit equivalent to lambda (equalling twice the size of lambda).

LAMBDA (λ): effect measure in the logarithmic form of loglinear analysis (equalling the log of tau, or $1/k$ of the log of the odds ratio, where k is the number of frequencies used to calculate the odds ratio).

LOGIT ANALYSIS: loglinear analysis predicting odds (or their logs) for a dependent variable.

LOGLINEAR ANALYSIS: scheme for predicting frequencies as a multiplicative function of their geometric mean and a set of taus, or the log of the frequencies as an additive function of the log of the mean and lambdas.

ODDS: ratio of two frequencies.

ODDS RATIO: ratio of odds.

TAU (τ): effect measure in the multiplicative form of loglinear analysis (equalling the kth root of an odds ratio calculated from k frequencies).

Exercises

10.1   A Loglinear Analysis of the Relationship between Sex, Occupation and Income

Use the data from Exercise 1.1 to perform a loglinear analysis of the relationship between the three variables based on a saturated model. If you have a calculator with a ln (natural logarithm) function, the simplest way is to use the setup of Table 10.3. Try also to calculate odds, and the odds ratios for partial effects, overall effect and interaction, and use the results to find tau and lambda.

How do the results of the saturated loglinear model compare with those reached by means of differences in proportions in Exercise 1.1? Do you see any possibilities for finding a simpler non-saturated model which may account for the data? As mentioned earlier, the frequencies given in the exercise are approximately one-tenth of those of the original data. Would the testing of unsaturated models in any way be influenced if we multiply each frequency with a factor of 10?

10.2   Sex, Seniority and Legislative Career

The data on Conservative members of the Norwegian Parliament has served as a basis for prediction and causal analyses by means of differences in proportions as well as regression coefficients (Exercises 1.2, 8.1, 8.4 and 9.1). Carry out a saturated loglinear analysis as well, and compare the results with those of the other prediction techniques. How do the interpretation of the results from the loglinear analysis differ from those made on the basis of a causal analysis of the same data?

Answers to Selected Exercises

1.1 Sex, Occupation and Income

On p. 192 the blanks in the sheet with model and tables have been filled in with the appropriate names and numbers. Two aspects of the results are worthy of special attention.

First of all, the partial effects of each causal variable turned out to be identical when controlled for the other independent variable in the trivariate table. In other words, there is no interaction between the independent variables. This saves us the trouble of having to calculate a weighted average of the partial effects in order to find the direct effect of a causal variable.

Secondly, this direct effect on income for sex as well as occupation turned out to be larger than the bivariate association. For sex the indirect effect is of the opposite sign as the direct effect, for occupation the same holds for the spurious effect on income. When the component due to a control variable serves to reduce the bivariate association by working in the opposite direction as the direct effect of the causal variable, the control variable is called a *suppressor variable*. In Section 4.2 this rather unusual and interesting situation is further discussed. There you will see that such a pattern tells us that the two causal variables in our model must be negatively related. You may check out this by calculating the bivariate association between sex and occupation.

1.2 Sex and Legislative Career

Model: Since the sex of a representative cannot be influenced by any of the other variables, and seniority may be assumed to affect rank rather than the other way round, the ordering of the variables becomes sex (causal variable), seniority (intervening variable) and rank (effect variable). The effect of sex on seniority among the representatives may be conceived as a result of the impact of sex in the recruitment process for Members of Parliament over the last decades.

Results: By means of bivariate and trivariate tables we find the

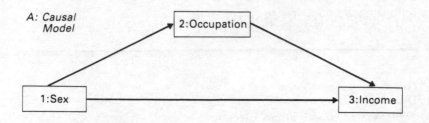

A: Causal Model

1: Sex → 2: Occupation → 3: Income

B: Bivariate association for 1: Sex & 3: Income

3: Income	Absolute frequencies 1: Sex M	F	Proportions 1: Sex M	F	Difference
H	34	10	0·64	0·22	0·42
L	19	35	0·36	0·78	−0·42
Sum	53	45	1·0	1·0	0·00

C: Bivariate association for 2: Occupation & 3: Income

3: Income	Absolute frequencies 2: Occupation W	B	Proportions 2: Occupation W	B	Difference
H	24	20	0·51	0·39	0·12
L	23	31	0·49	0·61	−0·12
Sum	47	51	1·0	1·0	0·00

D: Trivariate association for 1: Sex, 2: Occupation & 3: Income

1: Sex	Absolute frequencies M		F		Proportions M		F	
2: Occupation	W	B	W	B	W	B	W	B
3: Income H	16	18	8	2	0·76	0·56	0·31	0·11
L	5	14	18	17	0·24	0·44	0·69	0·89
Sum	21	32	26	19	1·0	1·0	1·0	1·0

E: Prop. High on 3: Income depending on 1 & 2

2: Occupation	1: Sex M	F	Difference
W	0·76	0·31	0·45
B	0·56	0·11	0·45
Difference	0·20	0·20	

F: Causal decomposition of bivariate associations

Components in association between	1: Sex & 3: Income	2: Occupation & 3: Income
Gross association:	0·42	0·12
Causal effect:	0·42	0·20
Direct effect:	0·45	0·20
Indirect effect:	−0·03	0
Spurious effect:	0	−0·08

following components for the association between the independent variables and the dependent:

	Labour	Conservatives
Gross association between sex and rank	−0·12	0·16
Direct effect of sex on rank	−0·24	0·12
Indirect effect of sex via seniority	0·12	0·04
Gross association between seniority and rank	0·39	0·47
Direct effect of seniority on rank	0·46	0·47
Spurious effect of seniority due to sex	−0·07	0·00

Comment: For both parties the indirect effect of sex on rank is positive (when male is defined as the 'high' value on the sex variable), indicating that male representatives are favoured by their higher seniority. In the Labour Party this indirect effect is more than offset by a tendency for female representatives to have a higher chance for being selected than male representatives on the same level of seniority, rendering the total causal effect negative. Within the Conservative Party also the direct effect indicates an advantage for male representatives.

This comment has been restricted to the results as they stand. We shall return to the above example later in the book, to discuss the need for considering alternative interpretations of the empirical pattern.

1.3 Opinions about Promotion Opportunity in the American Army

Model: It seems reasonable to assume that education affects rank, and that both these variables may influence satisfaction with promotion opportunities.

Results: With regard to the dependent variable, several possibilities exist, but here the proportion answering 'A very good chance' has been singled out for attention. For the Military Police, we find the following net associations with the dependent variable:

Education: $(0·27−0·58)×(241+165)/1{,}583 +$
$\qquad (0·21−0·33)×(470+707)/1{,}583$
$\qquad = (−0·31)×0·26+(−0·12)×0·74 = −0·08−0·09 = −0·17$
Rank: $\qquad (0·27−0·21)×(241+470)/1{,}583 +$
$\qquad (0·58−0·33)×(165+707)/1{,}583$
$\qquad = 0·06×0·45+0·25×0·55 = 0·03+0·14 = 0·17$

To find the gross associations we must calculate the bivariate frequency distributions. One way of doing this would be to reconstruct the data matrix by calculating the absolute frequencies from the bases and percentages in the chart. Another way is to obtain the proportions in the bivariate table by weighing together the relevant proportions in the trivariate table. For high education, this gives $0.27 \times 241/711 + 0.21 \times 470/711 = 0.09 + 0.14 = 0.23$, for low education $0.58 \times 165/872 + 0.33 \times 707/872 = 0.11 + 0.27 = 0.38$, and the bivariate association $0.23 - 0.38 = -0.15$. Following the same procedure we find the bivariate association between rank and satisfaction with promotion opportunity to be 0.12.

The results of the causal analysis for the Military Police branch of service, then, is that the gross association between education and satisfaction of -0.15 is the result of a direct effect of -0.17 and an indirect effect via rank of 0.02. The gross association of 0.12 between rank and satisfaction is explained as the result of a direct effect of 0.17 and a spurious effect due to education of -0.05.

Comment: In agreement with the interpretations made in the original report we find that having a high education increases the chances for being promoted, and at the same time decreases the chances for being satisfied with the promotion opportunities, as shown by the opposite signs of the indirect and direct effects.

2.1 Sex Differences in Legislative Career – Direct or Indirect Effect?

One set of possible intervening variables would include social background variables which might be considered as criteria of qualification for the leadership positions, such as education or occupational career. Another set of potential intervening factors would be political positions outside Parliament, especially in the party organisation. Possibly male representatives have been party members for a longer time, have reached higher positions in the party hierarchy, and so on. A third candidate for the role as intervening variable would be one often alluded to by male party leaders: lack of interest or downright reluctance to accept high-ranking positions on the part of the women.

2.2 Effect of Criminal Stereotype on Conviction of Homicide Defendants

In the study by Swigert and Farrel (1977) the following variables assumed to be prior to conformity to the 'normal primitive' stereotype were controlled for: sex, race, occupation, prior conviction severity. Sex and prior conviction severity turned out to have little effect on the chances of conforming to the stereotype, thus being without importance as causes of spurious effect between stereotype and final conviction. Intervening variables in the study were the retention of a private attorney, award of bail and trial format (jury or not). The last two turned out to be important mediators between stereotype and final conviction, rendering the direct effect equal to zero. The reader should consult the discussion in the article for more details.

2.3 Government Involvement and Income Inequality

The prior variable was economic development (measured as *GNP/C*), and the intervening variable rate of economic growth. The reasoning underlying such a model is given in the article by Stack (1978), which concludes that government involvement has the largest direct effect on income inequality among these three causal variables.

3.1 Robert Michels and the Iron Law of Oligarchy

On p. 196 is a causal diagram presenting one possible interpretation of the discussion of Michels. Based on the entire text, it contains aspects not covered in the excerpt. It may be suggested that the paths from variables 3 to 4, 7, 12 and 17, and from 3 to 6, 11 and 16 represent his reasoning in the excerpt fairly well, although it is not difficult to envisage alternative solutions.

3.2 Hypotheses on Social Differences in Political Participation

The hypotheses say nothing about causality, just association; but it would seem clear that if we were to assume a causal relationship, political participation would have to be the effect variable. As they stand, the hypotheses may be represented by what has been called a simple model for inventory of causes (Blalock 1969: 35). In the diagram occupation and income have been used as indicators of social status (in parenthesis the value assumed to increase the probability of being politically active).

The implication of such a model, that the causal variables are unrelated, will seldom seem appropriate. In our case it is clear that influence relations will exist between several of the social background variables. In the model a causal ordering for the variables is proposed and the influence relations assumed to be the most important indicated.

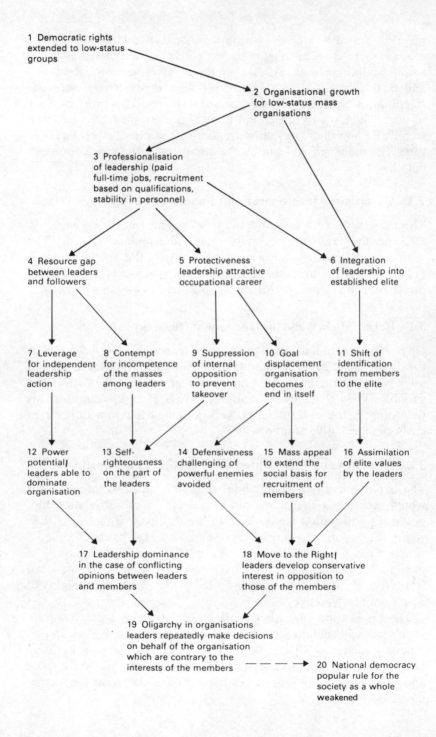

1 Democratic rights extended to low-status groups

2 Organisational growth for low-status mass organisations

3 Professionalisation of leadership (paid full-time jobs, recruitment based on qualifications, stability in personnel)

4 Resource gap between leaders and followers

5 Protectiveness leadership attractive occupational career

6 Integration of leadership into established elite

7 Leverage for independent leadership action

8 Contempt for incompetence of the masses among leaders

9 Suppression of internal opposition to prevent takeover

10 Goal displacement organisation becomes end in itself

11 Shift of identification from members to the elite

12 Power potential/ leaders able to dominate organisation

13 Self-righteousness on the part of the leaders

14 Defensiveness challenging of powerful enemies avoided

15 Mass appeal to extend the social basis for recruitment of members

16 Assimilation of elite values by the leaders

17 Leadership dominance in the case of conflicting opinions between leaders and members

18 Move to the Right/ leaders develop conservative interest in opposition to those of the members

19 Oligarchy in organisations leaders repeatedly make decisions on behalf of the organisation which are contrary to the interests of the members

20 National democracy popular rule for the society as a whole weakened

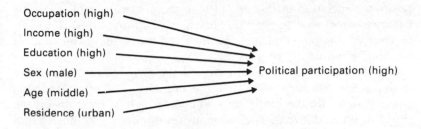

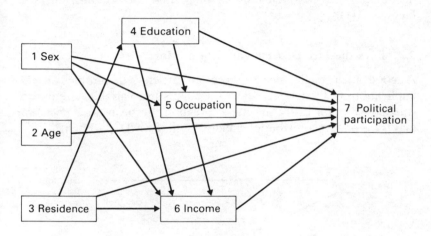

The case for revising this model further by adding or deleting arrows may well be argued. To explain as much as possible of the variation in participation we would pick the two variables with the strongest direct effects, which often will be causal variables weakly related to each other. Possible candidates: age and education. To explain the association between residence and participation we would choose a variable highly related to both, that is, one of nos 4–6 rather than 1 or 2.

4.1 Number of Parties and Responsiveness of Party Leadership

In Figure 3.5(b) number of parties and responsiveness of party leadership is related through a causal chain with an uneven number of negative effects (3), which produces a negative gross association.

In Figure 3.5(c) the effect of number of parties on loyalty is positive (two negative direct effects in the path connecting them). When comparing the two major American parties with European parties with regard to cohesion and rate of defections, the deduced positive association in this model may seem more tenable than the negative association implied by Hirschman's assumptions. But here, of course, other factors may be involved, such as presidential *vs* parliamentarian form of government.

Between loyalty and responsiveness the two indirect effects are both positive, while the direct effect is negative. The sign of the total causal effect will, therefore, depend upon which is the stronger, the direct or indirect effect. The same answer applies to the question of the relationship between number of parties and responsiveness in Figure 3.5(*c*).

4.2   Does the Fire Department Help or Hurt?

A good idea might be to write an article elaborating on the implications of the model, where the suppressor variable 'size of fire' is responsible for distorting the impression the bivariate association may give of the contribution made by the Fire Department.

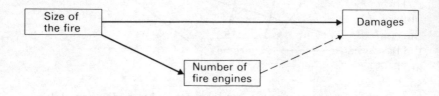

4.3   Deducing the Effect of Sex on List Position

Since the direct effect of sex is slightly larger than the bivariate association, the indirect effect must be negative, and small (*IE* = *BA* − *DE* = 0·06 − 0·07 = −0·01). Since the indirect effect equals the product of the two direct effects in the path from sex via list position to election success, we find the effect of sex on list position as −0·01/0·45 = −0·02, in other words, a negligible effect in favour of female candidates.

5.1   Attitude towards Premarital Sex

If we decide to order the variables causally in the sequence age, residence, education and attitude, we should arrive at the following causal interpretation of the relationship between the first three variables and the last one:

	Age	Residence	Education
Total causal effect:	−0·28	−0·09	0·11
Direct effect:	−0·25	−0·08	0·11
Indirect effect:	−0·03	−0·01	0
Spurious effect:	0	−0·04	0·07

(It might be a good idea to switch with regard to which value on the age and the residence variable is considered the 'high' value. With 'younger' and 'urban' defined as the high values, all effects become positive, which may make the results easier to grasp.)

5.2 Promotion Opportunity in the American Army

It would seem reasonable to rank branch of service as the second variable, being influenced by education and itself influencing rank (actual promotion) and the attitude towards promotion opportunity.

Since the analysis shows the data to be interaction-ridden, we have to weight the partial associations to arrive at the net association. Here we get into trouble, as the information in the heading of the table tells us that we are dealing with separate surveys for each branch of service instead of one representative sample. In relation to the composition of the American Army there would seem to be disproportionately many from the Military Police and disproportionately few from the Air Corps. To find the correct weights we, therefore, would have to obtain information on the approximate size of the two branches of service in the continental USA around 1944.

6.2 Reciprocal Causation

For the variable prior to the two reciprocally related, age, the decomposition in direct and indirect effect will remain unchanged. For residence, the negligible indirect effect will change to ambiguous effect under the new model; while for education, part of the spurious effect will now be ambiguous effect (to find out how much is spurious effect also under the revised model you have to see how the association between education and attitude is changed by controlling for age alone, compared to the bivariate association).

6.3 Sex and Legislative Career

In contrast to the results for the Conservative Party, the shift to trichotomies has little impact on the results for representatives from the Labour Party. Crude measures do not always distort the results, but without checking we will not know whether this is the case or not for the data at hand.

7.1 Sex and Income

One obvious methodological explanation is that the control for occupation is much too crudely done by just differentiating between manual and non-manual work, which does not take the hierarchical ordering of positions within each category into account.

Alternative substantive interpretations would include models introducing such intervening variables as education and seniority.

7.2 Effect of Sex a Result of Measurement Errors?

Since there are only three female representatives with high seniority, a change of value for one unit within this group will increase the proportion with high rank from 0·333 to 0·667, lowering the partial effect for sex among representatives with high seniority to 0·042. Multiplying with the weight 0·386 (from Table 1.6) the contribution to the overall effect from this group is found to be 0·02, as compared to 0·14 with the original distribution. One measurement error is enough to reduce the overall effect of sex on rank from 0·18 to 0·06. (Another point: the material is so small that it was possible to ensure complete accuracy in the measurement of the variables involved. So even if one measurement error might have great impact, it is not likely to have occurred.)

7.3 Effect of Marital Status a Result of Sampling Errors?

For men, the effect of marital status on political activity is 0·16. Calculating the variance we get the result 0·0030, which gives a standard deviation of 0·055 and a 95 per cent confidence interval of ±0·11. Since the interval around the sample result of 0·16 contains only positive values, we may assume the effect of marriage on political activity to be positive for all men in the population. For women, however, the effect is −0·11, with a confidence interval of ±0·16. In this case we see that the effect among women for the entire population may possibly be zero or even positive. The interpretation that the negative effect in the sample is due to random sampling error cannot be rejected.

7.4 Age as a Source of Spurious Effect?

Even if we do not know how strong the association between age and marital status is, the effect of age on political activity among the men is so weak that the age variable cannot possibly create spurious effect between marital status and activity of any importance. For the women, the effect of age on activity has the opposite sign from what we have assumed in our model in order to get negative spurious effect. It does not look as if age can explain the pattern of association between marital status and political activity for any of the sexes.

8.1 Sex and Legislative Career: a Prediction Analysis

The unweighted average for the partial effects of sex on rank is $(0\cdot21 + (-0\cdot07))/2 = 0\cdot07$, for seniority on rank $(0\cdot54 + 0\cdot26)/2 = 0\cdot40$. The interaction effect is $(0\cdot21 - (-0\cdot07))/2 = (0\cdot54 - 0\cdot26)/2 = 0\cdot14$. In this case the constant turns out to be $0\cdot00$, and we find each proportion as the sum of the relevant effects.

The bivariate association between sex and seniority (with sex as independent variable) is $0\cdot13$. If we use the unweighted effect of seniority on rank, we get an indirect effect of sex via seniority of $0\cdot13 \times 0\cdot40 = 0\cdot05$. Adding the unweighted effect of sex on rank $0\cdot07$ the sum of components becomes $0\cdot12$, which falls below the bivariate association between sex and rank of $0\cdot16$.

8.3 Predicting the Proportion Socialists

The proportions to be entered for the four variables (in the sequence from X_1 to X_4) are $0\cdot45$, $0\cdot15$, $0\cdot47$ and $0\cdot11$. Multiplying with the relevant effects the resulting predicted overall proportion of socialists should come close to the actual figure of $0\cdot51$ ($0\cdot506$). Changing the proportion of fathers who are workers with $+0\cdot15$, and the effect of own occupation on own vote with $-0\cdot20$, would bring the predicted proportion socialist down to $0\cdot43$.

8.4 Sex and Legislative Career: the Choice of Weights

When using the relative size of the control groups as weights, the direct effect of sex on rank is $0\cdot12$, and of seniority on rank $0\cdot47$. The direct effect of sex on seniority is $0\cdot13$. Using the effect transmittance design to find the indirect effect of sex we get a sum of components of

$0.12 + 0.13 \times 0.47 = 0.12 + 0.06 = 0.18$, which is somewhat above the bivariate association of 0.16.

Including the variance of the independent variable for each control group in the weight we obtain a completely accurate decomposition: $0.10 + 0.13 \times 0.46 = 0.10 + 0.06 = 0.16$.

9.1 A Regression Analysis

Coding male 1 and female 0 on the sex variable, and high 1 and low 0 on the seniority variable, the saturated regression coefficients are $b_0 = 0.14$, $b_1 = -0.08$, $b_2 = 0.26$ and $b_{12} = 0.28$ (with sex as the first and seniority as the second variable).

The effect of sex on the interaction variable is 0.62, the effect of seniority 0.72. The relatively strong interaction means that the decomposition is affected by a reordering of the values on the variables. For sex, the direct effect changes from -0.08 to 0.21, and the indirect effect from 0.24 to -0.05, if we recode the seniority variable.

The direct effect of sex in the simplified model becomes 0.10, and of seniority 0.46, the same as with Boyle's weighted average of differences in proportions in Exercise 8.4.

10.1 A Loglinear Analysis

The lambdas of the saturated model are: $X_1 = 0.18$, $X_2 = 0.04$, $X_3 = -0.19$, $X_1X_2 = -0.32$, $X_1X_3 = 0.55$, $X_2X_3 = 0.28$ and $X_1X_2X_3 = -0.05$ (with sex as X_1, occupation as X_2 and income as X_3).

If we delete the three-variable effect $X_1X_2X_3$, the fit to the data is still good (chi-square for the deviation between predicted and observed frequencies is as low as 0.16, which gives a probability higher than 0.5 for the observed frequencies being generated by the model). If we try the model $\{X_1X_2\}\{X_1X_3\}$, the fit is poor (probability 0.08), and for other unsaturated models, the result is even worse. The model $\{X_1X_2\}\{X_1X_3\}\{X_2X_3\}$ thus is the simplest model with a satisfactory fit between predicted and observed frequencies.

If the number of units is increased by a factor of 10, chi-square will also increase by this factor (from 0.16 to 1.6), reducing the probability that the observed frequencies have been generated under the model including all two-variable effects to 0.2. A larger sample thus makes it harder to find simple models which can account for the observed frequencies (just as it becomes easier to reject a null-hypothesis of no association).

Appendix:
The Computer Program NONCAN

The program NONCAN (non-metric causal analysis) performs causal analyses of up to ten dichotomous variables. By specifying the ordering of the variables, and whether the effect change or the effect transmittance design is to be used, the program calculates the tables necessary for a causal analysis (as shown in Figure 5.6). For each table (called a mastertable), a set of effect tables – one for each independent variable – gives the partial effects, their weights and the weighted overall effect (using the weights proposed by Boyle 1966). Standard deviation and significance level (*P*-value) for the effects are also reported.

On p. 204, a sample of the output from the program is given, using the actual data from Valen and Katz (1964: 177), which in a modified version were used in Table 5.1. The four-variable mastertable (corresponding to step 3 in Table 5.2), as well as the effect table for variable 1, father's occupation, is shown.

NONCAN has been developed at the Computer Centre of the University of Oslo, and can be obtained by writing to:

The Computer Centre
University of Oslo
PO Box 1059, Blindern
Oslo 3, Norway

MASTER TABLE

```
1 Father's occupation
:
:      2 Father's vote
:      :
:      :      3 Own occupation
:      :      :
:      :      :     4 Own vote
:      :      :   TOTAL socia PROP
==========================================
worke socia worke    135   121  .896
             - - -
  ''    ''  wcoll     38    25  .658
      ---------------
  ''  non-s worke     66    41  .621
             - - -
  ''    ''  wcoll     39     7  .179
==================
wcoll socia worke     32    30  .938
             - - -
  ''    ''  wcoll     19     5  .263
      ---------------
  ''  non-s worke    137    66  .482
             - - -
  ''    ''  wcoll    155    17  .110
==========================================
SUM   (N)            621
SUM     socia              312
PROPORTION   socia               .502
```

```
EFFECT OF:   1 Father's occupation
      ON:    4 Own vote     : socia

   2 Father's vote
   :
   :      3 Own occupation
   :      :
   :      :
   :      :  EFF  WEIGHT  E*W  SDEV  P-VAL
==========================================
socia worke  -.041  .226  -.009  .050  .206
      ------
  ''  wcoll   .395  .111   .044  .127  .001
===========
non-s worke   .139  .390   .054  .073  .029
      ------
  ''  wcoll   .070  .273   .019  .066  .146
==========================================
AVERAGE  EFF  .141
WEIGHTS  SUM       1.000
WEIGHTED NET EFFECT        .108
STANDARD DEVIATION              .038
P-VAL                                 .002
```

Further Reading

For those with no prior knowledge of social statistics, one of the many excellent general introductory texts (see, for example, Iversen 1979; or Blalock 1972) will be useful to gain a better understanding of probability, dispersion, variance, standard deviation, confidence interval and other statistical concepts which have been referred to in the text.

A survey of approaches to the analysis of non-metric data is given in Reynolds (1977). Rosenberg (1968) is an introduction to contingency table analysis in the Lazarsfeld tradition, whose history and main contributions are one of the topics in the interesting discussion by Marsh (1982) of survey research, the method for collecting the kind of data we have been analysing in this book. Davis (1980 and 1975, read in this order) are excellent introductions to causal analysis by means of contingency tables in general, and d-systems in particular.

Blalock (1961, 1969, 1971) discusses the problem of how to make causal inferences from non-experimental data within a path analytic framework. As an introduction to this tradition Asher (1976) may be used, while Kenny (1979) and Heise (1975) are more advanced texts. Excellent discussions of the experimental and quasi-experimental approach are found in Campbell and Stanley (1963) and Cook and Campbell (1979).

The texts on loglinear analysis by Knoke and Burke (1980) and Gilbert (1981) supplement each other well, and give references to the more advanced discussions.

An important topic not covered in this book is the analysis of diachronic data (data for the same variables from two or more points in time, for instance, panel studies or time series). Diachronic analyses of non-metric data are discussed in Davis (1978) with reference to d-systems, and in Knoke and Burke (1980) with reference to loglinear analysis.

References and Author Index

The numbers following each entry refer to the page numbers in the book where this item is referred to.

Amundsen, H. T. (1974), 'Binary variable multiple regression', *Scandinavian Journal of Statistics*, 1, pp. 59–70. **169**

Asher, H. B. (1976), *Causal Modeling*, Sage Quantitative Applications in the Social Sciences Series, 07-003 (Beverly Hills, Calif., and London: Sage). **158, 205**

Aubert, V. (1964), *Likhet og rett. Essays om forbrytelse og straff* (Oslo: Pax). **1, 4**

Barry, B. (1974), 'Review article: *Exit, Voice and Loyalty*', *British Journal of Political Science*, 4, pp. 79–107. **50**

Benson, O. (1969), *Political Science Laboratory* (Columbus, Ohio: Charles E. Merrill). **134**

Berelson, B., and Steiner, G. A. (1964), *Human Behavior. An Inventory of Scientific Findings* (New York: Harcourt, Brace & World). **54**

Blalock, H. M. (1961), *Causal Inferences in Nonexperimental Research* (Chapel Hill, NC: University of North Carolina Press). **25, 205**

Blalock, H. M. (1969), *Theory Construction. From Verbal to Mathematical Formulations* (Englewood Cliffs, NJ: Prentice-Hall). **195, 205**

Blalock, H. M. (1971), 'Theory building and causal inference', in H. M. Blalock and A. B. Blalock (eds), *Methodology in Social Research* (London: McGraw-Hill), pp. 155–98. **163, 205**

Blalock, H. M. (1972), *Social Statistics*, 2nd edn (New York: McGraw-Hill). **108, 205**

Boyle, R. P. (1966), 'Causal theory and statistical measures of effect: a convergence', *American Sociological Review*, 31, pp. 843–51. **139, 144, 145, 163, 168, 169, 171, 203**

Campbell, D. T., and Stanley, J. C. (1963), *Experimental and Quasi-Experimental Designs for Research* (Chicago: Rand McNally). **33, 205**

Coleman, J. A. (1964), *Introduction to Mathematical Sociology* (New York: The Free Press). **127, 144**

Cook, T. D., and Campbell, D. T. (1979), *Quasi-Experimentation* (Chicago: Rand McNally). **33, 205**

Costner, H. L., and Leik, R. K. (1964), 'Deductions from Axiomatic Theory', *American Sociological Review*, 29, pp. 819–35. **65**

Davis, J. A. (1971), *Elementary Survey Analysis* (Englewood Cliffs, NJ: Prentice-Hall). **134**

Davis, J. A. (1975), 'Analyzing contingency tables with linear flow graphs: *d*-systems', in D. Heise (ed.), *Sociological Methodology 1976* (San Francisco, Calif.: Jossey-Bass), pp. 111–45. **109, 136, 144, 145, 205**

Davis, J. A. (1976), 'Background characteristics of the US adult population 1952–1973: a survey-metric model', *Social Science Research*, 5, pp. 349–83. **136**

Davis, J. A. (1978), 'Studying categorical data over time', *Social Science Research*, 7, pp. 151–79. **136, 205**

Davis, J. A. (1980), 'Contingency table analysis: proportions and flow graphs', *Quality and Quantity*, 14, pp. 117–53. **136, 205**

Davis, J. A., and Schooler, S. R. (1974), 'Nonparametric path analysis – the multivariate structure of dichotomous data when using the odds ratio or Yule's Q', *Social Science Research*, 3, pp. 267–97. **187**

Dessens, J., and Jansen, W. (1978), 'Causal analysis of data from surveys: Goodman's procedure', *Quality and Quantity*, 12, pp. 331–56. **187**

Duncan, O. D. (1966), 'Path analysis: sociological examples', *American Journal of Sociology*, 72, pp. 1–16. **144**

Fienberg, S. M. (1977), *The Analysis of Cross-Classified Categorical Data* (Cambridge, Mass.: MIT Press). **187**

Foverskov, P. (1978), 'Women in Parliament: the causes of under-representation exemplified by Denmark and Norway in the 1960s', *European Journal of Political Research*, 6, pp. 53–69. **69, 111**

Gilbert, G. N. (1981), *Modelling Society. An Introduction to Loglinear Analysis for Social Researchers* (London: Allen & Unwin) **19, 136, 172, 180, 182, 185, 187, 205**

Goodman, L. A. (1973), 'Causal analysis of data from panel studies and other kinds of surveys', *American Journal of Sociology*, 78, pp. 1135–91. **169, 187**

Halsaa Albrektsen, B. (1977), *Kvinner og politisk deltakelse* (Oslo: Pax). **116, 120, 121**

Heise, D. R. (1975), *Causal Analysis* (New York: Wiley). **205**

Hellevik, O. (1979), 'Do Norwegian voters discriminate against women candidates for Parliament? A rejoinder', *European Journal of Political Research*, 7, pp. 285–300. **112**

Hellevik, O. (1983), 'Decomposing proportions and differences in proportions: approaches to contingency table analysis', *Quality and Quantity*, 18, pp. 79–111. **143**

Hirschman, A. O. (1970), *Exit, Voice, and Loyalty. Responses to Decline in Firms, Organizations, and States* (Cambridge, Mass.: Harvard University Press). **47**

Homans, G. C. (1964), 'Contemporary theory in sociology', in R. E. L. Faris (ed.), *Handbook of Modern Sociology* (Chicago: Rand McNally), pp. 951–77. **64**

Iversen, G. R. (1979), *Statistics for Sociology* (Dubuque, Iowa: C. Brown). **101, 108, 205**

Kalton, G. (1968), 'Standardization: a technique to control for extraneous variables', *Applied Statistics*, 17, pp. 118–36. **145, 146**

Kenny, D. A. (1979), *Correlation and Causality* (New York: Wiley). **205**

Knoke, D., and Burke, P. J. (1980), *Log-linear Models*, Sage Quantitative Applications in the Social Sciences series, 07-020 (Beverly Hills, Calif., and London: Sage). **128, 172, 182, 185, 187, 205**

Lafferty, W. M. (1981), *Participation and Democracy in Norway. The 'Distant Democracy' Revisited* (Oslo: Universitetsforlaget). **60**

Land, K. C. (1969), 'Principles of path analysis', in E. F. Borgatta and G. F. Bohrnstedt (eds), *Sociological Methodology 1969* (San Francisco, Calif.: Jossey-Bass), pp. 3–37. **44**

Lazarsfeld, P. F. (1955), 'Interpretation of statistical relations as a research operation', in P. F. Lazarsfeld and M. Rosenberg (eds), *The Language of Social Research* (New York: The Free Press), pp. 115–25. **42, 134**

Lazarsfeld, P. F., Berelson, B., and Gaudet, H. (1944), *The People's Choice* (New York: Duell, Sloan & Pierce). **xix**

Lazarsfeld, P. F., and Rosenberg, M. (eds) (1955), *The Language of Social Research* (New York: The Free Press). **23**

Linz, J. (1968), 'Robert Michels', in D. L. Sills (ed.), *International Encyclopedia of the Social Sciences* (London and New York: Macmillan/The Free Press), Vol. 10, pp. 463–9. **53**

Little, R. J. A., and Pullum, T. W. (1979), 'The general linear model and direct standardization. A comparison', *Sociological Methods and Research*, 7, pp. 475–501. **136, 145, 146**

Marsh, C. (1982), *The Survey Method. The Contribution of Surveys to Sociological Explanation* (London: Allen & Unwin). **205**

Martinussen, W. (1977), *The Distant Democracy: Social Inequality, Political Resources, and Political Influence* (London: Wiley). **41, 60**

May, J. D. (1965), 'Democracy, organization, Michels', *American Political Science Review*, 59, pp. 417–29. **53**

Michels, R. (1966), *Political Parties. A Sociological Study of the Oligarchical Tendencies of Modern Democracy* (New York: The Free Press). **52**

Nie, N. H., Hull, C. H., Jenkins, J. G., Steinbrenner, K., and Bent, D. H. (1975), *SPSS. Statistical Package for the Social Sciences* (New York: McGraw-Hill). **25, 156**

Reynolds, H. T. (1977), *The Analysis of Cross-Classifications* (New York: The Free Press). **136, 145, 147, 187, 205**

Rosenberg, M. (1962), 'Test factor standardization as a method of interpretation', *Social Forces*, 41, pp. 53–61. **134, 144**

Rosenberg, M. (1968), *The Logic of Survey Analysis* (New York: Basic Books). **205**

Skard, T. (1980), *Utvalgt til Stortinget. En studie i kvinners frammarsj og menns makt* (Oslo: Gyldendal). **23, 93**

Stack, S. (1978), 'The effect of direct government involvement in the economy on the degree of income inequality: a cross-national study', *American Sociological Review*, 43, pp. 880–8. **195**

Stinchcombe, A. L. (1968), *Constructing Social Theories* (New York: Harcourt, Brace & World). **41, 149**

Stouffer, S. A., Suchman, E. A., Devinny, L. C., Star, S. A., and Williams, R. M., Jr (1949), *The American Soldier. Adjustment during Army Life* (Princeton, NJ: Princeton University Press). **xix, 23**

Swigert, V. L., and Farrel, R. A. (1977), 'Normal homicides and the law', *American Sociological Review*, 42, pp. 16–32. **194**

Valen, H., and Katz, D. (1964), *Political Parties in Norway* (Oslo: Universitetsforlaget. **71, 129, 203**

Zetterberg, H. L. (1954), *On Theory and Verification in Sociology* (Totawa, NJ: Bedminster Press; 3rd edn 1965). **64**

Subject Index